ESSENTIAL
Japanese

Lynne Strugnell

ESSENTIAL JAPANESE

CONTENTS

CONTENTS

CONTENTS   v

ESSENTIAL JAPANESE

INTRODUCTION

For over a century, Berlitz language courses and books have helped people learn foreign languages for business, for pleasure, for travel – and helped people improve their ability to communicate with their fellow human beings all over the world. With more than 30 million students to date, Berlitz has maintained a tradition of excellence in language instruction that goes back to the founding of the company in 1878 by Professor Maximilian Berlitz.

Professor Berlitz's great innovation in the teaching of a foreign language was to modify the old practice of teaching grammar and vocabulary by rote, concentrating instead on the dynamic application of the living language from the moment a student begins his or her study. This Berlitz Essential book continues this successful method of foreign language teaching through dialog, phonetics and vocabulary.

Whether you're a beginner who's never studied a foreign language or a former student brushing up on old skills, Berlitz *Essential Japanese* will provide you with all the tools and information you need to speak a foreign tongue easily and effectively. Furthermore, the book is designed to permit you to study at your own pace, based on your level of expertise.

* Lively bilingual dialogs describe actual, everyday situations in which you might find yourself when travelling in a foreign country.

* Basic grammar is taught through actual phrases and sentences, which help you develop an instinctive sense of correct grammar without having to study long lists of rules and exceptions.

* An exercise section in each lesson gives you the opportunity to pinpoint your strengths and weaknesses, and enables you to study more efficiently.

* The glossary at the end of the book gives you an easy reference list of all the words used in the book.

HOW TO USE THIS BOOK

The best way to learn any language is through consistent daily study. Decide for yourself how much time you can devote to the study of *Essential Japanese* each day – you may be able to complete two lessons a day or just have time for a half-hour of study. Set a realistic daily study goal that you can easily achieve, one that includes studying new material as well as reviewing the old. The more frequent your exposure to the language, the better your results will be.

THE STRUCTURE OF THE BOOK

* Read the dialog at the beginning of each lesson aloud, slowly and carefully, using the translation.

* When you have read the dialog through enough times to get a good grasp of the sounds and sense of it, read the grammar and usage notes, paying particular attention to how the language builds its sentences. Then go back and read the dialog again.

* When studying the vocabulary list, it is useful to write the words down in a notebook. This will help you remember both the spelling and meaning, as you move ahead. You might also try writing the word in a sentence that you make up yourself.

* Try to work on the exercise section without referring to the dialog, then go back and check your answers against the dialog or by consulting the answer section at the end of the book. It's helpful to repeat the exercises.

By dedicating yourself to the lessons in the Berlitz *Essential Japanese* course, you will quickly put together the basic building blocks of Japanese, which will help you to continue at your own pace. You will find in this book all you need to know in order to communicate effectively in a foreign language; and you will be amply prepared to go on to master Japanese with all the fluency of a native speaker.

GUIDE TO PRONUNCIATION

One great advantage of learning Japanese over other languages is that the pronunciation is easy for speakers of English. It is straightforward, regular, and does not have the complications of different tones, strong stress patterns or unfamiliar sounds that some languages have. Each letter is pronounced in one way only, so you do not have to learn complex rules for combinations of letters. In fact, you probably already know how to pronounce most of the sounds if you are familiar with such words as **kimono, Honda, sumō, Yokohama, sushi, karate, geisha** and **Zen.**

THE VOWELS

"a" is pronounced as in **Kawasaki.**
"e" is pronounced as in **Zen.**
"i" is pronounced as in **kimono.**
"o" is pronounced as in **Hiroshima.**
"u" is pronounced as in **sumō.**

Remember that each vowel is always said in the same way, so the two "o" sounds at the end of **kimono**, for example, should be the same. Also, there is much less stress on individual syllables in Japanese than there is in English, so instead of saying **kiMOno** or **YokoHAma**, you should try saying the words evenly, without any particular stress.

The rule about vowels always being pronounced the same still holds when two vowels come together. Take them one by one, and pronounce them as in the guide above. For example, think of **geisha** as **ge-i-sha**, rather than "gay-sha."

Sometimes you will see a vowel with a line over the top (e.g. ō, ū). This means that the sound is equivalent to two vowels together, so it should be held for longer than a single vowel. In the placename **Kyōto**, for example, the first "o" lasts twice as long as the second one, so lean slightly on the first one as you say it. (In some texts, you may see these sounds written with double letters, for example **Kyooto**, rather than **Kyōto.**)

There are a few cases where the vowel sound almost disappears. One of the most common of these is the final "u" at the end of present tense verbs. These all end in -**masu**, but in practice it sounds more like "-mass." Another example is **desu** ("is/are"), which is pronounced rather like "dess."

CONSONANTS

Most of the consonant sounds are the same as in English, so pronounce them as they look. There are only a few differences, as follows.

The letter "g" is always pronounced hard as in "gain," not soft as in "gem."

The letter "f" represents a sound somewhere between "f" and "h." To make the sound, try saying **Fuji** without letting your top teeth touch your bottom lip, and you'll get the idea.

The letter "r" represents a sound which is halfway between "l" and "r." Try saying **Narita** (the name of Tokyo's international airport), but flick the tip of your tongue on the roof of your mouth on all three consonants, that is, on "r" as well as on "n" and "t."

Sometimes you will see words with double consonants in the middle (e.g. a<u>tt</u>a, ki<u>pp</u>u, ga<u>kk</u>ō, za<u>ssh</u>i). As with the vowels, these doubled sounds should be held for twice the length of a single sound. For example, **atta** ("had") is pronounced like the middle part of "th<u>at</u> <u>tap</u>."

Japanese written in the roman alphabet is phonetic, in other words it is written almost exactly as it sounds, so it isn't necessary to provide you with a phonetic guide to pronouncing each line in the text. However, just to make sure you're on the right track, here are some words taken from Lesson 1, along with a guide to how to pronounce them. Try saying them aloud.

> **arigatō** (thank you): ah-ree-gah-toe
> **Nihon** (Japan): nee-hon
> **hajimemashite** (how do you do?): hah-jee-meh-mash-teh
> **shitsurei** (excuse me): she-tsoo-reh-ee
> **iie** (no): ee-ee-eh
> **hai** (yes): hah-ee

THE WRITING SYSTEM

Although spoken Japanese is relatively easy to learn, the written language is one of the most complex in the world (which is one reason why this book uses the Roman alphabet!). It is made up of three quite different writing systems, **kanji, hiragana** and **katakana** characters, which are used in combination.

Some examples of kanji characters and the way they are pronounced have been given in each lesson. In addition, you will find some more information on **kanji, hiragana and katakana** in Appendix 2.

NIHON E YŌKOSO!
WELCOME TO JAPAN!

Mike Nelson has just arrived at Narita airport, outside Tokyo. He's expecting to be met by Mr. Watanabe, a teacher at the high school where Mike will be teaching.

Mike	**Shitsurei desu ga, Watanabe san desu ka.** Excuse me, but are you Mr. Watanabe?
Stranger	**Watashi desu ka? Iie, chigaimasu.** Me? No, I'm not.
Mike	**Sō desu ka. Dōmo sumimasen.** Oh, I see. I'm sorry.

Mr. Watanabe, who's late, guesses that this large foreigner must be Mike Nelson. He hurries over.

Watanabe	**Sumimasen, Neruson san desu ka.** Excuse me, are you Mr. Nelson?
Mike	**Hai, sō desu. Neruson desu.** Yes, that's right. I'm Nelson.

Watanabe	Hajimemashite, **Watanabe desu. Yokohama Gakuin Kōkō no Watanabe desu. Nihon e yōkoso!** How do you do? I'm Watanabe, Watanabe from Yokohama High School. Welcome to Japan!
Mike	**Ā, Watanabe san, hajimemashite.** Ah, Mr. Watanabe, how do you do?
Watanabe	**Watashi no meishi desu. Dōzo.** Here's my business card.
Mike	**Dōmo arigatō.** Thank you.
Watanabe	(pointing to suitcases) **Neruson san no sūtsukēsu desu ka.** Are these your suitcases, Mr. Nelson?
Mike	**Hai, sō desu.** Yes, they are.
Watanabe	**Ja, dōzo, kochira e.** Well, this way, please.

It's a long drive to Yokohama, but they finally get there. Mike has been trying hard to stay awake.

Watanabe	**Hai, Neruson san, Yokohama desu. Neruson san? Neruson san?** Well, this is Yokohama! Mr. Nelson? Mr. Nelson?

But all he gets in response is a gentle, peaceful snoring.

STRUCTURE AND USAGE NOTES

1. SAN – MR., MRS., MISS AND MS.

The word **san** is used as a term of respect after all names, so this one word is the equivalent of Mr., Ms., Mrs. and Miss. It is even used after first names, so don't be surprised if you are called **Tom san** or **Susan san**. Remember that, as **san** is a term of respect to other people, you never use it with your own name. Notice how Mr. Watanabe used **san** in his first line in the dialog, but Mike didn't use it in his reply.

Watanabe	**Neruson san desu ka.** Are you Mr. Nelson?

Mike	Hai, sō desu. Neruson desu.
	Yes, that's right. I'm Nelson.

2. DESU – "TO BE"

In Japanese it is not necessary to learn long lists of different verb endings, because the verb does not change with the person, and so **desu** can mean "I am/you are/he is/she is/it is/we are/they are." It is usually obvious from the situation which of these meanings is intended. Notice that the verb always comes at the end of a Japanese sentence.

Gakusei desu.
(I) am a student.

Enjinia desu.
(He) is an engineer.

Amerikajin desu.
(I) am an American.

Watanabe san desu ka.
Are (you) Mr. Watanabe?

3. KA – FORMING QUESTIONS

To form a question, simply add **ka** to the end of the sentence. You don't need to make any other changes. Because **ka** always indicates a question, it is not necessary to use a question mark after it.

Gakusei desu.	**Gakusei desu ka.**
I'm/He's a student.	Are you/Is he a student?
Yokohama desu.	**Yokohama desu ka.**
(This) is Yokohama.	Is (this) Yokohama?
Kanadajin desu.	**Kanadajin desu ka.**
I'm/She's Canadian.	Are you/Is she Canadian?

If **ka** is not spoken because the sentence is left unfinished, then you need to use a question mark.

Mike	Shitsurei desu ga, Kanadajin desu ka.
Stranger	Kanadajin? Iie, chigaimasu. Watashi wa Amerikajin desu.

In this case, **Kanadajin?** is an abbreviation of **Kanadajin desu ka.**

4. THE PARTICLE – NO

You will come across a number of small words in Japanese which do not have a meaning in themselves, but which serve to show the relationship between different parts of a sentence, or the function of a word or phrase within a sentence. These small words are called "particles," and usually come *after* the word to which they refer. One such word is **no**, which acts rather like the English "-'s" to show belonging or possession. It links the owner to the owned.

Takahashi san no sūtsukēsu
Ms. Takahashi's suitcase

Suzuki san no meishi
Mr. Suzuki's business card

watashi no gakkō
my school

gakkō no namae
the school's name

However, the usage of **no** is much wider than simply possession, and it can be used to join any two nouns where the first one describes, or gives more information about, the second one.

Amerika no kaisha
an American company

Nihon no kuruma
Japanese cars

Yokohama no gakkō
schools in Yokohama [Lit: Yokohama's schools]

You can use **no** more than once in the same phrase.

watashi no gakkō no sensei
the teachers at my school [Lit: my school's teachers]

Nihongo no sensei no namae
the Japanese (language) teacher's name

Mr. Watanabe introduces himself as **Yokohama Gakuin Kōkō no Watanabe desu**, literally "I'm Yokohama High School's Watanabe," or more colloquially, "I'm Watanabe, of Yokohama High School."

5. PLURALS

Good news! Japanese does not usually differentiate between singular and plural except where absolutely necessary, so you don't need to learn new forms for plurals. You'll find that it is generally obvious from the context whether a singular or plural is meant. In other situations you'll find it's not really necessary to differentiate.

Saitō san? Enjinia desu.	**Saitō san to Katō san? Enjinia desu.**
Mr. Saitō? He's an engineer	Mr. Saitō and Mr. Katō? They're engineers.
Watashi no meishi desu. Dōzo.	**Saitō san to Watanabe san no meishi desu.**
Here's my business card.	These are Mr. Saitō's and Mr. Watanabe's business cards.

6. ARTICLES – "THE" AND "A"

The next piece of good news is that there are no articles ("a/an/the") in Japanese, so where they may exist in English, simply ignore them when changing the sentence to Japanese.

Gakusei desu ka.
Are you (a) student?

Amerika no kaisha desu.
It's (an) American company.

Sumimasen ga, Nihongo no sensei desu ka.
Excuse me, but are you (the) Japanese language teacher?

7. ANOTHER PARTICLE – E

The particle e can often be translated as "to" or "towards," as it indicates the direction of movement towards something, but unlike in English, it comes *after* the name of the place towards which you're going.

Tōkyō e yōkoso.
Welcome to Tokyo.

Kochira e, dōzo.
This way, please.

VOCABULARY

Amerika: the United States of America
Amerikajin: an American
arigatō: thank you [more informal than **dōmo arigatō**]
chigaimasu: that's incorrect, wrong [from the verb **chigau**]
dai ik-ka: lesson one
desu: I am, you are, he is, she is, it is, we are, they are
dōmo arigatō: thank you
dōmo sumimasen: I'm sorry, I apologize
dōzo: please (go ahead), here you are [when giving something]
e: to, towards
enjinia: engineer
ga: but
gakkō: school
gakuin: institute, school, place of learning
gakusei: student
hai: yes
hajimemashite: how do you do?
iie: no
ja: well, in that case
-jin: person (of a country)
ka: [sentence ending to indicate a question]
kaisha: company, office
Kanada: Canada
Kanadajin: a Canadian
kochira: this way
kōkō: high school [short for **kōtō gakkō**]
kuruma: car
meishi: business card
namae: name
Nihon: Japan
Nihongo: Japanese language
no: [particle showing possession, similar to English "-'s"]
san: Mr., Mrs., Ms., Miss
sensei: teacher, professor
shitsurei desu ga: I'm sorry to trouble you, but ...; excuse me, but ...
sō desu: that's right, that's so
sō desu ka: I see, is that so?
sumimasen: excuse me, I'm sorry

sūtsukēsu: suitcase
to: and [to join nouns]
watashi: I, me
watashi no: my
yōkoso: welcome

TEST YOURSELF

1. *Read through the dialog at the beginning of the lesson again, and then say if the following statements are true or false.*

    1. Watanabe san wa sensei desu. T/F

    2. Watanabe san no gakkō wa Yokohama Gakuin Kōkō desu
       T/F

    3. Maiku san no namae wa Maiku Neruson desu. T/F

2. *Answer the questions about yourself with **Hai,** sō **desu** or **Iie, chigaimasu.***

    1. Shitsurei desu ga, Neruson san desu ka.

    2. Amerikajin desu ka.

    3. Gakusei desu ka.

    4. Sensei desu ka.

3. *How would you say the following sentences in Japanese?*

    1. How do you do?

    2. I'm American.

    3. Is this a Japanese car?

    4. Yes, that's right.

    5. No, it's not.

4. *Make up some questions and answers, using the pictures and cues given below. (Notice that in Japan, a small circle is generally used instead of a check mark as a symbol for "yes" or "correct.") Here is an example to help you.*

Example: Yokohama High School?
　　　　A. **Yokohama Gakuin**
　　　　　Kōkō desu ka.
　　　　B. **Iie, chigaimasu.**

1. Mike's suitcase?

2. A student?

3. A teacher?

4. Mr. Watanabe's car?

5. An engineer?

6. An American?

5. *Introduce yourself to Mr. Tanaka, of Fujimura Company, by filling in the blanks in the conversation below with appropriate words. (If you don't belong to a company, college, or other organization, then just give your name.)*

You   Shitsurei _____ ___, Tanaka ____ _____ _____.

Tanaka   Hai, sō desu.

You   _____, _____ no _____ desu.

Tanaka   _____, Fujimura no Tanaka desu.

You   Watashi no _____ desu. Dōzo.

Nihon is the Japanese word for "Japan." It is made up of the kanji characters for "sun" and "source/origin," giving the meaning "source of the sun." These two characters together can also be pronounced **Nippon**.

MINA SAN, OHAYŌ GOZAIMASU.

GOOD MORNING, EVERYONE.

It's Mike's first day of work at Yokohama High School, and Mr. Watanabe is introducing him to some of the staff.

Watanabe **Mina san, ohayō gozaimasu.**
Good morning, everyone.

Everyone **Ohayō gozaimasu.**
Good morning.

Watanabe **Neruson san, kochira wa Itō sensei desu.**
Mr. Nelson, this is Mr. Itō.

Itō **Hajimemashite, Itō desu.**
How do you do? I'm Itō.

Mike **Maiku Neruson desu. Yoroshiku onegai shimasu.**
I'm Mike Nelson. Pleased to meet you.

Watanabe **Kochira wa Takahashi san desu. Takahashi san wa jimu no hito desu.**
This is Ms. Takahashi. She's a clerk.

Takahashi	**Hajimemashite. Takahashi desu. Dōzo yoroshiku.**
	How do you do? I'm Takahashi. Pleased to meet you.

Mr. Watanabe then shows Mike around the office.

Watanabe	**Kore wa watashi no tsukue desu. Sore wa Takahashi san no tsukue desu.**
	This is my desk. That's Ms. Takahashi's desk.
Mike	**Watashi no tsukue wa doko ni arimasu ka.**
	Where's my desk?
Watanabe	**Neruson san no wa soko ni arimasu.**
	Yours is there.
Takahashi	**Watanabe san, chigaimasu. Sumimasen ga, sore wa Neruson san no tsukue ja arimasen. Saitō san no desu.**
	Mr. Watanabe, that's not right. Excuse me, but that isn't Mr. Nelson's desk. It's Ms. Saitō's.
Watanabe	**Saitō san? Saitō san wa dare desu ka.**
	Ms. Saitō? Who's Ms. Saitō?
Takahashi	**Atarashii pāto desu. Kyō kara desu.**
	She's the new part-time worker. From today.
Watanabe	**Sō desu ka. Atarashii pāto desu ka. Ja, Neruson san no tsukue wa?**
	I see. The new part-time worker. Well, what about Mr. Nelson's desk?
Takahashi	**Wakarimasen.**
	I don't know.
Watanabe	**Itō san! Neruson san no tsukue wa doko ni arimasu ka.**
	Mr. Itō! Where's Mr. Nelson's desk?
Itō	**Sono tsukue ja arimasen ka.**
	Isn't it that desk?
Watanabe	**A, sore desu ka. Neruson san, sore desu.**
	Ah, is it that one? Mr. Nelson, it's that one.
Mike	**Dōmo arigatō.**
	Thank you.

STRUCTURE AND USAGE NOTES

1. OHAYŌ GOZAIMASU – "GOOD MORNING" AND OTHER GREETINGS

Here are some useful phrases for greetings and partings.

Ohayō gozaimasu
Good morning

Konnichiwa
Good day/Hello

Konbanwa
Good evening

Shitsurei shimasu
Goodbye [Lit: Excuse me]

Oyasumi nasai
Good night

2. THE PARTICLE – WA

The job of the particle **wa** is to point out the main topic of a sentence and, like all particles, it comes after the word or phrase to which it refers. You can think of it as meaning "As for ..." or "Regarding ..."

Maiku san wa Amerikajin desu.
Mike is an American. [Lit: As for Mike, he's an American.]

Yokohama Gakuin Kōkō wa ōkii desu.
Yokohama High School is big.

Ogawa san wa Nihongo no sensei desu.
Ms. Ogawa is a Japanese teacher. [Lit: As for Ms. Ogawa, she's a Japanese teacher.]

Saitō san wa dare desu ka.
Who's Ms. Saitō? [Lit: With regard to Ms. Saitō – who is she?]

Watanabe san no uchi wa ōkii desu ka.
Is Mr. Watanabe's house big? [Lit: Regarding Mr. Watanabe's house – is it big?]

Sensei no namae wa Ogawa san desu ka.
Is the teacher's name Ms. Ogawa?

3. KORE, SORE, ARE AND DORE – "THIS," "THAT" AND "WHICH ONE?"

In English, we divide things into the two groups of "this" and "that," but in Japanese there are three groups: **kore,** meaning "this thing" or "these things" near me; **sore,** meaning "that thing" or "those things" near you; and **are** meaning "that thing" or "those things" over there, away from both of us. (Don't be tempted to pronounce that last one like the English "are." Remember that it should be said more like "ah-reh.")

Kore wa atarashii purintā desu ka.
Is this a new printer?

Neruson san no sūtsukēsu wa kore desu ka.
Your suitcase, Mr. Nelson – is it this one?

Sore wa pāto no sensei no tsukue desu.
That's the part-time worker's desk.

Itō san no uchi wa are desu.
Mr. Itō's house is that one over there.

The corresponding question word is **dore.**

A: **Itō san no kuruma wa dore desu ka.**
Which is your car, Mr. Itō?

B: **Sore desu.**
It's that one.

4. KOKO, SOKO, ASOKO AND DOKO – "HERE," "THERE" AND "WHERE?"

Another set of words beginning with **ko-, so-, a-** and **do-** relate to location: **koko** means "here," near me; **soko** means "there," near you; and **asoko** means "over there," away from both of us. The question word **doko** means "where?" Sentences describing the location of something usually use the verb **arimasu** ("to be/exist"), and the particle **ni** follows the word or phrase showing the place where something exists, so it can often be translated as "at" or "in."

Kyō no shinbun wa koko ni arimasu.
Today's newspapers are over here.

Denwa wa soko ni arimasu. Dōzo.
The telephone's there. Please (go ahead and use it).

Eki wa asoko ni arimasu ka.
Is the station over there?

Asoko no kuruma wa dare no kuruma desu ka.
That car over there – whose (car) is it?

Ginkō wa doko ni arimasu ka.
Where's the bank?

A. Jonson san wa doko kara desu ka.
Where are you from, Mr. Johnson?

B. Shikago kara desu.
I'm from Chicago.

(It is also possible to use **desu** instead of **arimasu** to show location. See the next note.)

5. ARIMASU VS. DESU – "BE," "BE LOCATED," "EXIST"

Both **arimasu** and **desu** mean "is/are," but there is a difference in the way they are used. **Desu** is used when one thing is, or equals, another.

Koko wa Yokohama eki desu.
This is Yokohama station.

Neruson san wa atarashii sensei desu.
Mr. Nelson is a new teacher.

Kore wa watashi no meishi desu. Dōzo.
This is my business card. Please (take it).

The verb **arimasu** means that something exists, so it is often used to describe the location of something. As we saw above, in this case it is preceded by **ni**, a particle pointing out place or location.

Daigaku wa Ōsaka ni arimasu.
(My) university is (located) in Osaka.

Ogawa san no kaisha wa Tōkyō ni arimasu.
Mr. Ogawa's company is (located) in Tokyo.

Denwa wa doko ni arimasu ka.
Where's the telephone (located)?

When describing the location of something, **ni arimasu** can often be replaced by **desu**. The nuance is slightly different, but the English translation is usually the same.

Ginkō wa doko desu ka.	Ginkō wa doko ni arimasu ka.
Where's the bank.	Where's the bank?
[Lit: What place is the bank?]	[Lit: In what place is the bank located?]
Gakkō wa asoko desu.	Gakkō wa asoko ni arimasu.
The school is over there.	The school is over there.
[Lit: The school is that place over there.]	[Lit: The school is located in that place over there.]

The verb **arimasu** can often be translated as "there is/are," or "have."

Denwa wa arimasu ka.
Do you have a telephone?/Is there a telephone?

Answers to this kind of "yes or no" question are **Hai, arimasu** ("Yes, I have./Yes, there is."), **Iie, arimasen** ("No, I haven't./No, there isn't."), or **Wakarimasen** ("I don't know.").

A. Denwa wa arimasu ka.
   Do you have a telephone?/Is there a telephone?
B. Iie, arimasen.
   No, we don't./No, there isn't.

A. Saitō san, kyō no shinbun wa arimasu ka.
   Ms. Saitō, do you have today's paper?
B. Hai, arimasu. Dōzo.
   Yes, I do. Here you are.

6. JA ARIMASEN – "ISN'T," "AREN'T"

Ja arimasen is the negative of **desu**, so it means "isn't," or "aren't." **Ja** is a contraction of **de wa**. (You may also hear the alternative forms **de wa arimasen, ja nai desu** and **de wa nai desu**, which all mean "isn't" or "aren't.")

Amerikajin ja arimasen. Igirisujin desu.
I'm not American. I'm British.

Sensei ja arimasen. Jimu no hito desu.
I'm not a teacher. I am an office worker.

Ōkii kōkō ja arimasen.
It's not a big high school.

A. Kono konpyūta wa atarashii desu ka.
   Is this computer new?

B. Iie, sō ja arimasen.
No, it isn't.

Are wa Watanabe san no kuruma ja arimasen ka.
Isn't that Mr. Watanabe's car?

7. SAITŌ SAN NO DESU – "IT'S MS. SAITŌ'S."

The word **no** can be used in place of a noun when it is obvious what you are talking about, in much the same way as "one" or simply "—'s" is used in English.

Kaisha no kuruma desu.	**Kaisha no desu.**
It's the company's car.	It's the company's.
Dare no shinbun desu ka.	**Dare no desu ka.**
Whose newspaper is it?	Whose is it?
Atarashii purintā wa arimasu ka.	**Atarashii no wa arimasu ka.**
Do you have a new printer?	Do you have a new one?
Ōsaka no daigaku wa ōkii desu.	**Ōsaka no wa ōkii desu.**
The university in Osaka is big.	The one in Osaka is big.

8. "YOU" AND "YOURS"

Although there is a word for "you" in Japanese (**anata**), you won't hear it used very often. Instead, the person's name is generally used, even when you are talking to him or her directly.

Neruson san no tsukue wa soko ni arimasu.
Your desk is there (Mr. Nelson).

Kore wa Neruson san no shinbun desu ka.
Is this your newspaper (Mr. Nelson)?

Maiku san no gakkō wa Yokohama ni arimasu ka.
Is your school in Yokohama (Mike)?

VOCABULARY

anata: you
are: that over there [noun]
arimasen: there isn't/aren't, don't have [from **aru**]
arimasu: be, exist, there is/are, have [from **aru**]
asoko: over there

atarashii: new
daigaku: university
dare: who?
denwa: telephone
doko: where?
dore: which one?
dōzo yoroshiku: happy to meet you
eki: train station
ginkō: bank
hito: person, people
Igirisu: England, Great Britain
Igirisujin: an English/British person
ja arimasen: isn't, aren't
jimu: office work
jimu no hito: office worker, clerk
kara: from
kochira: this person [used with introductions]
koko: here
konbanwa: good evening
konnichiwa: good day, hello [not used early in the morning]
konpyūtā: computer
kore: this [noun]
kyō: today
mina san: everyone
ni: in, at [particle indicating location]
ohayō gozaimasu: good morning
ōkii: big
oyasumi nasai: good night
pāto: part-time worker
purintā: printer
sensei: professor, doctor [used as a term of address to teachers, professors and doctors instead of **san**]
shinbun: newspaper
shitsurei shimasu: excuse me, goodbye
soko: there
sore: that [noun]
tsukue: desk
uchi: house, home
wa: [particle to indicate main topic of sentence]
wakarimasen: I don't know, I don't understand [from **wakaru**]
yoroshiku onegai shimasu: pleased to meet you

TEST YOURSELF

1. *Read through the dialog at the beginning of the lesson again, and then say if the following statements are true or false.*

   1. Takahashi san wa sensei ja arimasen.   T/F

   2. Atarashii pāto wa kyō kara desu.   T/F

   3. Pāto no namae wa Itō san desu.   T/F

2. *Answer the following questions about yourself.*

   1. Kyō no shinbun wa arimasu ka.

   2. Anata no kaisha [OR gakkō, daigaku] wa doko ni arimasu ka.

   3. Anata no uchi wa ōkii uchi desu ka.

   4. Atarashii kuruma wa arimasu ka.

   5. Anata wa doko kara desu ka.

3. *The words missing from this grid are all things that you might find in the office, and their English equivalents are listed below, although not in the right order. Complete the grid to discover what the missing word in the middle is.*

   business card

   computer

   desk

   telephone

   part-time worker

   printer

   person

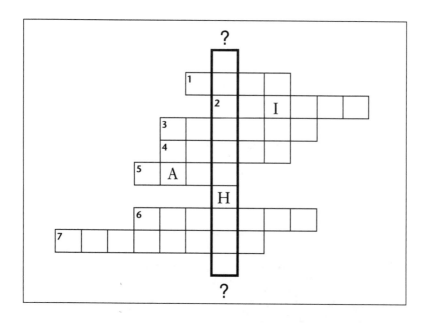

4. *How would you say the following sentences in Japanese?*

   1. Are you from Tokyo?

   2. My company is in New York.

   3. Excuse me, but where's the bank?

   4. The telephone's over there – please go ahead (and use it).

   5. That isn't my house.

5. *Fill in the blanks with an appropriate word from the lists below.*
   Each word can only be used once. Note that there are more words
   than you need.

no	kara	arimasen
dare	sō	asoko
ni	ja	wa
ka	are	namae

   1. Saitō san no daigaku wa doko _____ arimasu ka.

   2. Sumimasen ga, kyō no shinbun wa _____.

3. Denwa wa _____ ni arimasu.

4. Iie, watashi wa Amerikajin _____ arimasen.

5. Watanabe san _____ uchi wa atarashii desu ka.

6. Nihongo no sensei no _____ wa Itō sensei desu.

7. Tanaka san _____ enjinia desu ka.

8. Neruson san wa doko _____ desu ka.

The name of the port of Yokohama, just south of Tokyo, combines the characters for "next to/side" and "beach."

NANI O TABEMASU KA.
WHAT WILL YOU HAVE TO EAT?

Mr. Watanabe has invited Mike out for lunch at a small Japanese restaurant near the school. The menu is all in Japanese, which Mike can't read yet, so Mr. Watanabe questions him on what he likes.

Watanabe   **Neruson san wa nani o tabemasu ka.**
What are you going to eat?

Mike   **Hmm, wakarimasen. Kono resutoran wa, nani ga oishii desu ka.**
Hmm, I don't know. What's good at this restaurant?

Watanabe   **Sakana ga oishii desu. Sakana ga suki desu ka.**
The fish is good. Do you like fish?

Mike   **Hai, dai-suki desu.**
Yes, I like it very much.

Watanabe   **Ja, yaki-zakana teishoku wa dō desu ka. Sore wa yaki-zakana to gohan to tsukemono to miso shiru desu.**
Well, how about the grilled fish set meal? That's grilled fish and rice and pickles and miso soup.

Mike	Sore wa ii desu ne. Hai, watashi wa yaki-zakana teishoku ni shimasu. Watanabe san wa?
	That's good. Yes, I'll have the grilled fish set meal. And you?
Watanabe	Watashi wa sashimi teishoku ni shimasu. (to waiter) Sumimasen!
	I'll have the sashimi [raw fish] set meal. Excuse me!
Waiter	Hai, nani ni shimasu ka.
	Yes, what would you like?
Watanabe	Yaki-zakana teishoku to sashimi teishoku o kudasai.
	The grilled fish set meal and the sashimi set meal, please.

The waiter soon comes back with a tray of food each for Mr. Watanabe and Mike, and they tuck into it.

Mike	Itadakimasu.
	Bon appetit.
Watanabe	Itadakimasu.
	Bon appetit.
Mike	Kono miso shiru wa oishii desu ne. (noticing something decorating Mr. Watanabe's raw fish) E? Sore wa nan desu ka. Hana ja arimasen ka.
	This miso soup is good, isn't it. Eh? What's that? Isn't it a flower?
Watanabe	Hai, sō desu. Sono hana wa kiku desu.
	Yes, that's right. That flower's a chrysanthemum.
Mike	E? Nan desu ka? Kiku desu ka. Kiku o tabemasu ka.
	Eh? What? It's a chrysanthemum? You eat chrysanthemums?
Watanabe	Hai, tokidoki tabemasu. A, o-cha wa arimasen ne. O-cha o nomimasu ka.
	Yes, sometimes we do! Ah, there isn't any green tea, is there? Do you want some green tea?
Mike	Sumimasen ga, o-cha wa amari suki ja arimasen. Mizu o kudasai.
	I'm sorry, but I don't really like green tea. Could I have some water?
Watanabe	Hai, mizu desu ne. (to waiter) Sumimasen, o-cha to mizu o kudasai.
	Water – right. Excuse me, some green tea and some water, please.

STRUCTURE AND USAGE NOTES

1. SIMPLE PRESENT TENSE VERBS

As we have seen with **desu,** Japanese verbs do not change to agree with the person or persons doing the action, and there is usually no need even to mention any words for "you," "I," etc., so **tabemasu,** for example, can mean "I eat/you eat/he eats/she eats/we eat/they eat." Likewise, the negative, **tabemasen,** can mean "I/you/he/she/we/they don't eat." Here are some more present tense verbs for you to learn, with the negative forms. (Note that the final -**u** is almost silent, so the first word in the list, for example, is pronounced like **nomimass.**)

Present positive		Present negative	
nomimasu	drink	**nomimasen**	don't drink
ikimasu	go	**ikimasen**	don't go
kimasu	come	**kimasen**	don't come
wakarimasu	understand	**wakarimasen**	don't understand
arimasu	there is, have	**arimasen**	there isn't, don't have
kikimasu	listen, hear, ask	**kikimasen**	don't listen, hear, ask
yomimasu	read	**yomimasen**	don't read
oshiemasu	tell, teach	**oshiemasen**	don't tell, teach
mimasu	see, watch	**mimasen**	don't see, watch
shimasu	do	**shimasen**	don't do
hanashimasu	talk, speak	**hanashimasen**	don't talk, speak
tabemasu	eat	**tabemasen**	don't eat

Because this form of the present tense verb always ends in -**masu** in the positive, it is generally referred to as "the -**masu** form." There is another form, known as the plain form, or dictionary form, because it is the one used to list words in dictionaries (rather like the infinitive is used in English). The plain form of **tabemasu,** for example, is **taberu.** Both have exactly the same meaning, but the tone of **taberu** is much more informal, and the -**masu** form is the one used in everyday polite conversation. We will do some work with the plain form later in the book, but for the moment we will concentrate only on the -**masu** form, although you will find the plain form of new verbs given in the vocabulary lists at the end of each lesson. When you are learning a new verb, you should try to learn both the -**masu** form and the plain form.

2. THE OBJECT PARTICLE – O

Before we go any further with verbs, we need another particle, o, because this points out the direct object of the verb by following directly after it. In other words, it shows what the action of the verb is affecting.

Nihongo o hanashimasu.
I speak Japanese.

Tokidoki eiga o mimasu.
I sometimes watch movies.

Watanabe san wa Eigo o hanashimasen.
Mr. Watanabe doesn't speak English.

Mainichi rajio o kikimasu ka.
Do you listen to the radio every day?

Takahashi san wa sakana o tabemasen.
Ms. Takahashi doesn't eat fish.

Tokidoki sashimi o tabemasu.
I sometimes eat raw fish.

Nihongo no shinbun o yomimasu ka.
Do you read Japanese (language) newspapers?

Takahashi san wa mainichi Eigo no shinbun o yomimasu.
Ms. Takahashi reads an English (language) newspaper every day.

3. THE FUTURE

The **-masu** form is also used to refer to events happening in the future. If it is not clear from the context whether a present or future meaning is intended, then a time word such as "tomorrow/next week/at 2:00" can be used.

Watanabe san wa ashita Tōkyō e ikimasu.
Mr. Watanabe will go to Tokyo tomorrow.

Tomodachi wa asatte Igirisu kara kimasu.
The day after tomorrow, a friend is coming from Britain.

Nani o nomimasu ka.
What will you drink? [This sentence is also used to mean "What would you like to drink?"]

Konban nani o tabemasu ka.
What are you going to eat tonight?

Ashita, oshiemasen.
I'm not teaching tomorrow.

Konban eiga o mimasu ka.
Are you going to see a movie tonight?

Kyō nani o shimasu ka.
What are you going to do today?

Watashi wa kyō kaisha e ikimasen.
I won't be going to the office today.

4. KONO, SONO, ANO AND DONO – THE ADJECTIVES "THIS," "THAT" AND "WHICH?"

In English, the words "this," "that" and "which" can be used as pronouns or adjectives, but this is not the case in Japanese. We came across **kore, sore, are** and **dore** in Lesson 2, but these are used only as pronouns. In other words, they stand by themselves to represent something. There is another set of ko-, so- a- and do- words to use as adjectives: **kono, sono, ano** and **dono**. These words are always accompanied by a noun. Compare the pairs of sentences below.

Kono wain wa doko no desu ka.
Where is this wine from?

Kore wa doko no desu ka.
Where is this from?

Sono konpyūta wa atarashii desu.
That computer's new.

Sore wa atarashii desu.
That's new.

Sono shinbun o yomimasu ka.
Are you going to read that newspaper?

Sore o yomimasu ka.
Are you going to read that?

Ano hito wa dare desu ka.
Who's that person?

Are wa dare desu ka.
Who's that?

Itō san no kuruma wa dono kuruma desu ka.
Which car is Mr. Itò's car?

Itō san no kuruma wa dore desu ka.
Which is Mr. Itò's car?

Dono teishoku ni shimasu ka.
Which set meal are you going to have?

Dore ni shimasu ka.
Which are you going to have?

5. THE TAG QUESTION – NE

The particle **ne** at the end of a sentence plays the same role as tag questions in English, such as "isn't it?," "didn't he?," "aren't they?," "don't you?," "am I right?," etc. Such questions may be asking for confirmation, in which case they have rising intonation, or they may just be asking for agreement, in which case they have falling intonation.

Maiku san wa Amerikajin desu ne.
Mike is an American, isn't he?

Neruson san wa Eigo o oshiemasu ne.
Mr. Nelson will teach English, won't he?

Mainichi Nihongo no shinbun o yomimasu ne.
You read a Japanese newspaper every day, don't you?

Kono wain wa oishii desu ne.
This wine is good, isn't it!

Sono hito wa Itō san desu ne.
That person's Mr. Itō, right?

Kaigi wa asatte desu ne.
The meeting's the day after tomorrow, right?

Tomodachi no namae wa Fukuda san desu ne.
Your friend's name is Ms. Fukuda, isn't it?

6. THE SUBJECT PARTICLE – GA

The particle **ga** marks the subject of a sentence, especially when the information is being introduced for the first time. When the information is already known, and so is already the topic of conversation, then the topic marker **wa** is used. In some ways, the difference between **wa** and **ga** is similar to the difference betwen "the" and "a."

Asoko ni atarashii resutoran ga arimasu ne. Sono resutoran wa oishii desu.
There's a new restaurant over there, right? That restaurant [= the restaurant] is really good.

Konban Takahashi san no tomodachi ga kimasu ne. Sono tomodachi wa doko no hito desu ka. Kanadajin desu ka.
This evening Ms. Takahashi's friend is arriving, right? Where's the friend from? Is he Canadian?

A. Koko ni denwa ga arimasu ka.
Is there a telephone here?

B. Hai, denwa wa asoko ni arimasu.
Yes, the phone's over there.

Question words like **nani, doko** and **dare** by their very nature are asking about unknown information, so they can't be topics. Therefore, they always take **ga**, not **wa**, when they are the subject of a sentence.

Dare ga ashita Yokohama e ikimasu ka.
Who's going to Yokohama tomorrow?

Wain wa, nani ga arimasu ka.
What (kind of) wine do you have? [Lit: As for wine, what is there?]

Resutoran wa doko ga ii desu ka.
Where is there a good restaurant? [Lit: With regard to restaurants, where is good?]

There are certain verbs which usually take the subject particle **ga**, and one of these is **wakarimasu**, "to understand/know." The person understanding or knowing is marked by **wa**, and the thing understood or known is marked by **ga**.

Watanabe san wa Eigo ga wakarimasu ka.
Does Mr. Watanabe understand English?

(Watashi wa) Maiku san no tomodachi no namae ga wakarimasen.
I don't know Mike's friend's name.

Another verb which takes **ga** is **arimasu** when it indicates possession or the meaning "have."

Kono daigaku ni atarashii konpyūta ga arimasu.
This university has some new computers.

Maiku san wa kyō kaigi ga arimasu ne.
You have a meeting today, don't you, Mike? [Lit: As regards you, there is a meeting.]

7. SUKI DESU/KIRAI DESU – "I LIKE IT/I HATE IT"

Unlike English, the Japanese words for "like," "hate" and the various shades in between are not verbs, so they need to be followed by **desu**. The subject of such a sentence is the thing or person liked or disliked, and so is followed by **wa** or **ga**. Here are some sentences to show how to say the various degrees of like and dislike, which are **dai suki desu** ("I like very much"), **suki desu** ("I like"), **amari suki ja arimasen** ("I don't like very much"), **kirai desu** ("I dislike"), and **dai-kirai desu** ("I loathe").

(Watashi wa) sashimi ga dai-suki desu.
I love raw fish.

Hana wa, nani ga suki desu ka.
What kind of flowers do you like? [Lit: As for flowers, what do you like?]

Maiku san wa eiga ga suki desu ne.
Mike likes (going to) movies, doesn't he?

(Watashi wa) ano resutoran ga amari suki ja arimasen.
I don't like that restaurant very much.

Sakana ga kirai desu ka.
Don't you like fish? [Lit: Do you dislike fish?]

Ano sensei ga dai-kirai desu.
I loathe that teacher.

8. — O KUDASAI – ASKING FOR SOMETHING

The word **kudasai** means "please give me," although it sounds politer than that in Japanese, and can be translated into English in several different ways. When you want someone to give you something – for example in a restaurant, or when shopping – simply say what you want and add **o kudasai**.

Sumimasen, mizu o kudasai.
Excuse me, could I have some water, please?

A. **Nani o nomimasu ka.**
   What would you like to drink? [Lit: What will you drink?]
B. **Wain o kudasai.**
   Wine, please.

Mainichi Shinbun o kudasai.
I'd like the Mainichi Newspaper please.

Sashimi teishoku o kudasai.
I'd like the sashimi (raw fish) set meal, please.

9. ITADAKIMASU – TABLE MANNERS

The word **itadakimasu** is always said just before eating or drinking something, so it is like "Enjoy the meal" or the French "bon appetit." Do make sure you say this set phrase as it shows appreciation of what you are receiving. After a meal, the phrase **go-chisō sama deshita** is always said. This is a set phrase of thanks for the meal, whether you are at home, in a restaurant, or at someone else's house.

VOCABULARY

amari: not very [+ negative verb]
ano: that — over there [adjective]
asatte: the day after tomorrow
ashita: tomorrow
dai-kirai desu: hate, detest, loathe
dai-suki desu: like very much, love
dō: how?
— **wa dō desu ka:** how about —?
dono: which? [adjective]
eiga: movie, film
Eigo: English language
ga: [particle indicating subject of verb]
go-chisō sama deshita: thank you for the meal
gohan: cooked rice
hana: flower
hanashimasu: speak, talk [from **hanasu**]
ii: good, fine
ikimasu: go [from **iku**]
itadakimasu: good appetite, bon appetit
kaigi: a meeting
kikimasu: hear, listen, ask [from **kiku**]
kiku: chrysanthemum
kimasu: come [from **kuru**]
kirai desu: dislike
konban: this evening
kono: this [adjective]
mainichi: every day
mimasu: see, watch [from **miru**]

miso shiru: miso soup
mizu: water
nan/nani: what?
ne: isn't it, aren't they, don't you
— **ni shimasu:** I'll have/decide on —
nomimasu: drink [from **nomu**]
— **o kudasai:** could I have —, please?
o: [particle to indicate object of verb]
o-cha: green tea
oishii: tasty, delicious
oshiemasu: tell, teach [from **oshieru**]
rajio: radio
resutoran: restaurant
sakana: fish
sashimi: raw fish
shimasu: do [from **suru**]
sono: that [adjective]
suki desu: like
suki ja arimasen: don't like
sumimasen ga ...: I'm sorry but ...
tabemasu: eat [from **taberu**]
teishoku: set meal
tokidoki: sometimes
tomodachi: friend
tsukemono: pickles
wain: wine
wakarimasu: understand [from **wakaru**]
yaki-zakana: grilled fish
yomimasu: read [from **yomu**]

TEST YOURSELF

1. *Read through the dialog at the beginning of the lesson once more, and then say if the following statements are true or false.*

   1. Sono resutoran wa, sakana ga oishii desu. T/F

   2. Maiku san wa sashimi teishoku ni shimasu. T/F

   3. Maiku san wa miso shiru ga kirai desu. T/F

4. Nihonjin wa tokidoki kiku o tabemasu.   T/F

5. Maiku san to Watanabe san wa o-cha o nomimasu.   T/F

2. *If you were in a restaurant, how would you ask for:*

1. some water?

2. some green tea?

3. the grilled fish set meal?

4. some wine?

5. raw fish?

6. that [pointing to what someone else is having]?

3. *Look at the following pictures, and use them to make up questions and answers as in the example. (Remember that a small circle means a positive answer, and a cross means a negative answer.) If you are working with a partner, ask each other the questions and get true answers, then try to make up some new examples.*

Example:

Every day?
Q. Mainichi shinbun o yomimasu ka.
A. Hai, mainichi (shinbun o) yomimasu.

1. Tomorrow?

Q:

A:

2. Every day?

Q:

A:

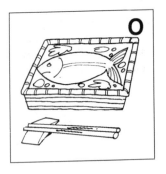

3. Today?

Q:

A:

4. Sometimes?

Q:

A:

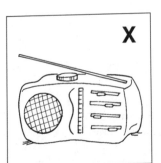

5. Every day?

Q:

A:

4. *Choose the appropriate particle – **wa, ga, o, no** or **e** – to complete the following sentences.*

1. Maiku san _____, nani _____ nomimasu ka.

2. Watashi _____ eiga _____ dai-suki desu.

3. Mainichi Eigo _____ shinbun _____ yomimasu ka.

4. Nihongo _____ wakarimasu ka.

5. Tanaka san _____ ashita Tōkyō _____ ikimasu ne.

6. Are _____ dare _____ kuruma desu ka.

5. *How would you say these sentences in Japanese?*

1. Do you understand English?

2. What are you doing this evening?

3. I don't really like raw fish.

4. What are you going to teach, Ms. Tanaka?

5. Which movie are you going to see this evening?

6. This university's big, isn't it?

大好 **Dai-suki** is made up of the characters for "big/great" and "like," so the two together mean "like very much/love."

GO-JI HAN NI AIMASHŌ.

LET'S MEET AT 5:30.

Ms. Takahashi wants to see a movie tonight, so she calls her boyfriend, Kenji Matsuda, who's a student, to see if he would like to go. However, he doesn't seem too enthusiastic about the idea.

Matsuda	**Moshi moshi, Matsuda desu ga.** Hello, this is Matsuda.
Takahashi	**Moshi moshi. Kenji? Keiko desu ga.** Hello. Kenji? This is Keiko.
Matsuda	**Ā, Keiko chan, konbanwa. Ima doko desu ka.** Ah, Keiko, evening. Where are you at the moment?
Takahashi	**Uchi ni imasu. Ne, Kenji, konban nani o shimasu ka.** I'm at home. Hey, Kenji, what are you doing this evening?
Matsuda	**Mada wakarimasen ga ...** I don't know yet, but ...

Takahashi	**Kenji, eiga wa dō desu ka. Eiga o mimashō.** Kenji, how about a movie? Let's see a movie.
Matsuda	**Eiga desu ka.** A movie?
Takahashi	**Hai, konban ii eiga ga arimasu. "Anata No Ashita"** **desu. Roku-ji han ni hajimarimasu. Ikimashō ka.** Yes, there's a good movie tonight. It's "Your Tomorrow." It starts at 6:30. Shall we go?
Matsuda	**Roku-ji han ni? Demo, ima roku-ji desu ne. Jikan ga** **arimasen.** At 6:30? But it's 6:00 now, isn't it? There isn't time.
Takahashi	**Ii desu. Takushii de ikimashō.** It's okay. Let's go by taxi.
Matsuda	**Demo ... sono eiga wa SF (ess efu) desu ne. Watashi** **wa SF ga amari suki ja arimasen.** But .... that movie is science-fiction, isn't it. I don't really like science-fiction.
Takahashi	**E? Suki ja arimasen ka. Demo ...** Eh? You don't like it? But ...
Matsuda	**Sore kara, ashita Eigo no tesuto ga arimasu. Konban** **tesuto benkyō o shimasu. Ja, ashita hanashimashō.** And also, I have an English test tomorrow. Tonight I'll study for the test. Well, let's talk tomorrow.
Takahashi	**E? Nan desu ka? Eigo no benkyō?** Eh? What? English study?
Matsuda	**Ja, shitsurei shimasu. Mata ashita.** Well, excuse me. Until tomorrow.

He hangs up, and Keiko Takahashi is left wondering about the cause
of his odd behavior. Somewhat upset, she decides to pour out her
woes to her friend, Yoko Abe, and calls to see if she's in.

Abe	**Moshi moshi, Abe desu ga.** Hello, this is Abe.
Takahashi	**Moshi moshi, Yoko san? Keiko desu. Ne, Yoko san,** **konban uchi ni imasu ka.** Hello, Yoko san? This is Keiko. Hey, are you at home this evening?
Abe	**Hai, imasu. Dō shite desu ka.** Yes, I am. Why?

Takahashi	Hanashi ga arimasu. Ima roku-ji jup-pun desu ne. Ja, takushii de ikimasu. Ii desu ka.
	I have something to talk about. It's 6:10 now, isn't it. Right, I'll come by taxi. Is that all right?
Abe	Hai, ii desu. Dōzo dōzo.
	Yes, it's fine. Come on over.
Takahashi	Arigatō. Ja, sugu ikimasu.
	Thanks. I'll come soon.

STRUCTURE AND USAGE NOTES

1. MOSHI MOSHI – TELEPHONE PHRASES

Here are some commonly-used sentences that you might need if you make a telephone call in Japanese.

Moshi moshi.
Hello? [This is usually said by both parties, and is a phrase used almost exclusively on the telephone.]

Tanaka san desu ka.
Is this Mr. Tanaka?

Tanaka san wa irasshaimasu ka.
Is Mr. Tanaka there? [The verb **irasshaimasu** is a very polite form of **imasu**, "to be."]

Tanaka san onegai shimasu.
Mr. Tanaka, please.

Harisu desu.
This is (Mr.) Harris.

Sumisu Enjiniaringu no Harisu desu.
This is (Mr.) Harris, from Smith Engineering.

The following phrases are all polite ways of finishing a telephone conversation. In English we tend to say "Goodbye" and then hang up, but in Japanese it is a longer process, and you can say any combination or all of these phrases to wind up the conversation.

Yoroshiku onegai shimasu.
[Lit: Please treat me well, or Please look kindly on me.]

Shitsurei shimasu.
Excuse me.

Gomen kudasai.
Pardon me for any inconvenience.

2. CHAN, SAN OR SAMA?

The usual way of addressing someone is to say **san** after their name, but you might also hear **chan** and **sama** sometimes. **Chan** is an informal, affectionate term of address, and is used to small children, younger members of the family, and young women. **Sama** is a very formal and polite form of address, and may be used, for example, to customers in a department store by the sales assistants.

3. IMASU AND ARIMASU – "TO BE"

The verbs **imasu** (from **iru**) and **arimasu** (from **aru**) both mean "to be/exist," but there is a very important difference between them. **Imasu** is used only to refer to the existence or location of animate objects, such as people, animals and fish, whereas **arimasu** is used only to refer to inanimate objects, such as tables, chairs and buildings. Compare the following pairs of sentences.

Kyō no shinbun wa doko ni arimasu ka.	**Watanabe san wa doko ni imasu ka.**
Where's today's newspaper?	Where's Mr. Watanabe?
Uchi ni terebi ga arimasen.	**Uchi ni inu ga imasen.**
We don't have a television at home.[Lit: At home, there isn't a television.]	We don't have a dog at home. [Lit: At home, there isn't a dog.]
Tōkyō ni wa, ii resutoran ga takusan arimasu.	**Tōkyō ni wa, gaijin ga takusan imasu.**
In Tokyo, there are a lot of good restaurants.	In Tokyo, there are a lot of foreigners.

4. MADA – "STILL" OR "NOT YET"

When **mada** is followed by a positive verb, it can be translated as "still" in the sense of something remaining as it was some time ago.

Gohan wa mada takusan arimasu.
There's still a lot of rice.

Maiku san wa mada gakkō ni imasu ka.
Is Mike still at the school?

Kōhii wa mada arimasu.
I still have some coffee.

When **mada** is followed by a negative verb, it can usually be translated as "(not) yet."

Nihongo ga mada wakarimasen.
I don't understand Japanese yet.

Takushii wa mada kimasen ne.
The taxi hasn't come yet, has it?

Kaigi wa mada hajimarimasen.
The meeting hasn't started yet.

The phrase **Mada desu** by itself means "Not yet."

5. MAKING SUGGESTIONS USING -MASHŌ

If you want to suggest doing something, then the way to express it is to change the final -**masu** of the verb to -**mashō**. This usually corresponds to "Let's —" in English.

Ashita Yokohama e ikimashō.
Let's go to Yokohama tomorrow.

Kā rajio o kikimashō.
Let's listen to the car radio.

Nihongo o benkyō shimashō.
Let's study Japanese.

Nihongo de hanashimashō.
Let's talk in Japanese.

Kōhii o nomimashō.
Let's have [Lit: drink] some coffee.

If you turn it into a question, then it becomes the equivalent of "Shall we —?" or "Shall I —?"

Kyō wa nani o shimashō ka.
What shall we do today?

Nani o tabemashō ka. Sakana ni shimashō ka.
What shall we eat? Shall we have fish?

Terebi o mimashō ka.
Shall we watch television?

6. TELLING THE TIME

To say the hours, first you'll need to know the numbers up to twelve.

1	ichi	5	go	9	kyū/ku
2	ni	6	roku	10	jū
3	san	7	shichi/nana	11	jū-ichi
4	yo/yon/shi	8	hachi	12	jū-ni

As you can see, there are different ways of saying the numbers 4, 7 and 9, and which one you use depends on what you are counting. In the case of saying the hour when telling the time, use the **yo** (4), **shichi** (7) and **ku** (9) alternatives. The hour is indicated by adding **-ji** to the number.

Ichi-ji desu.
It's one o'clock.

Yo-ji desu.
It's four o'clock.

Ima nan-ji desu ka. Shichi-ji desu ka.
What time is it now? Is it seven o'clock?

Next, the minutes. First, let's look at how to say plain numbers up to 99, then we'll add the word for "minutes." To begin with, here are the numbers from 11 to 19. You'll see that they are simply the equivalents of "ten-one, ten-two, ten-three," etc.

11	jū-ichi	14	jū-yon/shi	17	jū-shichi/nana
12	jū-ni	15	jū-go	18	jū-hachi
13	jū-san	16	jū-roku	19	jū-kyū/ku

To count in tens, think of the numbers as corresponding to "two tens, three tens, four tens," etc.

10	jū	40	yon-jū	70	shichi/nana-jū
20	ni-jū	50	go-jū	80	hachi-jū
30	san-jū	60	roku-jū	90	kyū/ku-jū

Finally, counting numbers in between is simply a matter of building up from what you already know. For example, think of the number twenty-one as "two-tens, one," or **ni-jū ichi.** Here are some more examples.

23	ni-jū-san	57	go-jū-nana	
34	san-jū-yon	68	roku-jū-hachi	
45	yon-jū-go	89	hachi-jū-kyū	

The word for "minutes" is **fun**, although this often changes to **pun** depending on the sound which precedes it. Here is a list of how to say the minutes up to ten.

1 minute	**ip-pun**	6 minutes	**rop-pun**
2 minutes	**ni-fun**	7 minutes	**nana-fun**
3 minutes	**san-pun**	8 minutes	**hap-pun**
4 minutes	**yon-pun**	9 minutes	**kyū-fun**
5 minutes	**go-fun**	10 minutes	**jup-pun**

When telling the time, the particle **ni** is used as an equivalent of "at." Here are some examples of times.

go-ji jup-pun ni
at 5:10

san-ji ni-jup-pun ni
at 3:20

roku-ji ni-jū-go-fun ni
at 6:25

hachi-ji yon-jū-go-fun ni
at 8:45

The word **han**, or "half," is often used instead of **san-jup-pun**.

jū-ji han ni
at 10:30

jū-ni-ji han ni
at 12:30

Here are some sentences to show how these time words are used.

Ni-ji han ni aimashō.
Let's meet at 2:30.

Ichi-ji no nyūsu o mimashō.
Let's watch the one o'clock news.

Takahashi san wa ashita no san-ji ni kimasu.
Ms. Takahashi will come at 3:00 tomorrow.

Shigoto wa hachi-ji go-jup-pun ni hajimarimasu.
Work begins at 8:50.

Nihon no ginkō wa ku-ji kara desu.
Japanese banks (are) open from 9:00.

A. **Kaigi wa nan-ji kara nan-ji made desu ka.**
   What time is the meeting? (Lit: From what time to what time ...?)
B. **Jū-ji kara jū-ichi-ji han made desu.**
   It's from 10:00 to 11:30.

7. TAKUSHII DE – "BY TAXI"

One use of the particle **de** is to show the instrument or means by which something is done. (We will meet another use of **de** in the next lesson.)

San-ji no densha de ikimashō.
Let's go by the 3:00 train.

Nihongo de hanashimashō.
Let's speak in Japanese.

Sushi o hashi de tabemasu ka.
Do you eat sushi with chopsticks?

Eiga no jikan wa, denwa de kikimasu.
I'll call and ask the time of the movie. [Lit: The time of the movie, I'll ask by telephone.]

Mainichi nyūsu o rajio de kikimasu.
I listen to the news every day on the radio.

8. BENKYŌ O SHIMASU – AND OTHER VERBS WHICH USE SHIMASU

There are a number of verbs which are made up of a noun with **shimasu**. Here are some of them. The object particle **o** is optional.

benkyō study, work	**benkyō (o) shimasu** to study
denwa a telephone	**denwa (o) shimasu** to telephone, call
shigoto work, employment	**shigoto (o) shimasu** to work
tenisu tennis	**tenisu (o) shimasu** to play tennis
hanashi a talk, conversation	**hanashi (o) shimasu** to have a conversation

Ashita, tomodachi to tenisu o shimasu.
I'm going to play tennis with a friend tomorrow.

Itō san wa tokidoki shichi-ji made shigoto shimasu.
Mr. Itō sometimes works until 7:00.

Nan-ji ni denwa shimashō ka.
What time shall I call you?

Neruson san wa ashita kara Nihongo no benkyō o shimasu.
Mr. Nelson will be studying Japanese from tomorrow.

9. KIMASU VS. IKIMASU – "COME" AND "GO"

The verbs **kimasu** ("come") and **ikimasu** ("go") are sometimes used in a slightly different way from English, as you can see in Keiko Takahashi's conversation with her friend Yoko Abe in the dialog. Keiko says **Takushii de ikimasu** and **Sugu ikimasu**, where in English we would say "I'll come by taxi," and "I'll come soon." This is because **ikimasu** means to leave where you are now, regardless of where you're going, whereas the English "go" means to leave where you are now and go anywhere except where the person you are speaking to is.

A. **Ashita, watashi no uchi ni kimasu ka.**
   Are you coming over to my house tomorrow?
B. **Hai, ikimasu. Nan-ji ni ikimashō ka.**
   Yes, I am. What time shall I come?

VOCABULARY

aimashō: let's meet [from **au**]
benkyō (o) shimasu: to study [from **benkyō suru**]
benkyō: study [noun]
chan: [used instead of **san** for girls and small children]
de: by [particle indicating means by which something is done]
demo: however, but [at the beginning of a sentence]
densha: train
dō shite: why?
dōzo dōzo: please do so, please go ahead
-fun/pun: minute
gaijin: foreigner
go: five
gomen kudasai: pardon me for causing any inconvenience
hachi: eight
hajimarimasu: to begin [from **hajimaru**]
-han: half past —
hanashi: a talk, conversation, chat
hanashi o shimasu: have a talk, chat [from **hanashi o suru**]

hanashimashō: let's talk [from **hanasu**]
hashi: chopsticks
ichi: one
ikimashō ka: shall we go? [from **iku**]
ima: now, at the moment
imasu: am, is, are [used with animate objects, from **iru**]
inu: dog
irasshaimasu: is, are [very polite form of **imasu**, from **irassharu**]
-ji: — o'clock
jikan: time, hour
jū: ten
jū-ichi: eleven
jū-ni: twelve
jup-pun: ten minutes
kā rajio: car radio
kyū/ku: nine
mada: still, (not) yet
made: until
mata: again, once more, another time
mata ashita: until tomorrow, see you tomorrow [informal]
mimashō: let's see [from **miru**]
moshi moshi: hello? [only on the telephone]
nan-ji: what time?
nana/shichi: seven
ni: at [when giving the time]
ni: two
nyūsu: the news
— onegai shimasu: could I speak to —?
roku-ji: six o'clock
roku: six
sama: Mr., Mrs., Ms., Miss [very polite]
san: three
SF (ess efu): science-fiction
shi/yo/yon: four
shichi/nana: seven
shigoto shimasu: to work
shigoto: work, employment
shitsurei shimasu: goodbye [on the telephone]
sore kara: and also
sugu: soon
takusan: a lot of, many, much
takushii de: by taxi
tenisu: tennis
terebi: television, TV

tesuto: a test
yon/yo/shi: four
yoroshiku onegai shimasu: goodbye [on the telephone] [Lit: please treat me well]

TEST YOURSELF

1. *Read through the dialog at the beginning of the lesson once more, and then say if the following statements are true or false.*

   1. Keiko san wa ima uchi ni imasen.   T/F

   2. Eiga wa roku-ji kara desu.   T/F

   3. Kenji san wa SF ga suki ja arimasen.   T/F

   4. Kenji san no Eigo no tesuto wa ashita desu.   T/F

   5. Konban Kenji san to Keiko san wa eiga o mimasen.   T/F

   6. Keiko san wa takushii de Yoko san no uchi e ikimasu. T/F

2. *How would you say the following times?*

   1. 4:00   2. 2:30   3. 9:45
   4. 11:40   5. 1:30   6. 6:15

3. *In tomorrow's English class, Mike will be teaching the students how to talk about their daily schedule, so he has just written out his own schedule to use as a sample. Look at the information below, and make up some sentences about what he does each day, and when, as in the examples.*

Example:

7:00	news on TV
10:10–12:10	teach English

Shichi-ji ni terebi no nyūsu o mimasu.
Jū-ji jup-pun kara jū-ni-ji jup-pun made Eigo o oshiemasu.

7:15	coffee
7:30–7:45	news on radio
8:00	go to station
8:45–4:45	work
6:00	read paper
7:00–8:30	study Japanese
9:30–11:00	TV

4. *How would you say the following sentences in Japanese?*

1. Let's meet at 7:30.

2. I'm going to study Japanese from tomorrow.

3. Shall we watch the news on TV?

4. What time does tomorrow's meeting begin?

5. Let's go to the station by taxi.

6. Is there any wine left?

5. *Ms. Takahashi is still irritated at the response of her boyfriend on the telephone, and in a fit of daring she decides to call Mike Nelson to see if he would like to see the movie with her. Complete their conversation by filling in the blanks.*

Mike   (Hello?) _____ _____, Neruson desu ga.

Takahashi   (Hello?) _____ _____, Neruson san?
Takahashi desu. Takahashi Keiko.

Mike   Ā Takahashi san, (good evening) _____.

Takahashi   (Good evening.) _____. Ne, Neruson
san, (you like movies, don't you?) _____ ____
_____ _____ ___.

Mike   (Yes, I do.) _____, _____ _____.

LESSON 4   45

Takahashi	Neruson san wa ashita (do you have some time?) _____ _____ _____ ____. Eiga o mimasen ka.
Mike	Ii desu ne. Nani o mimasu ka.
Takahashi	"Anata no Ashita" o mimasu ga.
Mike	(That's a good movie, isn't it.) _____ ____ ____ _____ _____ _____. SF desu ne.
Takahashi	(Yes, it is.) _____, _____ _____. SF wa dō desu ka.
Mike	Hai, SF ga dai-suki desu. (What time shall we meet?) _____ _____ _____ ____.
Takahashi	Roku-ji wa dō desu ka. (The movie starts at 6:30.) _____ ____ _____ ____ _____.
Mike	Ja, roku-ji ni (let's meet) _____.
Takahashi	Dewa, (until tomorrow.) _____ _____.
Mike	Hai, (until tomorrow.) _____ _____. Shitsurei shimasu.

勉強　Benkyō is made up of the kanji characters for "hard work/effort" and "strong," and the combination means "study."

MONDAI GA ARIMASU YO!
I HAVE A PROBLEM!

Keiko Takahashi has just hailed a taxi to take her to her friend's house, which is near Yamate station.

Takahashi **Yamate eki made onegai shimasu.**
To Yamate station, please.

Taxi driver **Hai, wakarimashita.**
Yes, got it.

They arrive at Yamate station, and Ms. Takahashi gives the driver instructions from there to Yoko's house.

Taxi driver **Hai, Yamate eki desu yo.**
We're here at Yamate station.

Takahashi **Mō eki desu ka. Ja, koko o migi ni magatte kudasai.**
The station already? Well, please turn right here.

Taxi driver **Koko desu ka.**
Here?

Takahashi	Hai, sō desu. Sore kara, massugu itte kudasai. Asoko ni ōkii tatemono ga arimasu ne. Yes, that's right. And then, please go straight ahead. There is a large building over there, right?
Taxi driver	Hidari-gawa desu ka. On the left-hand side?
Takahashi	Hai, sō desu. Asoko de ii desu. Asoko de tomete kudasai. Ikura desu ka. Yes, that's right. Over there is fine. Please stop there. How much is it?
Taxi driver	Sen ni-hyaku en desu. One thousand, two hundred yen.
Takahashi	Ja, kore, ni-sen en desu. Here's two thousand yen.
Taxi driver	Hai, hap-pyaku en no o-tsuri desu. Dōzo. Right, eight hundred yen change. Here you are.
Takahashi	Dōmo arigatō. Thank you.

She gets out of the taxi, and walks the last few meters to Yoko Abe's house. She opens the door to the house and calls out.

Takahashi	Gomen kudasai. Hello? Excuse me!
Abe	Ā, Keiko san. Konbanwa. Dōzo, agatte kudasai. Surippa, dōzo. Ah, Keiko. Good evening. Please come in. [Lit: Please come up.] Here, have some slippers.
Takahashi	(taking off her shoes, and stepping into the slippers provided) O-jama shimasu. Excuse me for disturbing you.
Abe	Dōzo, kochira e. Kōhii wa ikaga desu ka. This way. Would you like some coffee?
Takahashi	Itadakimasu. Yes, please.
Abe	Tokorode, Keiko san, ano hanashi wa? Nan no hanashi desu ka. Mondai ga arimasu ka. By the way, Keiko, that chat ... What did you want to talk about? Do you have a problem?

Takahashi Kenji desu yo! Dō shimashō ka. Kenji wa mō watashi
ga suki ja nai desu yo!
It's Kenji! What shall I do? Kenji doesn't like me any
more!

STRUCTURE AND USAGE NOTES

1. ASKING FAVORS USING ONEGAI SHIMASU

The phrase **onegai shimasu** can be used instead of **kudasai** when you
are asking for something.

Kōhii o onegai shimasu./Kōhii o kudasai.
Coffee, please.

Mizu o onegai shimasu./Mizu o kudasai.
Could I have some water, please?

It can also mean "Please do that," when used in response to someone
offering to do something for you.

A. **Ashita denwa shimashō ka.**
Shall I phone (you) tomorrow?
B. **Hai, onegai shimasu.**
Yes, please.

A. **Eigo de hanashimashō ka.**
Shall I speak in English?
B. **Onegai shimasu.**
Please.

A. **Namae to jūsho o kakimashō ka.**
Shall I write down my name and address?
B. **Hai, onegai shimasu.**
Yes, please.

2. SHOWING EMPHASIS WITH YO

The particle **yo** at the end of a sentence doesn't have any meaning in
itself, but is used to give the sentence emphasis, so it acts like an
exclamation mark in English. Compare the following pairs of
sentences.

Watashi no sūtsukēsu desu.   **Watashi no sūtsukēsu desu yo.**
It's my suitcase.   Hey, it's *my* suitcase!

Nihon no kuruma desu.	Nihon no kuruma desu yo.
It's a Japanese car.	It's a *Japanese* car!

Ii desu.	Ii desu yo.
It's okay.	Hey, it's okay!

3. MŌ – "ALREADY" AND "(NOT) ANY MORE"

When **mō** is used with a positive verb, it corresponds to the English "already," indicating that something is not in the same condition as it was a while ago.

Mō jū-ji desu.
It's already 10:00.

Mō Kyōto desu ka.
Are we in Kyoto already?

Kenji san wa mō daigakusei desu ka.
Is Kenji at university [Lit: a university student] already?

When **mō** is used with a negative verb, it corresponds to "(not) any more."

Mō sono resutoran e wa ikimasen.
I'm not going to that restaurant any more.

Mondai wa mō arimasen.
I don't have any problems any more.

4. -TE KUDASAI – MAKING REQUESTS

So far we have only come across the -masu form of verbs, and now it is time to introduce the -te form, so-called because it always ends in -te. The -te form has many uses, and in some ways corresponds to the "-ing" form in English (and like the "-ing" form, it has no tense, and cannot exist by itself to form a sentence). In this lesson you'll learn how to use the -te form to make requests.

The formation of the -te form is very regular, but it is somewhat involved, so although we have given a brief explanation of the rules, you might prefer simply to learn the -te form of verbs by heart from the list below.

To find out how to make the -te form, first you need to know the plain form, or dictionary form, of the verb, which you have come across so far only in the vocabulary lists at the end of each lesson. Japanese verbs can be divided into two groups. One group is of verbs which end in **-iru** or **-eru** in the plain form. To make the **-masu** form, the **-ru** ending is dropped. Look at the list below showing the dictionary form, **-masu** form and **-te** form of some **-iru/-eru** verbs.

dictionary form	meaning	-masu form	-te form
tabe-ru	eat	tabemasu	tabete
oshie-ru	teach, tell	oshiemasu	oshiete
i-ru	be, exist	imasu	ite
mi-ru	see, watch	mimasu	mite
tome-ru	stop, halt	tomemasu	tomete

The other group is of verbs which drop the final **-u** from the dictionary form, and then add **-imasu** to make the **-masu** form. This group contains all verbs which do *not* end in **-eru** or **-iru**, and also a few verbs which do. As you can see from the list of **-u** verbs below, the **-te** form ending varies depending on the sound which comes before it.

dictionary form	meaning	-masu form	-te form
yom-u	drink	yomimasu	yonde
nom-u	read	nomimasu	nonde
ar-u	be, exist	arimasu	atte
hajimar-u	begin	hajimarimasu	hajimatte
wakar-u	understand	wakarimasu	wakatte
a-u	meet	aimasu	atte
chiga-u	differ	chigaimasu	chigatte
mats-u	wait	machimasu	matte
hanas-u	speak, talk	hanashimasu	hanashite
kik-u	hear, ask	kikimasu	kiite
kak-u	write	kakimasu	kaite

(**Iku** is an exception to the rule for **-ku** verbs.)

ik-u	go	ikimasu	itte

The only two irregular verbs are **kuru** ("come") and **suru** ("do").

kuru	come	kimasu	kite
suru	do	shimasu	shite

When the **-te** form is followed by **kudasai**, it is a way of asking someone to do something.

Yukkuri hanashite kudasai.
Please speak slowly.

Yukkuri itte kudasai.
Please go slowly.

Namae to jūsho o kaite kudasai.
Please write your name and address.

Go-ji han ni kite kudasai.
Please come at 5:30.

Konban denwa shite kudasai.
Please call me this evening.

Sensei no hanashi o kiite kudasai.
Listen to what the teacher has to say.

Hon o mite kudasai.
Please look at your books.

5. ANOTHER USE OF THE PARTICLE DE – TO SHOW LOCATION

The particle **de** is used to indicate the place where something happens, so it can usually be translated as "at" or "in." (You may remember from Lesson 2 that the particle ni also points out location, but **ni** is only used to indicate the place where something or someone exists, so it is only used with the verbs **iru/imasu** and **aru/arimasu**.)

Ano atarashii resutoran de tabemashō.
Let's eat at that new restaurant.

Doko de aimashō ka.
Where shall we meet?

Ashita uchi de benkyō shimasu.
I'm going to study at home tomorrow.

Koko de machimasu.
I'll wait here.

Itō san wa Amerika de Eigo o benkyō shimasu.
Mr. Itō is going to study English in America.

6. UNDERSTANDING DIRECTIONS

It is not always easy to find your way around a city in Japan, as only the largest streets are given names, and addresses are based on numbered areas, with the numbers not always running consecutively. This means that it is almost impossible to find someone's house or office building just from the address if you are not familiar with the area, and so you will need to ask for directions. If you are going by taxi, then you will probably have to give directions to the taxi driver, unless you are going to a famous landmark that he is likely to know. Otherwise, you should get a friend or co-worker to draw a map or write directions in Japanese, and then you can just hand this to the taxi driver.

Here are some useful sentences for giving and understanding directions.

Koko made onegai shimasu.
(as you hand over the map and directions of where you want to go)
To this place, please.

Massugu itte kudasai.
Please go straight ahead.

Mō sukoshi massugu itte kudasai.
Please go a little further ahead.

Koko de migi ni magatte kudasai.
Please turn right here.

Shingō de hidari ni magatte kudasai.
Please turn left at the traffic lights.

Tsugi no shingō de migi ni magatte kudasai.
Please turn right at the next traffic lights.

Tsugi no kado de tomete kudasai.
Please stop at the next corner.

Koko de ii desu.
This [Lit: here] is fine.

Hidari-gawa ni arimasu.
It's on the left-hand side.

Gakkō wa migi-gawa ni arimasu.
The school is on the right-hand side.

7. HUNDREDS AND THOUSANDS

The word for "hundred" is **hyaku**, although the beginning of the word changes sometimes depending on the sound which comes before it. Here's how to count in hundreds.

100 **hyaku**	400 **yon-hyaku**	700 **nana-hyaku**
200 **ni-hyaku**	500 **go-hyaku**	800 **hap-pyaku**
300 **san-byaku**	600 **rop-pyaku**	900 **kyū-hyaku**

Numbers in Japanese are very regular, so to make any numbers in between, simply build up from what you already know. For example, 235 is the equivalent of "two hundreds, three tens, five," or **ni-hyaku san-jū-go**. Here are some more examples. See if you can work them out yourself before looking at the Japanese.

126 **hyaku ni-jū-roku**	491 **yon-hyaku kyū-ju-ichi**
345 **san-byaku yon-jū-go**	633 **rop-pyaku san-jū-san**
810 **hap-pyaku jū**	505 **go-hyaku go**

The word for "thousand" is **sen**, although, like the hundreds, there are some phonetic changes depending on the sound which precedes **sen**.

1,000 **sen**	4,000 **yon-sen**	7,000 **nana-sen**
2,000 **ni-sen**	5,000 **go-sen**	8,000 **has-sen**
3,000 **san-zen**	6,000 **roku-sen**	9,000 **kyū-sen**

Here are some more examples of large numbers.

2,350 **ni-sen san-byaku go-jū**
4,500 **yon-sen go-hyaku**
7,468 **nana-sen yon-hyaku roku-jū-hachi**
8,055 **has-sen go-jū-go**

A. **Sumimasen, kore wa ikura desu ka.**
   Excuse me, how much is this?
B. **Sore wa ni-sen go-hyaku go-jū en desu.**
   It's 2,550 yen.

A. **Ii hon desu ne. Amerika no hon desu ka.**
   Nice book, isn't it. Is it American?
B. **Hai, sō desu. Kono hon wa Amerika de ni-jū doru desu ga, Nihon de wa nana-sen go-hyaku en desu.**
   Yes, it is. In America this book is twenty dollars, but in Japan it's 7,500 yen.

8. VISITING SOMEONE'S HOME

If you are lucky enough to be invited to someone's home in Japan, there are a number of set phrases of greeting and a set procedure that you should know. Just inside the door is the **genkan**, an area where you leave your shoes before you step up to the level of the rest of the house. As the genkan is not really considered to be a part of the inside of the house, it is acceptable to open the door and step inside (although in newer houses or apartments you will need to ring the bell instead). Then call out:

Gomen kudasai.
Hello? Is there anyone home?

When you are invited in, step out of your shoes and up to the higher level of the house, being careful not to put your feet down on the floor of the genkan after you have taken your shoes off. Slippers are always provided. As you step up, say:

Shitsurei shimasu.
Excuse me.
or
O-jama shimasu.
Pardon me for disturbing you.

If you are shown into a Western-style room, then keep your slippers on, but if you go into a Japanese-style room with tatami-mat flooring, then step out of your slippers as you enter the room. You will then be invited to sit down, and probably offered some green tea.

A. **Dōzo, o-kake kudasai.** [or **Dōzo, suwatte kudasai.**]
   Please have a seat.
B. **Shitsurei shimasu.**
   Thank you.
A. **O-cha wa ikaga desu ka.**
   Would you like some green tea?
B. **Onegai shimasu.** [or **Itadakimasu.**]
   Yes, thank you.

VOCABULARY

agatte kudasai: please come in [Lit: please come up] [from **agaru**]

daigakusei: university student

de: at, in [particle indicating place where an action occurs]

dō shimashō ka: what shall I do?

doru: dollars

en: yen

-gawa: the — side

genkan: entrance area (in a house)

gomen kudasai: Excuse me, is anyone there?

hidari: the left

hidari-gawa: the left-hand side

hon: book

hyaku: hundred

ikaga desu ka: how about some ...? Would you like some ...? [polite form of **dō desu ka**]

ikura: how much (money)?

itadakimasu: yes, please [when offered food or drink]

itte kudasai: please go [from **iku**]

jūsho: address

kado: corner

kaite kudasai: please write [from **kaku**]

kōhii: coffee

machimasu: wait [from **matsu**]

made: as far as

magatte kudasai: please turn [from **magaru**]

massugu: straight ahead

migi ni: to the right

migi-gawa: right-hand side

mō: already, (not) any longer, another, further

mondai: problem

ni-hyaku: two hundred

o-jama shimasu: excuse me for disturbing you

o-kake kudasai: please take a seat

onegai shimasu: please [Lit: I have a request/favor]

o-tsuri: the change (money)

sen: thousand

shingō: traffic lights

suki ja nai: don't like [more informal than **suki ja arimasen**]

sukoshi: a little, a small amount

surippa: slippers

suwatte kudasai: please sit down [from **suwaru**]

tatemono: building

tokorode: by the way
tomete kudasai: please stop, halt [from **tomeru**]
tsugi no: the next
wakarimashita: I see, I've got it, I understand [from **wakaru**]
yo: [sentence ending to show emphasis]
yukkuri: slowly

TEST YOURSELF

1. Read through the dialog at the beginning of the lesson once more, and then say if the following statements are true or false.

1. Takahashi san wa Yamate eki made takushii de ikimasu.   T/F

2. Eki kara, takushii wa migi ni magarimasu.   T/F

3. Hidari-gawa ni ōkii tatemono ga arimasu.   T/F

4. O-tsuri wa ni-sen en desu.   T/F

5. Takahashi san wa kōhii o nomimasen.   T/F

6. Takahashi san wa mondai ga arimasu.   T/F

2. Imagine you are going to visit the home of a Japanese friend, and fill in the missing lines in the conversation below. First, open the door to the genkan and see if anyone is home.

You _____

Friend   Ā dōzo, agatte kudasai. Surippa, dōzo.

You _____

Friend   Ja, kochira e. Dōzo, suwatte kudasai.

You _____

Friend   Kōhii wa ikaga desu ka.

You _____

3. *Imagine you are standing at the points on the map marked with an X, and you want to get to the buildings which are also marked. Ask a passer-by where the places are, and give the answers too.*

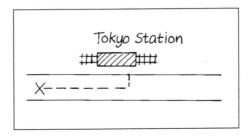

Example: You: **Sumimasen ga, Tōkyō eki wa doko desu ka.**
Passer-by: **Massugu itte kudasai. Hidari-gawa ni arimasu.**

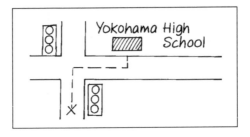

1.

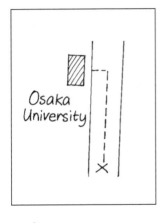

2.

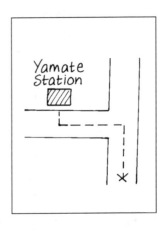

3.

4. *You are having a day out shopping. Ask the store assistant the price of the goods you want to buy, and give the responses too. Write the numbers out in full, as in the example.*

Example:
A.   Sumimasen ga, kono hana wa ikura desu ka.
B.   Sen go-hyaku en desu.

1.

_____

_____

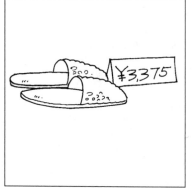

2.

_____

_____

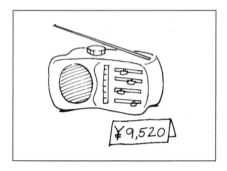

3.
_____

_____

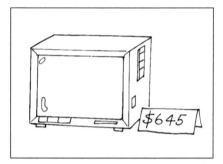

4.
_____

_____

What are the following numbers?

5. Has-sen ni-hyaku go-jū-go _____

6. Sen hyaku ni-jū _____

7. Go-sen kyū-jū-san _____

8. Nana-sen san-byaku-san _____

5. *How would you say these sentences in Japanese?*

1. Please turn left at the next traffic lights.

2. I'll watch TV at home tomorrow.

3. Are there any problems?

4. Please write your name and address here.

5. Excuse me, but how much is that book?

6. There's a large school on the left-hand side, right?

7. By the way, what are you doing tomorrow?

8. Would you like some coffee?

Mondai is a compound of the characters for "ask about/question" and "topic/subject." The two together mean "problem/question."

DAI IK-KA KARA DAI GO-KA MADE NO FUKUSHŪ

REVIEW OF LESSONS 1 TO 5

Read Dialogs 1 to 5 aloud, and try to understand the meaning without referring back to the English translations in previous lessons.

Dialog 1: NIHON E YŌKOSO!

Mike	Shitsurei desu ga, Watanabe san desu ka.
Stranger	Watashi desu ka? Iie, chigaimasu.
Mike	Sō desu ka. Dōmo sumimasen.
Watanabe	Sumimasen, Neruson san desu ka.
Mike	Hai, sō desu. Neruson desu.
Watanabe	Hajimemashite, Watanabe desu. Yokohama Gakuin Kōkō no Watanabe desu. Nihon e yōkoso!
Mike	Ā, Watanabe san, hajimemashite.
Watanabe	Watashi no meishi desu. Dōzo.
Mike	Dōmo arigatō.

Watanabe	(pointing to suitcases) Neruson san no sūtsukēsu desu ka.
Mike	Hai, sō desu.
Watanabe	Ja, dōzo, kochira e.

QUESTIONS:

1. Watanabe san no shigoto wa nan desu ka.

2. Watanabe san no gakkō wa doko desu ka.

3. Maiku san wa doko no hito desu ka.

Dialog 2: MINA SAN, OHAYŌ GOZAIMASU.

Watanabe	Mina san, ohayō gozaimasu.
Everyone	Ohayō gozaimasu.
Watanabe	Neruson san, kochira wa Itō sensei desu.
Itō	Hajimemashite, Itō desu.
Mike	Maiku Neruson desu. Yoroshiku onegai shimasu.
Watanabe	Kochira wa Takahashi san desu. Takahashi san wa jimu no hito desu.
Takahashi	Hajimemashite. Takahashi desu. Dōzo yoroshiku.
Watanabe	Kore wa watashi no tsukue desu. Sore wa Takahashi san no tsukue desu.
Mike	Watashi no tsukue wa doko ni arimasu ka.
Watanabe	Neruson san no wa soko ni arimasu.
Takahashi	Watanabe san, chigaimasu. Sumimasen ga, sore wa Neruson san no tsukue ja arimasen. Saitō san no desu.
Watanabe	Saitō san? Saitō san wa dare desu ka.
Takahashi	Atarashii pāto desu. Kyō kara desu.
Watanabe	Sō desu ka. Atarashii pāto desu ka. Ja, Neruson san no tsukue wa?
Takahashi	Wakarimasen.
Watanabe	Itō san! Neruson san no tsukue wa doko ni arimasu ka.
Itō	Sono tsukue ja arimasen ka.

| Watanabe | A, sore desu ka. Neruson san, sore desu. |
| Mike | Dōmo arigatō. |

QUESTIONS:

1. Takahashi san no shigoto wa nan desu ka.

2. Maiku san wa, tsukue ga arimasu ka.

3. Atarashii pāto no namae wa nan desu ka.

Dialog 3: NANI O TABEMASU KA.

Watanabe	Neruson san wa nani o tabemasu ka.
Mike	Hmm, wakarimasen. Kono resutoran wa, nani ga oishii desu ka.
Watanabe	Sakana ga oishii desu. Sakana ga suki desu ka.
Mike	Hai, dai-suki desu.
Watanabe	Ja, yaki-zakana teishoku wa dō desu ka. Sore wa yaki-zakana to gohan to tsukemono to miso shiru desu.
Mike	Sore wa ii desu ne. Hai, watashi wa yaki-zakana teishoku ni shimasu. Watanabe san wa?
Watanabe	Watashi wa sashimi teishoku ni shimasu. (to waiter) Sumimasen!
Waiter	Hai, nani ni shimasu ka.
Watanabe	Yaki-zakana teishoku to sashimi teishoku o kudasai.
Mike	Itadakimasu.
Watanabe	Itadakimasu.
Mike	Kono miso shiru wa oishii desu ne. (noticing something decorating Mr Watanabe's raw fish) E? Sore wa nan desu ka. Hana ja arimasen ka.
Watanabe	Hai, sō desu. Sono hana wa kiku desu yo.
Mike	Nan desu ka? Kiku desu ka. Kiku o tabemasu ka.
Watanabe	Hai, tokidoki tabemasu. A, o-cha wa arimasen ne. O-cha o nomimasu ka.
Mike	Sumimasen ga, o-cha wa amari suki ja arimasen. Mizu o kudasai.

Watanabe   Hai, mizu desu ne. (to waiter) Sumimasen, o-cha to
mizu o kudasai.

QUESTIONS:

1. Maiku san wa sakana ga kirai desu ka.

2. Watanabe san wa sakana ni shimasu ka.

3. "Kiku" wa nan desu ka.

4. Maiku san wa nani o nomimasu ka.

Dialog 4: GO-JI HAN NI AIMASHŌ.

Matsuda	Moshi moshi, Matsuda desu ga.
Takahashi	Moshi moshi. Kenji? Keiko desu ga.
Matsuda	Ā, Keiko chan, konbanwa. Ima doko desu ka.
Takahashi	Uchi ni imasu. Ne, Kenji, konban nani o shimasu ka.
Matsuda	Mada wakarimasen ga ...
Takahashi	Kenji, eiga wa dō desu ka. Eiga o mimashō.
Matsuda	Eiga desu ka.
Takahashi	Hai, konban ii eiga ga arimasu. "Anata No Ashita" desu. Roku-ji han ni hajimarimasu. Ikimashō ka.
Matsuda	Roku-ji han ni? Demo, ima roku-ji desu ne. Jikan ga arimasen.
Takahashi	Ii desu. Takushii de ikimashō.
Matsuda	Demo ... sono eiga wa SF desu ne. Watashi wa SF ga amari suki ja arimasen.
Takahashi	E? Suki ja arimasen ka. Demo ...
Matsuda	Sore kara, ashita Eigo no tesuto ga arimasu. Konban tesuto benkyō o shimasu. Ja, ashita hanashimashō.
Takahashi	E? Nan desu ka. Eigo no benkyō?
Matsuda	Ja, shitsurei shimasu. Mata ashita.

Abe	Moshi moshi, Abe desu ga.
Takahashi	Moshi moshi, Yoko san? Keiko desu. Ne, Yoko san, konban uchi ni imasu ka.
Abe	Hai, imasu. Dō shite desu ka.
Takahashi	Hanashi ga arimasu. Ima roku-ji jup-pun desu ne. Ja, takushii de ikimasu. Ii desu ka.
Abe	Hai, ii desu. Dōzo dōzo.
Takahashi	Arigatō. Ja, sugu ikimasu.

QUESTIONS:

1. Takahashi san wa doko kara denwa shimasu ka.

2. Nani ga roku-ji han ni hajimarimasu ka.

3. Keiko san to Kenji san wa konban aimasu ka.

4. Takahashi san wa nani de Abe san no uchi e ikimasu ka.

Dialog 5: MONDAI GA ARIMASU YO!

Takahashi	Yamate eki made onegai shimasu.
Taxi driver	Hai, wakarimashita.
Taxi driver	Hai, Yamate eki desu yo.
Takahashi	Mō eki desu ka. Ja, koko de migi ni magatte kudasai.
Taxi driver	Koko desu ka.
Takahashi	Hai, sō desu. Sore kara, massugu itte kudasai. Asoko ni ōkii tatemono ga arimasu ne.
Taxi driver	Hidari-gawa desu ka.
Takahashi	Hai, sō desu. Asoko de ii desu. Asoko de tomete kudasai. Ikura desu ka.
Taxi driver	Sen ni-hyaku en desu.
Takahashi	Ja, kore, ni-sen en desu.
Taxi driver	Hai, hap-pyaku en no o-tsuri desu. Dōzo.
Takahashi	Dōmo arigatō.

Takahashi	Gomen kudasai.
Abe	Ā, Keiko san. Konbanwa. Dōzo, agatte kudasai.
	Surippa, dōzo.
Takahashi	O-jama shimasu.
Abe	Dōzo, kochira e. Kōhii wa ikaga desu ka.
Takahashi	Itadakimasu.
Abe	Tokorode, Keiko san, ano hanashi wa? Nan no hanashi desu ka. Mondai ga arimasu ka.
Takahashi	Kenji desu yo! Dō shimashō ka. Kenji wa mō watashi ga suki ja nai desu yo!

QUESTIONS:

1. Ōkii tatemono wa dochira-gawa ni arimasu ka.

2. Takahashi san no uchi kara Abe san no uchi made takushii de ikura desu ka.

3. O-tsuri wa hap-pyaku en desu ka.

4. Takahashi san wa Abe san no uchi de nani o nomimasu ka.

TEST YOURSELF

1. Join the words in the left-hand column with their opposites on the right. Be careful – there are two words too many in the right-hand column.

	gakusei
migi	kimasu
kono	kara
kirai	watashi
e	tokidoki
itadakimasu	hidari
koko	ohayō gozaimasu
iie	sono
ikimasu	sukoshi
konbanwa	hai
oshiemasu	go-chisō sama
sensei	ōkii
takusan	benkyō shimasu
anata	suki
	soko

2. *Read the following numbers out loud.*

   1. ¥5,650
   2. $310
   3. 12:25
   4. ¥3,995
   5. $4,500
   6. 10:40

3. *Which is the odd man out in each of the groups of words below? Underline the word which doesn't fit with the others, as in the example.*

   Example:

   gakkō

   <u>takushii</u>   (the only one which is not a building)

   kaisha

   ginkō

   eki

1.	2.	3.	4.	5.
doko	hachi	ashita	sakana	daigaku
nani	jū	inu	gohan	jimu no hito
dare	ni	kyō	tsukemono	enjinia
koko	nana	asatte	sushi	sensei
nan-ji	ano	konban	hashi	pāto

4. *Join up the phrases to make complete sentences.*

   1. Denwa de   ni shimasu.
   2. Takushii de   arimasu ka.
   3. Keiko san wa mondai ga   suki desu ne.
   4. Nan-ji ni   desu ka.
   5. Wain wa mada   aimashō ka.
   6. Ashita Yokohama   hanashimasu.
   7. Dōzo   e ikimashō ka.

8. Watashi wa sashimi teishoku   suwatte kudasai.

9. Maiku san no gakkō wa doko   takusan arimasu.

10. Eiga ga   eki made ikimasu.

5. *Answer the following questions about yourself.*

1. Namae wa nan desu ka.

2. Sakana ga suki desu ka.

3. Ashita kaisha (gakkō, daigaku) e ikimasu ka.

4. Tokidoki tenisu o shimasu ka.

5. Anata no uchi wa doko desu ka.

6. Nihongo ga wakarimasu ka.

7. Anata no uchi ni inu ga imasu ka.

8. Mainichi terebi o mimasu ka.

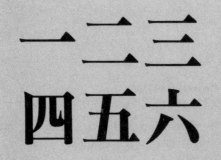

These are the characters for the numbers one to six, the lessons you have covered so far. They are pronounced **ichi, ni, san, yon** or **shi, go, roku.**

DAI NANA-KA

ATAMA GA ITAI!
MY HEAD HURTS!

Today is Saturday. Mr. Watanabe had a late night out last night, and he has just woken up, feeling somewhat the worse for wear. He goes downstairs and greets his wife.

Okusan	**Ohayō gozaimasu. Atama wa dō desu ka.** Good morning. How's your head?
Watanabe	**Itai yo! Atama ga itai! Ima nan-ji?** It hurts! My head hurts! What time is it?
Okusan	**Osoi desu yo. Mō jū-ni-ji jup-pun mae desu. Kōhii wa?** It's late. It's already ten to twelve. Coffee?
Watanabe	**A, ii ne. Tomoko to Fumiko to Hiro wa doko ni iru?** Ah, great. Where are Tomoko and Fumiko and Hiro?
Okusan	**Tomoko wa tonari no uchi de, tomodachi to issho ni terebi o mite imasu. Fumiko wa ni-kai de gakkō no Eigo no shukudai o shite imasu.** Tomoko is watching TV with her friend next door. Fumiko is doing her English homework upstairs.

Watanabe	**Hiro wa?** And Hiro?
Okusan	**Hiro wa gakkō de yakyū no renshū o shite imasu. Mō sugu kaerimasu. Hai, kōhii. Atsui desu yo. Ki o tsukete.** Hiro's doing baseball practice at school. He'll be home soon. Right, coffee. It's hot. Be careful.
Fumiko	(running downstairs) **O-tōsan, ohayō!** Morning, Dad!
Okusan	**Fumiko, ki o tsukete. O-tōsan wa kōhii o nonde iru yo.** Fumiko, take care. Your father is drinking his coffee.
Watanabe	**Fumiko, Eigo no shukudai wa dō? Muzukashii?** Fumiko, how's your English homework? Difficult?
Fumiko	**Iie, muzukashiku nai yo. Eigo ga suki desu.** No, it isn't difficult. I like English.
Okusan	**A, mō hiru-gohan no jikan desu ne. Fumiko, Tomoko o yonde. Mada tonari ni imasu.** Ah, it's time for lunch. Fumiko, call Tomoko. She's still next door.
Fumiko	**Hai.** Okay.
Okusan	(to her husband) **Ne, kyō no gogo wa minna de Kawasaki ni ikimasu ne.** So, we're all going to Kawasaki this afternoon, right?
Watanabe	**Ē? Kawasaki? Dō shite?** Eh? Kawasaki? Why?
Okusan	**Oboete imasen ka. Kyō wa haha no tanjōbi desu yo ne.** Don't you remember? Today is my mother's birthday, isn't it?
Watanabe	**O-kāsan no tanjōbi? A, atama ga itai! Mata neru yo! Oyasumi nasai!** Your mother's birthday? Oh, my head hurts! I'm going back to bed! Goodnight!

STRUCTURE AND USAGE NOTES

1. ADJECTIVES ENDING IN -I

There are two types of adjective in Japanese: those that end in -i, and those that are followed by -na when they come before nouns. Predictably, they are generally referred to as "-i adjectives" and "-na adjectives." For now, we will concentrate on -i adjectives, and look at -na adjectives in the next lesson.

We have already come across several -i adjectives, and you will find these listed below along with some other common -i adjectives which it will be useful for you to learn.

ii	good, fine	atarashii	new, fresh
warui	bad, wrong	atsui	hot
hayai	fast, early	samui	cold (weather)
osoi	slow, late	muzukashii	difficult
takai	high, expensive	itai	painful
yasui	cheap	ōkii	big
oishii	delicious, tasty	chiisai	small

Just as in English, these words can come before the word they are describing, or stand alone.

Kore wa oishii sakana desu ne.
This is delicious fish, isn't it?

Kono sakana wa oishii desu ne.
This fish is delicious, isn't it?

Kore wa muzukashii shukudai desu.
This is difficult homework.

Kono shukudai wa muzukashii desu.
This homework is difficult.

Here are some more examples of sentences with -i adjectives.

Kyō wa atsui desu ne.
Hot today, isn't it?

Chotto osoi desu ne. Mō kaerimashō.
It's a bit late, isn't it? Let's go home.

Ano atarashii resutoran no teishoku wa yasui desu yo. Soko de tabemashō.
Hey, the set meals at that new restaurant are cheap. Let's eat there.

Kono hon wa go-sen en desu ka. Chotto takai desu ne.
This book is five thousand yen? A bit expensive, isn't it?

Sono chiisai rajio wa ikura desu ka.
How much is that small radio?

The -i group of adjectives have a different form for negatives and for past tenses, so in some ways they act more like verbs than adjectives. In fact, they can stand alone without **desu** and still make sentences which are complete grammatically, although the tone is pretty informal and familiar, and it is better to add **desu**. (For example, in the dialog at the beginning of the lesson, Mr. Watanabe says **Atama ga itai**, or, literally, "My head is painful." In more formal company, he would say **Atama ga itai desu**.)

To make a negative sentence, that is, to say when something isn't big, or isn't expensive, or isn't good, drop the final -i and add -ku **arimasen**. (You may also come across the endings -ku nai desu and -ku nai n' desu, which mean the same thing. **Nai** is the plain form of **arimasen**.)

Positive	Negative	Meaning
takai	takaku arimasen	isn't expensive
ōkii	ōkiku arimasen	isn't large
chiisai	chiisaku arimasen	isn't small
muzukashii	muzukashiku arimasen	isn't difficult
itai	itaku arimasen	isn't painful
warui	waruku arimasen	isn't bad
atsui	atsuku arimasen	isn't hot

The adjective **ii** ("good") has an alternative form **yoi**, and its negative is formed from this: **yoku arimasen**.

Kyō wa amari atsuku arimasen ne.
It's not very hot today, is it?

Watashi no shigoto wa muzukashiku arimasen.
My work isn't difficult.

Atama wa mō itaku arimasen.
My head doesn't hurt any more./I don't have a headache any more.

Sono kaisha wa amari ōkiku nai desu ne.
That company isn't very big, is it?

Kono purintā wa yoku arimasen yo.
This printer is no good.

2. MORE ON TELLING THE TIME

Jū-ni-ji jup-pun mae, or "ten minutes before twelve," is an alternative to saying jū-ichi-ji go-jup-pun, or "eleven fifty." The word mae means "before" or "in front of," so you can use it to talk about the minutes *to* the hour. Here are some more times using mae.

Kaigi wa ku-ji jū-go-fun mae ni hajimarimasu.
The meeting starts at a quarter to nine.

Hachi-ji jup-pun mae ni denwa shimasu.
I'll call you at ten to eight.

Ni-ji chotto mae ni kite kudasai.
Please come a little before two o'clock.

In the same way, you can use **sugi** ("past/after") with the minutes past the hour, although the meaning is usually clear without it.

Jū-ji jup-pun sugi desu.
It's ten past ten.

Mō ichi-ji sugi desu.
It's already gone one o'clock.

3. PRESENT PROGRESSIVE TENSE

Another use of the -te form of the verb is to form the present progressive tense, that is, the one we use to describe an event that's happening at the moment. This is done by adding the verb **iru/imasu** after the -te form.

Tomoko wa ima nani o shite imasu ka.
What's Tomoko doing at the moment?

Hiro wa mada nete imasu.
Hiro is still sleeping.

Kenji wa konban uchi de Eigo no benkyō o shite imasu.
Kenji is studying English at home this evening.

Takahashi san wa ima denwa de tomodachi to hanashite imasu.
Ms. Takahashi's talking to a friend on the phone at the moment.

(on the phone) **Eki no mae de matte imasu. Sugu kite kudasai!**
I'm waiting in front of the station. Hurry up! [Lit: Please come soon.]

Hiro wa tenisu no renshū o shite imasen. Kyō wa yakyū desu yo.
Hiro isn't doing tennis practice. Today it's baseball.

The -te iru form is also used to describe actions that continue over a long period of time.

Maiku san wa Nihon no kōkō de Eigo o oshiete imasu.
Mike teaches [Lit: is teaching] English at a Japanese high school.

Sono kaisha de mō hataraite imasen. Ima ginkō de hataraite imasu.
I don't work at that company any more. Now I work [Lit: am working] at a bank.

A. **Takahashi san no tomodachi wa doko ni sunde imasu ka.**
   Where does your friend live, Ms. Takahashi?
B. **Yokohama ni sunde imasu.**
   She lives [Lit: is living] in Yokohama.

4. HAHA VS. O-KĀSAN – FAMILY WORDS

A clear distinction is made in Japan between people in your "in-group" and people outside the group, and this is reflected in the language used to refer to them. The in-group and out-group will differ depending on the situation. If you are talking to someone at work about your family, then naturally the family members will be your in-group, and the person you are talking to will be outside this group. However, if you are talking about colleagues at your company to someone from a different company, then you use more familiar terms to refer to them, while using more polite, formal words to refer to people from the company of the person you are talking to.

There are different ways of referring to members of someone else's family, usually by adding the polite o- or go- to the beginning of the word, but sometimes by using different words altogether. Because this makes it obvious that you are talking about the other person's family, it is not necessary to use the words for "my" or "your."

My family	Your family	
kazoku	go-kazoku	family
haha	o-kāsan	mother
chichi	o-tōsan	father
kanai/tsuma	okusan	wife
shujin/otto	go-shujin	husband
ane	o-nēsan	older sister
ani	o-niisan	older brother
imōto	imōtosan	younger sister
otōto	otōtosan	younger brother

Ani wa ginkō de hataraite imasu ga, otōto wa mada daigakusei desu.
My older brother works in a bank, but my younger brother is still at university [Lit: is a university student].

O-nēsan wa Igirisu de benkyō shite imasu ne.
Your older sister is studying in Britain, isn't she?

Ashita haha to issho ni Tōkyō ni ikimasu.
I'm going to Tokyo (together) with my mother tomorrow.

Chichi no kaisha wa Kawasaki ni arimasu.
My father's company is in Kawasaki.

The polite forms are also used when addressing older members of one's own family. (Younger children are generally addressed by their older brothers and sisters using their names.)

O-kāsan, atama ga itai!
Mom, I have a a headache!

O-tōsan, o-nēsan wa mada tonari no uchi ni iru?
Dad, is Sis still next door?

5. INFORMAL SPEECH LEVELS

A more informal level of speech tends to be used within the family, or with very close friends, and this is characterised by use of the plain form of the verb instead of the -masu form, and leaving off **desu** after -i adjectives. In everyday conversation, you will be safer using the polite -masu form of verbs, as use of the plain form can sound too familiar if used inappropriately, but it is useful for you to be able to recognise such forms. Below are some of the sentences from the main dialog, and how they would be if spoken to someone outside the family.

Atama ga itai.	**Atama ga itai desu.**
My head hurts./I have a headache.	
Ima nan-ji?	**Ima nan-ji desu ka.**
What time is it?	
A, ii ne.	**A, ii desu ne.**
Great.	
... doko ni iru?	**... doko ni imasu ka.**
Where are ...?	
Eigo no shukudai wa dō?	**Eigo no shukudai wa dō desu ka.**
How's your English homework?	

| Muzukashii? | Muzukashii desu ka. |
| Is it difficult? | |

| Iie, muzukashiku nai yo. | Iie, muzukashiku arimasen yo. |
| No, it's not difficult. | |

| Tomoko o yonde. | Tomoko o yonde kudasai. |
| Please call Tomoko. | |

| Mata neru yo. | Mata nemasu yo. |
| I'm going back to sleep./I'm going to sleep again. | |

6. FIRST NAMES AND FAMILY NAMES

First names are not generally used in Japan except within the family, with children, or with very close friends. Even colleagues who have worked together for many years tend to call each other by their family names. For your information, below is a list of common boys' and girls' first names. Notice that girls' names often end in -ko.

Girls' names	Boys' names
Keiko	Jiro
Tomoko	Ichiro
Michiko	Taro
Yoko	Hiroyuki
Yasuko	Shusaku
Sachiko	Jun
Akiko	Hidehiko
Kimiko	Yasuo
Yuki	Takeshi
Mari	Tatsuo

VOCABULARY

ane: (my) older sister
ani: (my) older brother
atama: head
atama ga itai: I have a headache, my head hurts
atsui: hot
chichi: (my) father
chiisai: small
chotto: a little, a bit
go-kazoku: (your) family
go-shujin: (your) husband

gogo: afternoon
haha: (my) mother
hataraite imasu: is working [from **hataraku**]
hayai: fast, early
hiru-gohan: lunch
imōto: (my) younger sister
imōtosan: (your) younger sister
issho ni: together
itai: painful
kaerimasu: return, go/come home [from **kaeru**]
kanai/tsuma: (my) wife
Kawasaki: industrial city near Tokyo
kazoku: family
ki o tsukete (kudasai): take care, be careful [from **tsukeru**]
mae: before, in front of
matte imasu: is waiting [from **matsu**]
minna de: altogether, everyone together
mite imasu: is watching [from **miru**]
muzukashii: difficult
muzukashiku nai: isn't difficult
neru: to sleep, go to bed
ni-kai: second floor, upstairs
nonde iru: is drinking [from **nomu**]
o-kāsan: (your) mother [or when addressing one's own mother]
o-nēsan: (your) older sister [or when addressing one's own older sister]
o-niisan: (your) older brother [or when addressing one's own older brother]
o-tōsan: (your) father [or when addressing one's own father]
oboete imasen ka: don't you remember? [from **oboeru**]
okusan: (your) wife
oshiete imasu: is teaching [from **oshieru**]
osoi: late, slow
otōto: (my) younger brother
otōtosan: (your) younger brother
otto/shujin: (my) husband
renshū: practice
samui: cold
shukudai: homework
sugi: past, after
sunde imasu: is residing, living [from **sumu**]
takai: high, expensive
tanjōbi: birthday
tonari: next to, by the side

tsuma/kanai: (my) wife
warui: bad, wrong
yakyū: baseball
yasui: cheap
yonde: call [short for **yonde kudasai,** from **yobu**]

TEST YOURSELF

1. *Read through the dialog at the beginning of the lesson once more, and then say if the following statements are true or false.*

   1. Ima jū-ichi-ji go-jup-pun desu.   T/F

   2. Tomoko chan to Fumiko chan to Hiro chan wa ima uchi ni imasu.   T/F

   3. Watanabe san no kōhii wa atsuku arimasen.   T/F

   4. Fumiko san wa Eigo o benkyō shite imasu.   T/F

   5. Okusan no o-kāsan no tanjōbi wa kyō desu.   T/F

   6. Okusan no o-kāsan wa Kawasaki ni sunde imasu.   T/F

2. *Make a comment about the things in the first column, choosing an appropriate word from the second column, as in the example.*

   Example: **Kono resutoran wa yasui desu ne!**

Kono	sushi	wa	chiisai	desu ne!
	shukudai		yasui	
	resutoran		muzukashii	
	densha		takai	
	kaisha		oishii	
	inu		hayai	
	tatemono		ōkii	

3. *A co-worker is trying to make conversation, but you are busy, and not in the mood for a chat. Irritated, you contradict everything he says, as in the example below.*

Example: A. **Nyū Yōku wa ima atsui desu ne.**

B. **Iie, amari atsuku arimasen yo.**

1. Nihongo wa muzukashii desu ne.

2. Anata no kuruma wa atarashii desu ne.

3. Ano atarashii resutoran wa oishii desu ne.

4. Sono konpyūtā wa ii desu ne.

5. Ima chotto samui desu ne.

4. *The principal at Yokohama High School is looking for someone to help him with some school duties this lunchtime, but discovers that all the staff seem to be busy. Using the information on the staff board below, answer his questions about what everyone is doing at the moment, as in the example.*

Example: *Principal* **Watanabe san wa imasu ka.**
       You **Iie, imasen.**
     Principal **Nani o shite imasu ka.**
       You **Watanabe san wa ima kaigi o shite imasu.**

NAMAE	DOKO?
Watanabe	meeting
Itō	lunch
Sakai	reading students' homework
Nelson	teaching English class
Takahashi	studying English
Ogawa	doing baseball practice

5. *How would you say these sentences in Japanese?*

1. Today's Japanese homework is difficult, isn't it?

2. It's my mother's birthday tomorrow.

3. I'll be home before twelve o'clock.

4. Where does your older brother live?

5. Mike is teaching English in Kawasaki today.

6. I'm sorry, but Keiko isn't in at the moment. She's watching a movie on TV next door. Shall I call her?

 The word **Eigo**, combining the kanji characters for "England" and "word," means "the English language." The suffix **-go** can be added to the name of any country to give that country's language.

IYA DESU NE!

HORRIBLE, ISN'T IT!

Mr. Watanabe has reluctantly agreed to go shopping with his wife, as she has persuaded him that he needs a new suit. They are now in the menswear department of a large department store in Ginza, Tokyo's central shopping area.

Okusan	**Sūtsu wa doko deshō ne.** (to sales assistant) **Anō, sumimasen, sūtsu wa doko desu ka.** I wonder where the suits are. Uh, excuse me, where are the suits?
Assistant	**Sūtsu desu ka. Koko o mō sukoshi massugu itte kudasai. Migi-gawa ni gozaimasu.** The suits? Go a little further along here. They're on the right-hand side.
Okusan	**Arigatō. A, koko desu ne. Kono gurē no sūtsu wa ii desu ne.** Thank you. Ah, here they are. This gray suit is nice, isn't it?

Watanabe	Gurē wa dame. Suki ja nai yo.
	Gray's no good. I don't like it.
Okusan	Sō desu ka. Ja, kono burū no wa dō desu ka. (looking inside at the label) A, kono dezainā wa yūmei desu yo. Ii desu ne.
	I see. Well, how about this blue one? Ah, this designer is famous. It's nice, isn't it?
Watanabe	Yūmei-na dezainā desu ka. Takai deshō. Motto yasui sūtsu ga ii desu. A, kore wa ii.
	A famous designer? It's probably expensive. A cheaper suit is fine. Ah, this one's okay.
Okusan	Sore wa ii desu ga, saizu wa chotto chiisai desu ne. (to sales assistant) Sumimasen, motto ōkii saizu wa arimasu ka.
	That one's nice, but it's a bit small, isn't it? Excuse me, do you have a larger size?
Assistant	Gozaimasu. Kochira e dōzo.
	We do. This way, please.

Mr. Watanabe goes off to try on the suit, and while the rest of the family are waiting for him, Mrs. Watanabe suddenly sees one of her old schoolfriends.

Okusan	A, Sachiko san, konnichiwa! O-hisashiburi desu ne.
	Ah, Sachiko, hello! I haven't seen you for ages!
Friend	A, Michiko san, konnichiwa. O-genki desu ka.
	Michiko, hello. How are you?
Okusan	Hai, genki desu. Arigatō. Sachiko san wa?
	I'm fine, thank you. And you?
Friend	Hai, o-kage sama de.
	Yes, fine, thank you.
Okusan	Kyō wa konde imasu ne.
	It's crowded today, isn't it?
Friend	Sō desu ne. Iya desu ne. Kaimono wa suki desu ga, Ginza no depāto wa itsumo konde imasu ne. Michiko san wa yoku Ginza e kimasu ka.
	Yes, it is. Horrible, isn't it! I like shopping, but the Ginza department stores are always crowded, aren't they? Do you often come to Ginza?

Okusan	Tokidoki kimasu. Watashi mo kaimono wa suki desu ga, kyō wa shujin no atarashii sūtsu o mite imasu ...
	Sometimes. I like shopping too, but today my husband is looking at new suits ...
Friend	A, wakarimashita. Go-shujin to issho desu ka. Sore wa taihen deshō!
	Oh, I see, you're (shopping) with your husband. That's tough, isn't it!
Okusan	Sō desu! (Mr. Watanabe comes out of the room where he changed suits) A, shujin desu. Dō desu ka. Saizu wa daijōbu desu ka.
	It is! Ah, there he is. How is it? Is the size all right?
Watanabe	Saizu wa daijōbu desu ga, dezain wa chotto ...
	The size is okay, but the design is a bit ...

STRUCTURE AND USAGE NOTES

1. USES OF DESHŌ

The word **deshō** has its origins in **desu**, but it has different nuances depending on the situation and intonation used. When it is used in a question, and followed by **ka**, it is the equivalent of "I wonder ..." so it makes the question less direct.

Kore wa nan desu ka.	**Kore wa nan deshō ka.**
What's this?	I wonder what this is?
Sono hito wa Watanabe san no o-tōsan desu ka.	**Sono hito wa Watanabe san no o-tōsan deshō ka.**
Is that (person) Mr. Watanabe's father?	I wonder if that (person) is Mr. Watanabe's father?
Kaigi wa nan-ji desu ka.	**Kaigi wa nan-ji deshō ka.**
What time is the meeting?	I wonder what time the meeting is?

When it is used with rising intonation, it is asking for the agreement of the person being spoken to, so it is similar to **ne**, but softer and less direct.

Are wa Watanabe san no uchi deshō.
That's Mr. Watanabe's house, right?

Asoko no kodomo wa Fumiko chan deshō.
That child over there is Fumiko, isn't it?

Nihongo wa muzukashii deshō.
Japanese is difficult, isn't it?

Kyō wa tanjōbi deshō.
Today is your birthday, am I right?

Sono dezainā wa yūmei deshō.
That designer is famous, isn't she?

When the intonation is falling at the end of the sentence, it shows that the speaker is almost, but not completely, sure of his facts, so is making an assumption. This kind of sentence is often translated into English using words such as "probably," "must be," "almost certainly."

Hokkaidō wa ima samui deshō.
It's probably cold in Hokkaido now.

Sono saizu wa daijōbu deshō.
I guess that size will be okay.

Pāto no shigoto mo, benkyō mo shite imasu ka. Sore wa taihen deshō.
You're doing part-time work and studying? That must be tough.

Deshō can also be used instead of **desu** when you want to be extra polite.

Sumimasen ga, Tanaka san deshō ka.
Excuse me, but would you be Mr. Tanaka?

Chotto sumimasen, eki wa doko deshō ka.
Excuse me, where might the station be?

2. VOCABULARY FOR CLOTHING

Much of the vocabulary for Western-style clothing has been taken from English, so if you want to buy an item of clothing and you don't know the word, try saying the English equivalent with Japanese pronunciation, and the chances are that you will be correct.

burausu	blouse	**sūtsu**	suit
sētā	sweater	**nekutai**	necktie
sukāto	skirt	**shatsu**	shirt
jaketto	jacket	**kōto**	coat
beruto	belt	**T-shatsu**	T-shirt
wanpiisu	dress ("one-piece")	**G-pan**	jeans ("jean pants")
kutsu	shoes	**zubon**	pants, trousers

3 GOZAIMASU – "WE HAVE"

As we saw in the previous lesson when talking about family members, vocabulary can differ markedly in Japanese, depending on who you are talking to, the degree of formality of the situation and even the relative age of the people talking. In situations which demand a high degree of courtesy, such as a sales assistant in a department store talking to a customer, or staff in a prestigious hotel talking to a guest, the speaker is likely to use the very formal and humble **gozaimasu** instead of **arimasu**.

A. Kono hoteru ni wa, fakkusu ga arimasu ka.
Do you have a fax in this hotel?
B. Hai, gozaimasu.
Yes, we do.

In the same way, **de gozaimasu** is used in formal situations instead of **desu**.

A. Sumimasen, kono sētā wa ikura desu ka.
Excuse me, how much is this sweater?
B. Sore wa kyū-sen en de gozaimasu.
It's ¥9,000.

4. GURĒ, BURŪ – AND OTHER COLORS

Some of the words for colors are -i adjectives.

kuroi	black
shiroi	white
aoi	blue, green, blue/green
akai	red

Asoko no shiroi tatemono wa hoteru desu ka.
That white building over there – is it a hotel?

Sono akai kuruma wa dare no desu ka.
Whose is that red car?

These words can be turned into nouns by dropping the final -i.

Kono kuroi sukāto wa ii desu ne. Watashi wa kuro ga suki desu.
This black skirt is nice, isn't it? I like black.

Ki o tsukete kudasai. Shingō wa aka desu.
Be careful. The traffic lights are red.

Other color words are nouns, so when they are used in front of the word they are describing, they need to be followed by **no**.

chairo	brown
kiiro	yellow
midori	green
murasaki	purple

(**Kiiro** also has the alternative form **kiiroi**, acting like an -i adjective.)

Sono chairo to midori no nekutai wa ikura desu ka.
How much is that brown and green necktie?

Kono kiiro no hana no namae wa nan desu ka.
What's the name of these yellow flowers?

A third set of color words are those that have been borrowed from English. These tend to be used to describe man-made things rather than those found in nature. For example, a sweater may be **guriin**, but the park in spring would be **midori**; jeans may be **burū**, but the sky is **aoi**. These words also have to be followed by **no** when they are used before the word they are describing.

burū	blue
gurē	gray
orenji	orange
guriin	green
buraun	brown
pinku	pink

Mata pinku no wanpiisu o kaimasu ka.
You're going to buy another pink dress?

Kono burū no sētā wa dō desu ka.
How about this blue sweater?

5. YŪMEI-NA DEZAINĀ – -NA ADJECTIVES

In the previous lesson you learned about -i adjectives. Now we will look at -na adjectives, so-called because they are always followed by -na when they come before a noun to describe it. Here are some of the most common -na adjectives.

iya-na	horrible	kirei-na	pretty, clean
dame-na	no good, useless	yūmei-na	famous
taihen-na	terrible, tough	shizuka-na	quiet, peaceful
shinsetsu-na	kind	kantan-na	simple, brief
suki-na	like	kirai-na	dislike
genki-na	healthy, cheerful	hen-na	strange, odd

Ima no shigoto wa taihen desu.
My current job is really tough.

Sono burū no burausu wa kirei desu ne.
That blue blouse is pretty, isn't it?

Atarashii jimu no hito wa itsumo genki desu ne.
The new office worker is always cheerful, isn't she?

To make a negative statement, use **ja arimasen**, the negative of **desu**.

Ogawa san no atarashii uchi wa amari shizuka ja arimasen ne.
Mr. Ogawa's new house isn't very quiet, is it?

Tomoko san no Eigo no sensei wa amari shinsetsu ja arimasen.
Tomoko's English teacher isn't very kind.

These adjectives are followed by -na to join them to the thing they are describing.

Hen-na hito desu ne!
He's a weird person, isn't he!

Kantan-na repōto o kaite kudasai.
Please write a brief report.

Kyō no sora wa kirei-na ao desu ne.
The sky today is a beautiful blue, isn't it?

A. **Saitō san no kaisha wa yūmei desu ka.**
   Is Ms. Saitō's company famous?
B. **Hai, totemo yūmei-na kaisha desu yo.**
   Yes, it's a really famous company.

Suki-na sakana wa nan desu ka.
What (kind of) fish do you like?

Fumiko wa genki-na kodomo desu ne.
Fumiko is an energetic child, isn't she?

The words **ōkii** ("big") and **chiisai** ("small") can also become -na adjectives (drop the final -i first) when they come before a noun.

Sore wa totemo ōkii/ōki-na hoteru desu ne.
That's a really big hotel, isn't it?

Tomoko chan no gakkō wa chiisai/chiisa-na gakkō desu ka.
Is your school a small school, Tomoko?

6. MOTTO YASUI, MOTTO ŌKII – "CHEAPER" AND "BIGGER"

To describe something as "bigger," "smaller," "more expensive," "cheaper," etc., in Japanese, simply put **motto** ("more") in front of the appropriate word, which is the equivalent of saying "more big," "more small," "more quiet."

Sumimasen ga, motto chiisai no wa arimasu ka.
Excuse me, but do you have a smaller one?

Kono buraun no jaketto wa suki desu ga, sono kuroi no wa motto suki desu.
I like this brown jacket, but I like that black one more.

Tsugi no tesuto wa motto muzukashii deshō.
The next test will probably be more difficult.

Sumimasen, motto yukkuri hanashite kudasai.
Excuse me, but could you please speak more slowly?

7. SORE WA II DESU GA – JOINING SENTENCES WITH "BUT"

The word **ga** can be used to join two sentences which are in contrast, so it is much like the English "but." However, remember that in Japanese **ga** ends the first part of the sentence before the comma, whereas the English equivalent "but" begins the second part of the sentence.

Maiku san wa kimasu ga, Takahashi san wa kimasen.
Mike is coming, but Ms. Takahashi isn't.

Kono burū no sētā wa suki desu ga, sono guriin no wa iya desu ne.
I like this blue sweater, but that green one is horrible, isn't it?

Tōkyō no depāto wa itsumo konde imasu ga, Chiba no wa amari konde imasen.
The department stores in Tokyo are always crowded, but the ones in Chiba aren't (very crowded).

Tomoko wa mada chiisai kodomo desu ga, mainichi shinbun o yomimasu.
Tomoko is still a small child, but she reads the newspaper every day.

Ani wa Tōkyō ni sunde imasu ga, ane wa Chiba ni sunde imasu.
My older brother lives in Tokyo, but my older sister lives in Chiba.

Sometimes **ga** is used to link two sentences even though there isn't a very strong element of contrast.

Watashi wa kaimono ga totemo suki desu ga, Takahashi san wa dō desu ka.
I really enjoy shopping – how about you, Ms. Takahashi?

Watashi wa ashita Yokohama e ikimasu ga, Saitō san mo issho ni ikimasen ka.
I'm going to Yokohama tomorrow – do you want to come along too, Ms. Saitō?

Asatte wa haha no tanjōbi desu ga, nani o kaimashō ka.
It's Mom's birthday the day after tomorrow. What shall we buy her?

8. O-GENKI DESU KA – "HOW ARE YOU?"

This phrase, literally meaning "Are you well?", is a common greeting, but note that the honorific beginning o- should not be used in your answer, because you are talking about yourself. To make your response even more courteous, thank the person for asking by using the set phrase **o-kage sama de.**

A. **O-genki desu ka.**
How are you?
B. **Hai, o-kage sama de, genki desu.**
Thank you, I'm fine.

9. ITSUMO, TOKIDOKI – "ALWAYS," "SOMETIMES" AND OTHER WORDS OF FREQUENCY

Here are some of the most commonly-used words of frequency that you might find useful. They usually come before the verb, but they can also be used to begin the sentence or phrase.

itsumo	yoku	tokidoki	amari	zenzen
always	often	sometimes	not often	never, not at all

Ani wa ima daigakusei desu ga, zenzen benkyō shimasen.
My elder brother is a university student now, but he never does any work.

Rajio no nyūsu o itsumo kikimasu ga, terebi no nyūsu wa amari mimasen.
I always listen to the news on the radio, but I don't often watch it on TV.

A. **Maiku san wa gakkō de yoku Nihongo de hanashimasu ka.**
Do you often speak in Japanese at the school, Mike?
B. **Hai, yoku hanashimasu.**
Yes, often.

Itsumo ginkō no tonari no resutoran de hiru-gohan o tabemasu.
We always eat lunch at the restaurant next to the bank.

VOCABULARY

beruto: belt
Chiba: satellite city of Tokyo
daijōbu: fine, all right
dame-na: no good, useless
de gozaimasu: is, are [formal]
depāto: department store
deshō: I wonder if, probably, must be
dezain: design
dezainā: designer
fakkusu: fax
G-pan: jeans
ga: but [when joining two sentences]
genki: healthy, energetic
gozaimasu: have [formal]
hen-na: odd, strange
Hokkaidō: northernmost of the four main islands of Japan
hoteru: hotel
ii desu ga: it's fine, but ...
itsumo: always
iya-na: horrible
jaketto: jacket
kaimashō ka: shall we buy? [from **kau**]
kaimono: shopping [noun]
kantan-na: brief, simple
kirei-na: pretty, clean
kodomo: child
konde imasu: is crowded [from **komu**]
kōto: coat
kutsu: shoes
mo: too, also
motto yasui: cheaper
motto; more
nekutai: necktie
o-genki desu ka: how are you?
o-hisashiburi: it's been a long time
o-kage sama de: thank you for asking [set phrase in response to o-genki desu ka]
repōto: report

saizu: size
sētā: sweater
shatsu: shirt
shinsetsu-na: kind, gentle
shizuka-na: quiet, peaceful
sora: sky
sukāto: skirt
suki ja nai: don't like [informal]
sūtsu: suit
T-shatsu: T-shirt
taihen-na: terrible, awful
tokidoki: sometimes
totemo: very, extremely
wanpiisu: dress
yoku: often
yūmei-na: famous
zenzen: never [+ negative verb]

Colors:
aka(i): red
ao(i): green
buraun: brown
burū: blue
chaiiro: brown
gurē: gray
guriin: green
kiiro(i): yellow
kuro(i): black
midori: green
murasaki: purple
orenji: orange
pinku: pink
shiro(i): white

TEST YOURSELF

1. *Read through the dialog at the beginning of the lesson again, and then say if the following statements are true or false.*

1. Watanabe san to okusan wa ima depāto ni imasu.　T/F

2. Watanabe san wa gurē no sūtsu wa suki ja arimasen.　T/F

3. Burū no sūtsu no dezainā wa yūmei ja arimasen.　T/F

4. Okusan wa kaimono ga suki desu ga, tomodachi wa suki ja arimasen.　T/F

5. Watanabe san no okusan wa yoku Ginza e ikimasu.　T/F

6. Yasui sūtsu no saizu wa daijōbu desu ga, Watanabe san wa dezain ga suki ja arimasen.　T/F

2. *Ms. Takahashi is out shopping with a friend, and at the moment she's looking at blouses. Choose the appropriate word from the parentheses to complete their conversation.*

Takahashi	Suki-na burausu ga arimasen ne.
Friend	Kore wa dō desu ka. Kono (**aka/akai**) hana (**no/na**) burausu wa kirei deshō.
Takahashi	(**Ii/Iya**) desu. Aka ga kirai desu.
Friend	Sō desu ka. Tokorode (**dō shite/daijōbu**) atarashii burausu o (**kaerimasu/kaimasu**) ka. A, wakarimashita. Konban Neruson san to issho ni eiga o (**machimasu/mimasu**) ne.
Takahashi	Sō desu yo. Ima yo-ji han desu (**ga/wa**), roku-ji han ni Neruson san ni (**aimasu/imasu**). Dō shimashō ka. Jikan ga arimasen ne.
Friend	Ja, wanpiisu wa dō desu ka.
Takahashi	Sō ne. Wanpiisu ni shimashō. A, (**kono/kore**) dezainā wa dai-suki desu. Demo takai (**arimasu/deshō**).
Friend	Iie, mite kudasai yo. (**Takai/takaku**) arimasen.
Takahashi	Ja, kore wa ii. Kore ni shimasu.

3. *Make comments about the items in the pictures, as in the example.*

Example: like
Suki-na kuruma desu ne!

1. pretty!

2. full of energy!

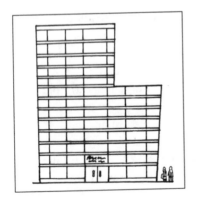

3. high!

4. famous!

5. strange!

4. *Look at the three short sentences in each group below, and then choose the two which can be joined together with ga ("but") to make one long sentence, as in the example.*

Example: **a. Kodomo ja arimasen.**
b. Hiro-chan wa mada chiisai kodomo desu.
c. Konpyūtā ga dai-suki desu.

b+c: Hiro-chan wa mada chiisai kodomo desu ga, konpyūtā ga dai-suki desu.

1. a. Kono gurē no sūtsu wa suki desu.
    b. Gurē wa suki ja arimasen.
    c. Chotto ōkii desu.

2. a. Sakana wa tokidoki tabemasu.
    b. O-cha wa amari suki ja arimasen.
    c. Watashi wa kōhii o yoku nomimasu.

3. a. Eiga wa go-ji ni hajimarimasu.
    b. Chotto hayai deshō.
    c. Oishii deshō.

4. a. Asatte imasu.
    b. Asatte kimasen.
    c. Watashi wa ashita kaisha ni imasen.

5. a. Purintā wa dame desu.
    b. Watashi no konpyūtā wa daijōbu desu.
    c. Konpyūtā wa daijōbu ja arimasen.

5. How would you say these sentences in Japanese?

1. I wonder if that person over there is Mr. Saitō.

2. Could you write a briefer report, please?

3. The black jacket is probably a bit small.

4. The train is very crowded today, isn't it?

5. I don't really like Tokyo, but Yokohama is nice.

6. My mother works at a famous department store in Tokyo.

 The name of Japan's capital city, Tōkyō, uses a combination of the characters for "east" and "capital."

DAI KYŪ-KA

SHŪMATSU WA DŌ DESHITA KA.
HOW WAS THE WEEKEND?

It's Monday morning, and as Mr. Watanabe waits on the station platform for the train to work, he bumps into Mike.

Watanabe **A, Neruson san, ohayō gozaimasu.**
Ah, Mr. Nelson, good morning.

Mike **Ohayō gozaimasu. Kyō wa, densha wa konde imasu ne.**
Good morning. The trains are crowded today, aren't they!

Watanabe **Sō desu ne. Getsuyōbi wa itsumo sō desu ne. Tokorode, shūmatsu wa dō deshita ka. Dokoka e ikimashita ka.**
Yes, they are. It's always like this on Mondays, isn't it? By the way, how was your weekend? Did you go anywhere?

Mike **Ē, totemo tanoshikatta desu. Tomodachi futari to issho ni, yama e ikimashita. Doyōbi no asa itte, kinō no yoru kaerimashita. Dakara kesa chotto tsukarete imasu.**

	Yes, it was extremely enjoyable. I went to the mountains together with two friends. We went on Saturday morning, and came back yesterday evening. That's why this morning I'm a bit tired.
Watanabe	**Ii desu ne. Doko ni ikimashita ka.**
	That's nice. Where did you go?
Mike	**Nihon Arupusu no onsen ni ikimashita. Machi no namae wa wasuremashita kedo, totemo kirei-na tokoro deshita.**
	We went to a hot spring in the Japan Alps. I've forgotten the name of the town, but it was a really pretty place.
Watanabe	**Onsen! Ii ne. Soto no onsen mo arimashita ka.**
	A hot spring! Nice. Was there an outside hot spring bath too?
Mike	**Arimashita. Doyōbi no yoru mo, nichiyōbi no asa mo hairimashita. Tenki wa chotto samukatta kedo, onsen no yu wa taihen atsukatta desu.**
	Yes, there was. We went in Saturday evening and Sunday morning. The weather was a bit cold, but the spring water was extremely hot.
Watanabe	**Ryokan ni tomarimashita ka.**
	Did you stay at an inn?
Mike	**Hai, sō desu. Konde imashita ga, wakai onna no hitotachi ga takusan tomatte imashita yo.**
	Yes, we did. It was crowded, but there were a lot of young women staying there.
Watanabe	**Sō desu ka. Hanashi o shimashita ka.**
	I see. Did you get to talk?
Mike	**Iie, chansu ga arimasen deshita. Watashitachi o mite, minna hazukashikatta deshō.**
	No, there was no chance. They saw us, and all of them probably got embarrassed.
Watanabe	**Sore wa zannen deshita ne.**
	That was a pity!
Mike	**Ē, sō desu ne. Tokorode, Watanabe san wa nani o shimashita ka. Dokoka e ikimashita ka.**
	Yes, it was. By the way, what did you do, Mr. Watanabe? Did you go anywhere?
Watanabe	**Taihen deshita yo. Zenzen omoshiroku arimasen deshita. Kazoku to issho ni Tōkyō e itte, kaimono o shimashita ga, nichiyōbi no depēto wa, mō iya desu yo!**

	It was terrible. Completely uninteresting. I went with the family to Tokyo, and we did some shopping – department stores on a Sunday are horrible!
Mike	**Nanika kaimashita ka.**
	Did you buy anything?
Watanabe	**Ē, atarashii sūtsu o kaimashita kedo, hontō ni jikan ga kakarimashita. Kyō wa, watashi mo taihen tsukarete imasu yo.**
	Yes, I bought a new suit, but it really took (a long) time. Today I'm really exhausted too!

STRUCTURE AND USAGE NOTES

1. GETSUYŌBI – "MONDAY" AND OTHER DAYS OF THE WEEK

The days of the week are as follows:

getsuyōbi	Monday
kayōbi	Tuesday
suiyōbi	Wednesday
mokuyōbi	Thursday
kinyōbi	Friday
doyōbi	Saturday
- nichiyōbi	Sunday
nan-yōbi	what day?

Tokidoki doyōbi ni kaisha e ikimasu.
I sometimes go to the office on Saturdays.

Kinyōbi no yoru ni eiga o mimashō ka.
Shall we see a movie on Friday evening?

Getsuyōbi kara mokuyōbi made Tōkyō ni imasu ga, kinyōbi no asa Nagoya e kaerimasu.
I'm in Tokyo from Monday to Thursday, but I'll return to Nagoya on Friday morning.

Raishū no doyōbi to nichiyōbi ni umi e ikimasu ga, issho ni ikimasen ka.
Next Saturday and Sunday we're going to the ocean – would you like to come with us?

2. IKIMASHITA KA – "DID YOU GO?" AND OTHER PAST TENSE VERBS

To talk about something which happened in the past, simply end the verb with -**mashita** instead of -**masu**. (There are also plain forms of the past tense verbs, but we will look at those in the following lessons.) Note that the pronunciation of this past tense ending is like -**mash'ta**, that is, the final -**i**- is hardly sounded. Here are some examples of past tense verbs.

Plain form	-masu form	Past	Meaning
iku	ikimasu	ikimashita	went
kuru	kimasu	kimashita	came
tomaru	tomarimasu	tomarimashita	stayed
matsu	machimasu	machimashita	waited
hairu	hairimasu	hairimashita	entered
aru	arimasu	arimashita	there was/were
miru	mimasu	mimashita	saw, watched
matte iru	matte imasu	matte imashita	was waiting
mite iru	mite imasu	mite imashita	was watching
shite iru	shite imasu	shite imashita	was doing

Doyōbi no gogo ni, yakyū o mimashita ka.
Did you see the baseball (game) on Saturday afternoon?

Mainichi kanji no benkyō o shimashita ga, sugu wasuremashita.
I studied kanji (Chinese characters) every day, but I soon forgot them.

Itsu kaisha ni hairimashita ka.
When did you join [Lit: enter] your company?

Kinō kono atarashii kutsu o kaimashita ga, chotto chiisai desu.
I bought these new shoes yesterday, but they're a bit small.

Doyōbi ni kaimono ni ikimashita ne. Nanika kaimashita ka.
You went shopping on Saturday, right? Did you buy anything?

Ichi-jikan machimashita yo. Dō shimashita ka.
I waited an hour! What happened?

The past form of **desu** is **deshita** ("was/were").

Fumiko chan no Eigo no sensei no namae wa nan deshita ka.
What was the name of Fumiko's English teacher?

Nichiyōbi wa hontō ni iya-na tenki deshita ne.
It was really awful weather on Sunday, wasn't it?

Eiga wa dō deshita ka.
How was the movie?

Tanjōbi wa nan-yōbi deshita ka.
What day was your birthday?

Senshū Saitō san ni aimashita ne. Genki deshita ka.
You met Mr. Saitō last week, right? How was he?

Saying what you *didn't* do isn't so difficult. Just add **deshita** to the negative **-masen** form.

Present negative		Past negative	
kakimasen	don't write	**kakimasen deshita**	didn't write
ikimasen	don't go	**ikimasen deshita**	didn't go
tabemasen	don't eat	**tabemasen deshita**	didn't eat
shimasen	don't do	**shimasen deshita**	didn't do
kaimasen	don't buy	**kaimasen deshita**	didn't buy
kaerimasen	don't return	**kaerimasen deshita**	didn't return
shite imasen	isn't doing	**shite imasen deshita**	wasn't doing
matte imasen	isn't waiting	**matte imasen deshita**	wasn't waiting
kaite imasen	isn't writing	**kaite imasen deshita**	wasn't writing

Kare no hanashi ga zenzen wakarimasen deshita.
I didn't understand what he was saying at all.

Dō shite kaigi no repōto o kakimasen deshita ka.
Why didn't you write up the report of the meeting?

Nyū Yōku ni sunde imasen deshita yo. Rondon ni sunde imashita.
I wasn't living in New York. I was living in London.

Jikan ga amari kakarimasen deshita.
It didn't take very long.

Ichi-jikan machimashita ga, tomodachi wa kimasen deshita.
I waited an hour, but my friend didn't come.

The same principle applies to **desu** when making the past form of the negative ("wasn't/weren't"). In other words, find the negative (**ja arimasen**) and add **deshita**.

Sono ryokan wa amari suki ja arimasen deshita.
We didn't like that ryokan [inn] very much.

Kirei-na tokoro ja arimasen deshita.
It wasn't a pretty place.

Machi no namae wa Shirakawa ja arimasen deshita yo. Shirazawa deshita.
The name of the town wasn't Shirakawa. It was Shirazawa.

You may also come across the form **ja nakatta desu** instead of **ja arimasen deshita**. It means the same thing, but is derived from the plain form.

Watanabe san no tanjōbi wa kinō ja nakatta desu yo. Ashita desu.
Mr. Watanabe's birthday wasn't yesterday! It's tomorrow.

3. TANOSHIKATTA – "IT WAS ENJOYABLE," AND OTHER PAST TENSE ADJECTIVES

It has already been mentioned that -i adjectives sometimes act like verbs, and one way they show this is by having a different past tense, used when describing something that was in the past. To make the past form, drop the last -i and add -katta. Because this -katta ending already shows that it's the past tense, the final desu doesn't need to change. (If the adjective comes in the middle of a sentence, as in the first example below, then desu can be omitted.)

-i adjective	Past tense	Meaning
oishii desu	oishikatta desu	was delicious
tanoshii desu	tanoshikatta desu	was enjoyable
atsui desu	atsukatta desu	was hot
ii/yoi	yokatta desu	was good
hazukashii	hazukashikatta desu	was embarrassed, shy
ōkii desu	ōkikatta desu	was big

Hoteru wa yokatta (desu) ga, chotto takakatta desu.
The hotel was fine, but it was a little expensive.

Totemo oishikatta desu. Go-chisō sama deshita.
That tasted wonderful. Thank you for the meal.

Maiku san no tanjōbi no pātii wa hontō ni tanoshikatta desu yo. Takusan no tomodachi ga kimashita.
Mike's birthday party was really good [Lit: enjoyable]. Lots of (his) friends came.

Bideo wa omoshirokatta desu ka.
Was the video interesting?

Sensei no namae wa zenzen oboete imasen deshita. Dakara hontō ni hazukashikatta desu yo.
I couldn't remember the teacher's name at all. So it was really embarrassing!

To make the negative of -i adjectives in the past, in other words to talk about things which *weren't* hot or *weren't* expensive, etc., once again just add **deshita** to the present tense negative. This, you may remember, ends in **-ku arimasen**, so the past form ending is **-ku arimasen deshita.**

Kanji no tesuto wa amari muzukashiku arimasen deshita ne.
The kanji test wasn't very difficult, was it?

Maiku san no tanjōbi no pātii de o-sake o takusan nomimashita ga, atama wa zenzen itaku arimasen deshita.
I drank a lot of sake at Mike's birthday party, but I didn't have a headache at all.

Instead of the ending **-ku arimasen deshita**, you may also hear **-ku nakatta desu**, as **nakatta** is the plain form of **arimasen deshita.**

Sono hon wa amari omoshiroku nakatta desu ne.
That book wasn't very interesting, was it?

4. FUTARI – COUNTING PEOPLE

When we count things in English, we sometimes need to use special counters, such as "two *bars* of chocolate," "one *spoonful* of sugar," "three *cartons* of milk," "a *glass* of water," etc. This happens even more in Japanese, and there are, for example, special counters for things which are flat (newspapers, stamps, train tickets), things which are long and thin (bottles, rolled umbrellas, pencils), large animals (cows, horses), and many others. To count people, add the counter **-nin**, except in the cases of "one person" and "two people," which are irregular.

nan-nin?	how many people?		
hitori	one person	**roku-nin**	six people
futari	two people	**shichi-nin**	seven people
san-nin	three people	**hachi-nin**	eight people
yo-nin	four people	**ku-nin**	nine people
go-nin	five people	**jū-nin**	ten people

Sono chiisai gakkō de jū-nin no sensei ga oshiete imasu.
There are ten teachers teaching at that small school.

Imōto ga hitori to otōto ga futari imasu.
I have one younger sister and two younger brothers.

Ogawa san no kaisha de nan-nin hataraite imasu ka.
How many people are there working at Mr. Ogawa's company?

Sono ryokan ni hachi-nin dake tomatte imashita yo. Otoko no hito san-nin, onna no hito san-nin, kodomo hitori to watashi deshita.
There were only eight people staying at that inn - three men, three women, a child and me.

Kinō no yoru Nihongo no kurasu ga arimashita ga, futari dake kimashita. Dakara hontō ni tsukaremashita.
I had a Japanese class yesterday evening, but only two people came. So it was really tiring.

5. THE PARTICLE NI – "TO," "TOWARDS"

We have already come across the particle ni used with arimasu or imasu to show the location of something, but it can also be used like e to show movement to or towards a place.

Shūmatsu ni dokoka e/ni ikimashita ka.
Did you go anywhere on the weekend?

Takahashi san wa itsu Kyōto e/ni kaerimasu ka.
When is Ms. Takahashi going back to Kyoto?

Fumiko chan wa kinō amari genki ja arimasen deshita. Dakara gakkō e/ni ikimasen deshita.
Fumiko wasn't very well yesterday. That's why she didn't go to school.

6. ... MO ... MO – "BOTH ... AND ..."

Sentences with ... mo ... mo are the equivalent of "both ... and ..." when in the positive, and "neither ... nor ..." when in the negative.

O-sake mo biiru mo nomimashita ka. Dakara atama ga itai desu yo.
You drank (both) sake and beer? That's why you have a headache!

Takahashi san wa tenisu mo gorufu mo jōzu desu ga, watashi wa heta desu.
Ms. Takahashi is good at both tennis and golf, but I'm bad (at them).

Kōhii mo o-cha mo nomimasen.
I don't drink (either) coffee or green tea.

7. JOINING SENTENCES WITH -TE

The -te form of verbs can be used to link two or more sentences together, and can often be translated as "and." The -te form can be used in the middle of a sentence regardless of whether the event it describes happened in the past, is happening now or will happen in the future, because it is the verb at the *end* of the sentence that shows the overall tense of the sentence.

> Doyōbi no asa ni Tōkyō e ikimashita. +
> Atarashii sūtsu o kaimashita. =
> Doyōbi no asa ni Tōkyō e itte, atarashii sūtsu o kaimashita.
> On Saturday morning I went to Tokyo, and bought a new suit.

> Shūmatsu ni tomodachi to issho ni yama e ikimasu. +
> Onsen no ryokan ni tomarimasu. =
> Shūmatsu ni tomodachi to issho ni yama e itte, onsen no ryokan ni tomarimasu.
> On the weekend I'm going to the mountains with a friend, and staying at an inn at a hot spring.

Here are some more examples of how the -te form is used in this way.

Ashita Pari ni itte, asatte wa Roma ni ikimasu. Tsukaremasu yo!
I go to Paris tomorrow, and Rome the next day. I'm going to be tired!

Tanaka san wa mainichi tenisu no renshū o shite, totemo jōzu desu.
Mr. Tanaka practices tennis every day, and is really good [Lit: skillful].

Mokuyōbi ni atarashii Nihongo no kurasu ni haitte, totemo omoshirokatta desu.
On Monday I joined a new Japanese class, and it was really interesting.

Kinō no yoru, uchi ni ite, bideo o mimashita.
Yesterday evening, I stayed at home and watched a video.

The equivalent form for **desu** is **de**.

> Getsuyōbi no yoru wa yakyū no renshū desu. +
> Kayōbi wa tenisu no renshū desu. =
> Getsuyōbi no yoru wa yakyū no renshū de, kayōbi wa tenisu no renshū desu.
> Monday evening is baseball practice, and Tuesday is tennis practice.

Takahashi san no imōtosan wa kirei desu. +
Takahashi san no imōtosan wa shinsetsu desu. =
Takahashi san no imōtosan wa kirei de, shinsetsu desu.
Ms. Takahashi's younger sister is pretty, and kind.

Maiku san wa sensei desu. +
Yokohama Gakuin Kōkō de oshiete imasu. =
Maiku san wa sensei de, Yokohama Gakuin Kōkō de oshiete
imasu.
Mike is a teacher, and he teaches at Yokohama High School.

Watashi wa Eigo ga heta desu. +
Hazukashii desu. =
Watashi wa Eigo ga heta de, hazukashii desu.
I'm embarrassed because I'm bad at English. [Lit: I'm bad at
English, and I'm embarrassed.]

8. NIHON NO ARUPUSU NO ONSEN – A CULTURAL NOTE

There are natural hot springs (onsen) all over Japan, and staying at a
nearby ryokan, or traditional Japanese-style inn, and relaxing in the
hot waters of the springs is a very popular weekend pursuit. Most
ryokan have several segregated baths inside the building, but some
also have rock pools outside which are fed by the natural hot water,
and it is very pleasant to relax in the steaming water, surrounded by
beautiful views of mountains, especially in the winter when snow is
lying on the ground. Visiting hot springs used to be popular mainly
among the older generation, but more and more young people are
now beginning to enjoy this healthy pastime.

9. JOINING SENTENCES WITH KEDO – "BUT"

The word kedo (and its more formal variations keredo and
keredomo) is used to join sentences together with the meaning "but,"
and always ends the first part of the sentence, before the comma. It
can sometimes be used instead of ga ("but"), but kedo is the only one
that can be used in the sense of "although."

Tenisu wa dai-suki desu kedo, amari jōzu ja arimasen.
Although I really like tennis, I'm not very good.

Shūmatsu ni umi ni ikimashita kedo, taihen samukatta desu. Dakara
tanoshiku arimasen deshita.
We went to the ocean on the weekend, but it was very cold. So it
wasn't much fun.

Ogawa san wa mainichi mainichi gorufu no renshū o shimasu kedo, mada heta desu.
Although Mr. Ogawa practices golf day after day, he's still no good.

When an -i adjective is followed by **kedo**, the **desu** which usually comes after such an adjective can be omitted.

Atama wa chotto itai kedo, daijōbu desu.
My head hurts a little, but I'm okay.

Sono o-sake wa oishii kedo, chotto takai desu.
That sake is delicious, but it's very expensive.

10. A BRIEF NOTE ON THE PLAIN FORM

As you've seen in earlier lessons, all verbs have a plain form (e.g. **taberu, kaeru, wakaru**) which can be used in informal situations such as with very close friends, and the more polite **-masu** form (**tabemasu, kaerimasu, wakarimasu**) for general use. However, it is the verb at the end of the sentence which determines the overall tone. So as long as this final verb is in the **-masu** form, any verb which occurs in the middle of the sentence can be in the plain form and still sound courteous. Here are some examples.

Takahashi san wa gorufu ga jōzu da kedo, watashi wa jōzu ja arimasen yo.
You're good at golf, Ms. Takahashi, but I'm not!

Watanabe san no kazoku wa ashita yama no onsen ni iku kedo, Watanabe san wa ikimasen.
Mr. Watanabe's family are going to a hot spring in the mountains tomorrow, but Mr. Watanabe isn't going.

Sushi wa tokidoki taberu kedo, amari suki ja arimasen.
Although I eat sushi sometimes, I don't really like it very much.

Ōsaka kara Tōkyō made kuruma de jikan ga kakaru deshō.
It must take a long time from Osaka to Tokyo by car.

We will look at the plain form of negatives and past tenses in the next few lessons.

VOCABULARY
arimashita: was/were [from **aru**]
asa: morning
atsukatta: was hot [from **atsui**]

bideo: video
biiru: beer
chansu: chance, opportunity
dakara: so, therefore
dake: only
deshita: was/were [from desu]
dō shimashita ka: what happened?
dokoka: somewhere, anywhere
doyōbi: Saturday
ē: yes [informal]
futari: two (people)
getsuyōbi: Monday
gorufu: golf
hairimashita: went in, entered [from hairu]
hazukashikatta: was embarrassed, shy [from hazukashii]
heta: bad at, unskillful
hitori: one (person)
hitotachi: people
hontō ni: really, truly
ikimashita: went [from iku]
itsu: when?
itte: go and ... [from iku]
-jikan: — hours
jōzu: skillful, good at
kaerimashita: went home [from kaeru]
kaimashita: bought [from kau]
kakarimashita: took (time), lasted [from kakaru]
kanji: Chinese written characters
kayōbi: Tuesday
kedo: but, although
kesa: this morning
kinō: yesterday
kinyōbi: Friday
kissaten: coffee shop
konde imashita: was crowded [from komu]
kurasu: class
machi: town, city
... mo ... mo: both ... and .../neither ... nor ...
mokuyōbi: Thursday
nan-nin: how many people?
nan-yōbi: what day?
nanika: something, anything
ni: to, towards
nichiyōbi: Sunday

Nihon Arupusu: Japan Alps, mountain range in central Japan
-nin: [counter for people]
Nyū Yōku: New York
o-sake: sake, rice wine
omoshiroi: interesting, amusing
omoshiroku arimasen deshita: wasn't interesting [from **omoshiroi**]
onna no hito: woman
onna no hitotachi: women
onsen: hot spring
otoko no hito: man
pātii: party
raishū: next week
Rondon: London
ryokan: Japanese-style inn
sake: sake, rice wine
samukatta: was cold [from **samui**]
san-nin: three (people)
senshū: last week
shimashita: did [from **suru**]
shūmatsu: weekend
soto: outside
suiyōbi: Wednesday
-tachi: [plural ending for words associated with people]
tanoshikatta: was fun [from **tanoshii**]
tenki: weather
tokoro: place
tomarimashita: stayed [from **tomaru**]
tomatte imashita: was/were staying [from **tomaru**]
tsukarete imasu: is/are tired [from **tsukareru**]
umi: sea, ocean
wakai: young
wasuremashita: forgot [from **wasureru**]
watashitachi: us, we
yama: mountain
yoru: evening
yu: hot water
zannen: pity, unfortunate

TEST YOURSELF

1. Read through the dialog at the beginning of the lesson again, and then say if the following statements are true or false.

1. San-nin wa yama e ikimashita. T/F

2. Onsen wa Nihon Arupusu no kirei-na tokoro ni arimashita. T/F

3. Tenki mo, onsen no yu mo, atsukatta desu. T/F

4. Maiku san wa, wakai onna no hitotachi o mite, hazukashikatta desu. T/F

5. Watanabe san wa kaimono o shimashita ga, tanoshiku arimasen deshita. T/F

6. Watanabe san wa hitori de Tōkyō e ikimashita. T/F

2. *Mike has decided that it's time he became more organized, so he's putting all of his appointments down on his calendar. Look at what he did last week, and then ask questions and give answers about each evening's activities, as in the example below.*

Example: A. Getsuyōbi no yoru, nani o shimashita ka.
B. Uchi ni ite, terebi o mimashita.

Monday	Tuesday	Wednesday	Thursday	Friday	Saturday Sunday
at home – watch TV	6:30–7:30 tennis practice	call Mom	6:00–8:00 Japanese class	to restaurant with Ms. Takahashi	go to ocean!

3. *Unfortunately, last week was not the success it appeared to be. In fact, something went wrong every evening. Using the notes Mike wrote on the calendar, make sentences about what went wrong each evening, as in the example. Use* **kedo** *in your answers.*

Example: Getsuyōbi no yoru, uchi ni ite, terebi o mimashita kedo, zenzen omoshiroku arimasen deshita.

Monday	Tuesday	Wednesday	Thursday	Friday	Saturday Sunday
completely uninteresting!	I wasn't any good!	she wasn't in!	only me!	tasted awful!	extremely cold!
at home – watch TV	6:30–7:30 tennis practice	call Mom	6:00–8:00 Japanese class	to restaurant with Ms. Takahashi	go to ocean!

4. *Ms. Takahashi is telling her friend about her visit to the movies with Mike last week. What did she say? Below are some cues to help you piece together what she said. Use the -te form to join the sentences, as in the example.*

Example: (waited in front of the station – really cold!)
   Eki no mae de matte, hontō ni samukatta desu.

1. met Mike – went to Ginza – saw a movie

2. movie was SF – not interesting

3. went into coffee shop (**kissaten**) – drank coffee

4. we were speaking in English – difficult!

5. bad at English – was shy!

6. went home by taxi – expensive!

5. *How would you say these sentences in Japanese?*

1. When did you come back from the USA?

2. How many people went to the hot spring in the mountains?

3. It was really horrible weather.

4. We ate a lot of sushi and drank a lot of sake last night.

5. I read the paper this morning, but I've already forgotten the news.

6. Did you go anywhere on the weekend?

The word **onsen**, meaning "hot spring/spa," is a combination of the characters for "hot/warm" and "spring water".

NIHON NO KOTO, DŌ OMOIMASU KA.
WHAT DO YOU THINK OF JAPAN?

It's Friday evening, and everyone has gathered in the staff room for the formal welcome party for Mike and two other new members of staff. The other two new teachers have just given a short speech of self-introduction (**jiko shōkai**) and now it's Mike's turn.

Mike	**Mina san, hajimemashite. Watashi wa Maiku Neruson to mōshimasu. Amerika no Ohaio-shu kara kimashita. Watashi wa san-shūkan mae ni Nihon e kimashita. Gakkō no shigoto wa omoshiroi to omoimasu. Ganbarimasu. Yoroshiku onegai shimasu.**
	How do you do, everyone. I'm called Mike Nelson. I'm from Ohio. I came to Japan three weeks ago. I think the work in this school is going to be very interesting. I intend to do my best. Thank you.
Watanabe	**Yoku dekimashita, arigatō. Nihongo ga jōzu desu ne.** You did very well, thank you. Your Japanese is (very) good, isn't it?

Mike	Iie, mada mada dame desu. Hazukashikute, taihen deshita!
	No, it's still poor. It was terrible, because I was so embarrassed! [Lit: I was embarrassed, and it was terrible.]
Watanabe	Daijōbu deshita yo. A, Katō sensei desu. Neruson san wa mada atte inai deshō. Atama ga yokute, omoshiroi hito desu yo. Shōkai shimashō.
	It was fine. Ah, there's Mr. Katō [Lit: teacher Katō]. You probably haven't met him yet, have you? He's smart, and a very interesting person. I'll introduce you.

Mr. Watanabe introduces Mike to Mr. Katō, and they chat.

Katō	Neruson sensei, Nihon wa mada san-shūkan desu ne. Nihon no koto, dō omoimasu ka.
	Mr. Nelson, you've been in Japan for only three weeks, right? What do you think of Japan?
Mike	Totemo omoshirokute, dai-suki desu! Nihon wa ii kuni da to omoimasu.
	It's very interesting, and I like it very much. I think Japan is a great country.
Katō	Sō desu ka. Ii kotae desu ne. Tabemono mo daijōbu desu ka.
	I see. That's a good answer! Are you okay with the food?
Mike	Hai, Nihon ryōri wa totemo suki desu. Sashimi ya sushi ya soba wa zenbu taberu koto ga dekimasu.
	Yes, I like Japanese cooking very much. Sashimi, sushi, soba [noodles], I can eat all of it.
Katō	Sō desu ka. Ja, Nihon no seikatsu wa, mondai nai deshō! Anō, shumi wa nan desu ka. Supōtsu wa suki desu ka.
	I see. Well, you shouldn't have any problems with life in Japan! Uh, what are your interests? Do you like sport?
Watanabe	(laughing) Neruson sensei, ki o tsukete kudasai yo. Kore kara gakkō no sensei no yakyū chiimu no hanashi da to omoimasu. Katō sensei wa yakyū chiimu no manejā de, itsumo chiimu no koto dake o kangaete imasu.
	Mr. Nelson, please be careful! I think he's going to talk about the school's staff baseball team. Mr. Katō is the team's manager, and he only ever thinks about the team!

Katō	Sore wa uso desu yo! Neruson san, sensei no yakyū chiimu ga aru kedo, issho ni shimasen ka.
	That's not true! Mr. Nelson, we have a teachers' baseball team – would you like to play with us?
Mike	(hesitating) Watashi wa yakyū ga suki da kedo, hayaku hashiru koto ga dekimasen.
	I like baseball, but I can't run fast.
Katō	Daijōbu desu yo. Sa, tsugi no gēmu wa nichiyōbi no asa desu ga.
	That's fine. Right, the next game is on Sunday morning...
Mike	Nichiyōbi no asa?!
	Sunday morning?!
Watanabe	Ja, Neruson sensei, ganbatte kudasai!
	Well, Mr. Nelson, do your best!

STRUCTURE AND USAGE NOTES

1. JIKO SHŌKAI – INTRODUCING YOURSELF

If you find yourself at any kind of gathering in Japan where some of the people are meeting for the first time, then the newcomers will probably be asked to do a jiko shōkai, or short speech of self-introduction. The information you give may differ depending on the kind of occasion, but usually you would include your name and nationality, your job and company, or university and major subject of study if you are a student. As a foreigner, you can also mention how long you have been studying Japanese, when you came to Japan, and what you like about Japan. The speech usually finishes with a standard phrase of courtesy such as yoroshiku onegai shimasu.

Here are some sentences which you might like to include in a self-introduction.

[your name] to mōshimasu.
I'm called [name].

[company or university name] no [your name] desu.
I'm [name] from [company or university].

[country or city name] kara kimashita.
I'm from [country or city].

Ima [place-name] ni sunde imasu.
I now live in [placename].

[name] daigaku de [subject] o benkyō shite imasu.
I'm studying [subject] at [name] university.

[company name] ni tsutomete imasu.
I work at [company name].

2. ... GA JŌZU DESU – "IS GOOD AT ..."

With the words jōzu ("good at") and heta ("poor at"), it's the thing
that you are good or bad at that takes the subject particle ga. The
person who is good or bad at it is shown by wa.

Ogawa san wa Eigo ga jōzu desu ne.
Ms. Ogawa is good at English, isn't she?

Watashi wa ryōri ga amari jōzu ja arimasen.
I'm not very good at cooking.

Ane mo imōto mo piano ga jōzu desu ga, watashi wa heta desu.
Both my older sister and my younger sister are good at the piano, but
I'm hopeless.

3. HAZUKASHIKUTE – JOINING -I ADJECTIVES WITH -KUTE

In English when we want to link together several simple sentences,
we can just put "and" between them ("We went to Paris and we had
a good time"), but it is not the same in Japanese. In the last lesson we
saw how some sentences can be linked with the -te form of verbs
(Pari ni itte, tanoshikatta desu). It is similar when joining sentences
which end in -i adjectives: drop the final -i and then add -kute.

Omoshiroi eiga deshita. + Ii eiga deshita. =
Omoshirokute, ii eiga deshita.
It was a good, interesting movie. [Lit: It was an interesting and good
movie.]

Sūgaku wa muzukashii desu. + Sūgaku wa suki ja arimasen. =
Sūgaku wa muzukashikute, suki ja arimasen.
Mathematics is difficult, and I don't like it.

Here are some more examples of sentences joined with -kute. Note
that in some cases, the first part of the sentence is giving a reason for
what is stated in the second part.

Atama ga itakute, ku-ji han ni nemashita.
I had a headache, and (so) I went to bed at 9:30.

Hazukashikute, dame deshita.
It was no good because I was embarrassed. [Lit: I was embarrassed, and it was no good.]

Tenki ga warukute, zannen deshita.
It's a pity the weather was bad. [Lit: The weather was bad, and it was a pity.]

Sensei no kotae wa nagakute, wakarimasen deshita.
The teacher's answer was long, and I didn't understand it.

Atarashii rekishi no sensei wa atama ga yokute, kirei de, totemo shinsetsu na hito desu.
The new history teacher is smart and pretty, and a very kind person.

Sūgaku no jūgyō wa nagakute, omoshiroku arimasen deshita.
The math lesson was long and uninteresting.

Sono gurē no sūtsu wa takakute, kaimasen deshita.
That gray suit was expensive, and (so) I didn't buy it.

Mae no kaisha wa chiisakatta kedo, ima ōkikute, yūmei-na kaisha ni tsutomete imasu.
My previous company was small, but now I'm working at [Lit: am employed at] a large, well-known company.

4. THE PLAIN FORMS OF VERBS

As long as the final verb at the end of a sentence is in the polite form (-masu, -masen, -mashita, etc.), any verbs which come in the middle of the sentence can be in the plain form, and still not affect the overall tone. This means that the plain form can be used when sentences are joined with **kedo**, for example, or when they finish with **deshō**.

Piano ga dekiru kedo, amari jōzu ja arimasen.
I can (play) the piano, but I'm not very good.

Takahashi san wa Eigo ga wakaru deshō ka.
I wonder if Ms. Takahashi understands English.

Jūgyō wa sugu hajimaru kedo, minna wa doko ni imasu ka.
The lesson is going to begin soon – where is everyone?

Gēmu wa sugu owaru deshō.
The game will probably finish soon.

Basu wa mō sugu kuru deshō.
The bus should come soon.

The negative of the plain form ends in **-nai**. With **-iru/-eru** verbs (see Lesson 5, Structure and Usage Note 4), drop the final **-ru** and then add **-nai**. Here are some examples.

Plain form	Negative	Plain negative	Meaning
tabe-ru	tabe-masen	tabe-nai	doesn't eat
kangae-ru	kangae-masen	kangae-nai	doesn't think of
mi-ru	mi-masen	mi-nai	doesn't see
tsukare-ru	tsukare-masen	tsukare-nai	doesn't tire
wasure-ru	wasure-masen	wasure-nai	doesn't forget
oshie-ru	oshie-masen	oshie-nai	doesn't teach
i-ru	i-masen	i-nai	isn't in

Saitō san wa sakana o tabenai deshō.
Ms. Saitō doesn't eat fish, am I right?

Watashi wa ashita kaisha ni inai kedo, asatte hachi-ji han ni wa kaisha ni imasu.
I won't be in the office tomorrow, but I'll be in at 8:30 the day after tomorrow.

Terebi wa amari minai deshō.
You don't usually watch TV, do you?

Kao wa wasurenai kedo, namae wa sugu wasuremasu.
I don't forget faces, but I soon forget names.

With the other group of verbs – those that drop **-u** to make other forms – you need to add **-anai** to make the plain negative. (In cases where the stem ends with a vowel, **-wanai** is added.)

Plain form	Negative	Plain negative	Meaning
nom-u	nom-imasen	nom-anai	doesn't drink
hanas-u	hanash-imasen	hanas-anai	doesn't speak
omo-u	omo-imasen	omo-wanai	doesn't think
hashir-u	hashir-imasen	hashir-anai	doesn't run
ka-u	ka-imasen	ka-wanai	doesn't buy
mats-u	mach-imasen	mat-anai	doesn't wait
ik-u	ik-imasen	ik-anai	doesn't go
kak-u	kak-imasen	kak-anai	doesn't write
wakar-u	wakar-imasen	wakar-anai	doesn't understand

Takahashi san wa Eigo ga amari wakaranai kedo, Eigo no jūgyō de yoku ganbarimasu.
Ms. Takahashi doesn't really understand English, but she tries hard in English class.

Ani wa ikanai kedo, watashi wa ikimasu.
My older brother isn't going, but I am.

Itō san wa kōhii o nomanai deshō.
Mr. Itō doesn't drink coffee, does he?

Kaigi wa mada mada owaranai deshō.
The meeting probably isn't going to finish yet.

The irregular verbs are:

kuru	kimasen	konai	doesn't come
suru	shimasen	shinai	doesn't do
aru	arimasen	nai	there isn't

Kotae wa nai deshō.
There isn't an answer, is there?

Ogawa sensei wa kyō konai deshō. Dō shimashō ka.
Mr. Ogawa probably isn't coming today. What shall we do?

Supōtsu wa amari shinai kedo, terebi de yoku mimasu.
I don't do much sport, but I often watch it on TV.

The plain forms of **desu** are **da** (positive) and **dewa nai** or **ja nai** (negative).

Taiiku no sensei wa ii hito da kedo, chotto hen desu ne!
The physical education teacher is nice, but he's a bit strange, isn't he!

Sō ja nai deshō.
That's probably not so.

Muzukashii mondai ja nai kedo, chotto jikan ga kakarimasu.
It's not a difficult problem, but it will take a little time.

We will look at the plain form of past tenses in the next lesson.

5. MADA ATTE INAI – "NOT YET"

When something hasn't yet happened, it is often described using the -te imasen/-te inai form.

Hiru-gohan wa mada tabete imasen.
I haven't eaten lunch yet.

Rekishi no shukudai wa mada kaite inai deshō.
You haven't written your history homework yet, right?

Neruson san wa, sensei no yakyū chiimu ni mada haitte imasen ne.
You haven't joined the staff baseball team yet, have you Mr. Nelson?

Taiiku no sensei wa mada kite imasen.
The physical education teacher isn't here yet.

Fumiko chan ni mada denwa shite inai kedo, kore kara denwa shimasu.
I haven't called Fumiko yet, but I'll call her now.

6. TO OMOIMASU – "I THINK"

As in English, the phrase for "I think" – **to omoimasu** – is often added to the end of a sentence when giving an opinion. You'll see by comparing the pairs of sentences below that there's no need to make any changes to the sentence which is expressed as the thought, except that any verbs are put into the plain form, and -i adjectives don't need to be followed by **desu**. The word **to** before **omoimasu** is used to mark a quotation, so it is also used before verbs with meanings such as "say," "think," "ask," 'shout," etc.

Sore wa zannen desu.	**Sore wa zannen da to omoimasu.**
That's a pity.	I think that's a pity.
Takahashi san wa kimasen.	**Takahashi san wa konai to omoimasu.**
	I don't think Ms. Takahashi is coming. [Lit: I think ... isn't coming.]
Ms. Takahashi isn't coming.	
Neruson san wa ima Eigo no kurasu o oshiete imasu.	**Neruson san wa ima Eigo no kurasu o oshiete iru to omoimasu.**
Mr. Nelson is teaching an English class at the moment.	I think Mr. Nelson is teaching an English class at the moment.
Mondai wa arimasen.	**Mondai wa nai to omoimasu.**
	I don't think there are any problems.
There aren't any problems.	

Here are some other examples using **to omoimasu**.

Are wa uso da to omoimasu.
I don't think that's true. [Lit: I think that's untrue.]

Ano Furansu ryōri no resutoran wa zenzen oishiku nai to omoimasu.
I don't think that French restaurant is good at all.

Sono hito wa Nihon no koto ga zenzen wakaranai to omoimasu.
I don't think he understands anything about Japan.

Nihon de no seikatsu wa muzukashii to omoimasu ka.
Do you think living in Japan is difficult?

If you want to talk about what someone else is thinking, then it's usual to use **omotte imasu**.

Maiku san wa, Nihon wa ii kuni da to omotte imasu.
Mike thinks that Japan is a great country.

Takahashi san mo sō omotte imasu.
Ms. Takahashi thinks so too.

Maiku san wa Nihon no terebi wa amari omoshiroku nai to omotte imasu.
Mike thinks that Japanese television isn't very interesting.

Both **kangaeru** and **omou** may be translated into English as "think," but there is a difference between them. **Omou** is used when you are talking about an opinion or feeling, whereas **kangaeru** means "to consider/think about."

Nani o kangaete imasu ka.
What are you thinking about?

Chiimu no koto o kangaete imashita.
I was thinking about the team.

Takahashi san wa itsumo bōifurendo no koto o kangaete ite, chotto mondai desu.
Ms. Takahashi is always thinking about her boyfriend, and it's becoming a bit of a problem.

7. SASHIMI YA SUSHI YA – "SASHIMI AND SUSHI, ETC."

The word **ya**, like **to**, means "and" when used to join a list of items, but when **ya** is used, it implies that the items you have mentioned are just a sample, and that there are others on the list that you haven't mentioned. (To make this meaning more obvious, you can also add **nado**, "et cetera," if you wish.)

Sono gakkō de Eigo ya Furansugo ya Doitsugo (nado) o oshiete imasu.
At that school they teach English, French, German and the like.

Kyōto ya Nara (nado) e ikimashita.
I went to Kyoto, Nara, etc.

Kaisha ni yakyū chiimu ya basukettobōru chiimu ga arimasu.
At work we have a baseball team, a basketball team ...

8. ... KOTO GA DEKIMASU – "CAN/BE ABLE TO"

There are several ways of saying "can, am able to" in Japanese, but the easiest way is to add **koto ga dekimasu** to the plain form of the verb. It literally means "—ing is possible."

Maiku san wa kanji o kaku koto ga dekimasu ka.
Mike, can you write kanji characters?

Soko e wa, basu de iku koto ga dekimasen.
You can't get there by bus.

Sumimasen ga, ashita made ni kagaku no shukudai o owaru koto ga dekimasen.
I'm sorry, but I won't be able to finish my science homework by tomorrow.

Kore o zenbu taberu koto ga dekinai to omoimasu.
I don't think I can eat all this. [Lit: I can't eat all this, I think.]

Sumimasen ga, shigoto ga mada takusan atte, konban au koto ga dekinai to omoimasu.
I'm sorry, but I still have a lot of work to do, and (so) I don't think we'll be able to meet this evening.

In cases where it is obvious what the verb is going to be, it isn't necessary to mention it.

Nihongo ga dekimasu ka.
Can you (speak) Japanese?

Tenisu ga dekimasu ka.
Can you (play) tennis?

Piano ga dekimasu ka.
Can you (play) the piano?

9. ISSHO NI SHIMASEN KA – INVITATIONS, USING A NEGATIVE VERB

When you want to invite someone to do something, a polite way of doing so is to use a negative question, in other words, one ending in -masen ka.

Raishū no doyōbi wa tanjōbi nó pātii o shimasu ga, Maiku san mo kimasen ka.
I'm having a birthday party next Saturday – would you like to come, Mike?

Mō hiru-gohan no jikan desu ne. Issho ni tabemasen ka.
It's already lunchtime, isn't it? Would you like to eat with us?

Mo sukoshi nomimasen ka.
Would you like a little more to drink?

VOCABULARY
aru: there is/are [plain form of **arimasu**]
atama ga yokute: is clever and ...
atte inai: haven't met [from **au**]
basu: bus
basukettobōru: basketball
bōifurendo: boyfriend
chiimu: team
da: is/are [plain form of **desu**]
dekimashita: were able to [from **dekiru**]
dō omoimasu ka: what do you think?
Doitsugo: German language
Furansu: France
Furansugo: French language
ganbarimasu: I'll do my best [from **ganbaru**]
gēmu: game
hashiru: run
hayaku: quickly
hazukashikute: embarrassed and ...
jiko shōkai: self-introduction
jūgyō: lesson, class
kagaku: science
kangaete imasu: think about [from **kangaeru**]
kao: face
kotae: answer, response
koto ga dekimasu: can, be possible [from **dekiru**]

koto: thing, event, fact
kuni: country
mada mada dame desu: I'm still no good (at …)
made ni: by, by the time
mae ni: before, previously
manejā: manager
nado: and so on, et cetera
nagai: long
nai: there isn't/aren't [from **aru**]
Nihon no koto: about Japan
Ohaio-shu: the state of Ohio
omoshirokute: interesting and …
owaru: finish, end [verb]
piano: piano
rekishi: history
ryōri: cooking, cuisine
soba: noodles
san-shūkan: three weeks
seikatsu: life, living
shōkai shimashō: let me introduce you
-shūkan: — weeks
shumi: interest, hobby
sūgaku: mathematics
supōtsu: sport
sushi: raw fish with rice
tabemono: food
taiiku: physical education, training
to mōshimasu: am called [from **mōsu**]
to omoimasu: I think [from **omou**]
tsutomete imasu: be employed [from **tsutomeru**]
uso: untruth, story, lie
ya: and
yoku dekimashita: you did well [from **dekiru**]
yoku: well
zenbu: all

TEST YOURSELF

1. *Read through the dialog at the beginning of the lesson again, and then say if the following statements are true or false.*

   1. Maiku san wa ni-shūkan mae ni Nihon ni imashita.   T/F

   2. Katō sensei wa Maiku san no gakkō de oshiete imasen.   T/F

3. Watanabe san wa, Katō sensei wa omoshiroi hito da to omotte imasu.   T/F

4. Maiku san wa Nihon ryōri ga zenbu kirai desu.   T/F

5. Katō sensei wa sensei no yakyū chiimu no koto o hanashimasu.   T/F

6. Maiku san wa yakyū ga dekimasu.   T/F

2. *The other new teachers at the welcome party also had to introduce themselves. Here is some information about one of them. How do you think she introduced herself?*

Name: Yoko Fukuda

From: Kyoto

Teaches: French

Background: studied French at Osaka University, then went to France, and studied French again at a university in Paris

Interests: movies, sports

"Watashi wa Fukuda Yoko to _____. Hajimemashite.

Kyōto _____. Furansugo _____

_____. Ōsaka Daigaku de

_____. Sore kara

Furansu e _____, Pari _____ mata

_____. Shumi wa _____ to

_____. Dōzo yoroshiku onegai shimasu."

3. *It's already late on Friday afternoon, but the teachers at Mike's school have to stay behind for a teachers' meeting. Everyone around the table is finding it hard to concentrate, as the principal makes a long and boring speech. Make sentences about what each person is thinking, as in the example.*

Example: Takahashi: "It'll soon be 5:30."

            Takahashi san wa, mo sugu go-ji han da to omotte imasu.

1. Ms. Wada: "My boyfriend's waiting in front of the station."

2. Ms. Fukuda: "This is a strange school!"

3. Mr. Itō: "This coffee isn't very tasty."

4. Mike: "I don't understand Mr. Ogawa's Japanese very well."

5. Mr. Katō: "Mr. Watanabe is sleeping!"

6. Ms. Nakayama: "I can't meet Kenji tonight."

4. *Respond to the following comments by adding comments of your own, as in the example.*

Example: **Kono akai sētā wa takai desu ne.** (kirei ja nai)

Sō desu ne. Takakute, kirei ja arimasen ne.

1. Kagaku no jūgyō wa nagai desu ne. (omoshiroku nai)

2. Kono resutoran wa yasui desu ne. (oishii)

3. Doitsugo wa muzukashii desu ne. (suki ja nai)

4. Nakayama san wa atama ga ii desu ne. (kirei)

5. Kyō wa atsui desu ne. (ii tenki)

6. Kono basu wa hayai desu ne. (yasui)

5. *How would you say the following sentences in Japanese?*

1. Mr. Tanaka is always thinking about work.

2. The next lesson begins at 2:30, and finishes at 3:20, I think.

3. The fish was good, and I ate lots.

4. I don't like math, but I like science.

5. The train will probably come soon.

6. Can you read a Japanese newspaper?

学校 Gakkō, the word for "school," uses a combination of the kanji characters for "learning/study" and "school/correction."

MADA O-HITORI DESU KA
ARE YOU STILL SINGLE?

It's Saturday evening, and Mr. Watanabe has invited Mike Nelson to his house for a meal and to meet his family.

Mike	**Oishi-sō desu ne.** This looks good.
Okusan	**Dōzo, go-enryo naku tabete kudasai.** Please help yourself. [Lit: Please eat, without standing on ceremony.]
Mike	**Ja, itadakimasu.** Thank you.
Okusan	**O-hashi wa o-jōzu desu ne.** You're very good with chopsticks, aren't you?
Mike	**Arigatō. Demo hashi wa Amerika de mo tokidoki tsukaimasu yo.** Thank you. But we use chopsticks sometimes in America too, you know.

Okusan	Ē? Amerikajin mo o-hashi o tsukau n' desu ka.
	What? Americans use chopsticks too?
Mike	Ē, Nihon ryōri ya Chūka ryōri no resutoran ga takusan arimasu kara, tokidoki tsukaimasu.
	Yes, there are lots of Japanese and Chinese restaurants, so we sometimes use them.
Fumiko	Neruson san, Nihon ryōri no naka de, nani ga ichiban suki desu ka.
	Mr. Nelson, what do you like best among Japanese food?
Mike	Iroiro suki da kara, muzukashii shitsumon desu ne. Hmmmm. Ichiban suki-na no wa tenpura desu. Sushi mo dai-suki desu.
	I like all kinds, so that's a difficult question. Hmmm. The (food) I like best is tempura. I also really like sushi.
Okusan	Kyō wa o-sushi ga takusan arimasu kara, dōzo tabete kudasai!
	We have lots of sushi today, so please eat it up!
Fumiko	Neruson san wa yon-shūkan mae ni Nihon e kita n' deshō ne.
	You came to Japan four weeks ago, didn't you, Mr. Nelson?
Mike	Hai, sō desu. Chōdo yon-shūkan mae desu.
	Yes, that's right. Exactly four weeks ago.
Fumiko	Nihongo ga yoku dekiru ne! O-niisan wa ni-nen-kan Eigo o benkyō shite iru kedo, mada zenzen jōzu ja nai yo.
	You can speak Japanese well, can't you! My older brother has been studying English for two years, but he's still no good at it.
Hiro	Uso da! Boku wa kurasu no naka de ichiban da yo!
	That's not true! I'm number one in the class!
Mike	(laughing) Nihongo no benkyō wa kono yon-shūkan dake ja nai n' desu yo. Amerika no daigaku de mo, ni-nen-kan Nihongo o benkyō shita kara, ima sukoshi dekimasu.
	My study of Japanese hasn't been just these four weeks. I also studied for two years at a university in the USA, so I can speak a little.

Okusan	Sō desu ka. Ne, Neruson san, shitsurei desu ga, o-ikutsu desu ka.
	I see. Uh, Mr. Nelson, excuse me, but how old are you?
Mike	Yoku aru shitsumon desu ne. Watashi wa san-jū roku desu.
	That's a common question, isn't it? I'm thirty-six.
Okusan	San-jū-roku-sai desu ka. Mada o-hitori desu ka.
	Thirty-six years old? Are you still single?
Mike	Ima hitori desu. Mae ni kekkon shite ita kedo, ni-nen mae ni rikon shita n' desu.
	I am now. I was married before, but I got divorced two years ago.
Okusan	Sō desu ka. Hen-na shitsumon o shite, gomen nasai.
	Oh, I see. I'm sorry for asking a strange question.
Watanabe	Sa, Neruson san, biiru mo sukoshi dō desu ka.
	Well, Mr. Nelson, how about some more beer?

STRUCTURE AND USAGE NOTES

1. QUESTIONS FOREIGNERS ARE OFTEN ASKED

There are certain questions that you are likely to be asked over and over again in Japan, so it is as well to be able to answer them smoothly. Here are some of them, with possible responses.

Q. Nan-sai desu ka./O-ikutsu desu ka.
   How old are you?
A. Jū-nana-sai desu./Ni-jū-kyū-sai desu./Go-jū-sai desu.
   I'm seventeen./I'm twenty-nine./I'm fifty.

Q. Kuni wa dochira desu ka.
   What country are you from?
A. Amerika kara desu./Amerikajin desu.
   I'm from the USA./I'm American.

Q. Amerikajin desu ka.
   Are you American?
A. Hai, sō desu./Iie, Igirisujin desu.
   Yes, I am./No, I'm British.

Q. Nihon o dō omoimasu ka.
What do you think of Japan?
A. Dai-suki desu./Hito ga ōi desu ne./Ii kuni da to omoimasu.
I like it very much./It's very crowded, isn't it?/I think it's a great country.

Q. Itsu Nihon e kimashita ka.
When did you come to Japan?
A. Senshū no kayōbi ni kimashita./Ichi-nen mae ni kimashita.
Last Tuesday. [Lit: Last week's Tuesday.]/A year ago.

Q. Itsu made Nihon ni imasu ka.
When are you in Japan until?
A. Raishū no mokuyōbi made desu.
Until next Thursday. [Lit: Until next week's Thursday.]

Q. Nihon no jōsei/dansei o dō omoimasu ka.
What do you think of Japanese women/men?
A. Totemo kirei/shinsetsu/hansamu da to omoimasu.
They're very beautiful/kind/handsome.

Q. O-hashi wa daijōbu desu ka.
Are you okay with chopsticks?
A. Hai, daijōbu desu.
Yes, I'm fine.

Q. O-hashi wa jōzu desu ne.
You're good at (using) chopsticks.
A. Arigatō.
Thank you.

Q. Sashimi o taberu koto ga dekimasu ka.
Can you eat raw fish?
A. Hai, dai-suki desu.
Yes, I like it very much.

Q. Kekkon shite imasu ka./O-hitori desu ka.
Are you married?/Are you single?
**A. Hai, sō desu./Iie, mada desu./Iie, kekkon shite imasu./
Rikkon shite imasu.**
Yes, I am./No, not yet./No, I'm married./I'm divorced.

2. DESCRIBING HOW SOMETHING LOOKS

To describe how something looks or appears to be, add -sō to the appropriate adjective. With -i adjectives, you need to drop the final -i first. This is the equivalent of saying "it looks ..., seems ..."

Hashi wa muzukashi-sō da kedo, jitsu wa muzukashiku arimasen.
Chopsticks look difficult (to use), but in fact they're not (difficult).

Wada san no atarashii sūtsu o mite kudasai yo. Taka-sō desu ne.
Hey, look at Mr. Wada's new suit. It looks expensive, doesn't it!

Watanabe san no kodomotachi wa genki-sō desu ne.
Mr. Watanabe's children seem lively, don't they?

Maiku san wa yakyū ga jōzu-sō desu ne!
Mike looks good at baseball, doesn't he!

The -sō form of **ii/yoi** is irregular: **yosa-sō** ("looks good").

Kono kissaten wa yosa-sō desu yo. Hairimashō.
This coffee shop looks good. Let's go in.

Katō sensei wa atama ga yosa-sō desu ne.
Mr. Katō looks clever, doesn't he?

This pattern is also useful for describing how you think someone else is feeling, as it is generally considered that you can't really *know* how they're feeling, only how they *appear* to be feeling.

Fumiko chan wa tomodachi ga takusan iru kedo, itsumo sabishi-sō desu ne.
Fumiko has lots of friends, but she always looks lonely, doesn't she?

Watanabe san wa atama ga ita-sō desu ne. Daijōbu deshō ka.
Mr. Watanabe looks as if he has a headache. I wonder if he's all right.

Maiku san wa kyō ureshi-sō desu ne.
Mike looks happy today, doesn't he?

3. PLAIN FORM + NO DESU

When a sentence ends in **no desu**, or more colloquially **n' desu**, it often indicates that the speaker is explaining something, or asking for an explanation of something. It is also sometimes used to indicate emphasis, so it can be shown in the corresponding English with an exclamation mark. **N' desu** can follow the plain form of a verb, an -i adjective, or a -na adjective (with -na). Pronounce it as if the n' ends the previous word (e.g. **takai n' desu = takain desu**).

Iroiro-na mondai ga arimasu ne. Dō suru n' desu ka.
There are all sort of problems, aren't there? What are you going to do?

Nani o shite iru n' desu ka.
What are you doing?

Kono terebi wa mō dame-na n' desu yo. Atarashii no o kaimashō.
This TV is no good any more! Let's buy a new one.

Dō shite atarashii konpyūtā o tsukawanai n' desu ka.
Why don't you use the new computer?

Densha wa taihen konde iru n' desu ne. Takushii de ikimashō ka.
The trains are really crowded. Shall we go by taxi?

Totemo takai n' desu yo. Dakara kawanai n' desu.
It's really expensive! That's why I'm not buying it.

4. ICHIBAN – SUPERLATIVES

If you want to say that something is biggest, or best, or fastest, or most beautiful, then all you need do is add **ichiban** before the relevant adjective. Think of it as meaning "most," or more literally "number one."

Nihon de ichiban takai yama wa Fuji-san desu.
The highest mountain in Japan is Mount Fuji.

Tenpura wa ichiban oishii to omoimasu.
I think tempura tastes the best.

Kurasu no naka de, dare ga ichiban wakai desu ka.
Who's the youngest in the class?

Nihonjin no namae no naka de, nani ga ichiban ōi desu ka.
Which Japanese name is most common? [Lit: Among Japanese names, what is most numerous?]

Ichiban suki-na tokoro wa doko desu ka.
What is your favorite place?

5. PLAIN FORM OF PAST TENSE VERBS

In the previous lesson we looked at the plain form of present tense verbs (**taberu, nomu, ikanai**). There are also plain forms of the past tenses. In the positive ("went," "did," "ate," "drank," etc.), it is formed like the -te form, but ends in -ta instead.

Present plain	-te form	Past plain	Meaning
iku	itte	itta	went
kuru	kite	kita	came
suru	shite	shita	did
tsukau	tsukatte	tsukatta	used
aru	atte	atta	there was/were
iru	ite	ita	was/were
omou	omotte	omotta	thought
wakaru	wakatte	wakatta	understood
au	atte	atta	met

Dō shita n' deshō.
I wonder what happened.

Sensei wa doko ni itta n' desu ka
Where's the teacher gone?

Kyō wa kinyōbi da to omotta kedo, chigaimasu ne!
I thought it was Friday today, but it isn't, is it!

Chōdo ichi-nen mae ni Nihon e kita kedo, Nihongo wa mada mada jōzu ja nai n' desu.
I came to Japan exactly a year ago, but my Japanese still isn't very good.

Kaigi de wa, iroiro-na shitsumon ga atta kedo, ii setsumei ga amari arimasen deshita.
There were all kinds of questions at the meeting, but there weren't really any answers.

Doko de atta n' desu ka.
Where did you meet her/him?

Ano hito no kao wa wakatta kedo, namae o wasurete imashita.
I knew her/his face, but I didn't remember her/his name.

With the negative past ("didn't go," "didn't do," "didn't eat," etc.), change the present negative -nai ending to -nakatta.

Present plain	Negative plain	Negative past plain	Meaning
iku	ikanai	ikanakatta	didn't go
kuru	konai	konakatta	didn't come
wakaru	wakaranai	wakaranakatta	didn't understand
tsukau	tsukawanai	tsukawanakatta	didn't use
suru	shinai	shinakatta	didn't do
aru	nai	nakatta	there wasn't
iru	inai	inakatta	wasn't in
yomu	yomanai	yomanakatta	didn't read
kaku	kakanai	kakanakatta	didn't write
taberu	tabenai	tabenakatta	didn't eat

Takahashi san wa dō shite kinō no ban konakatta n' deshō ka.
I wonder why Ms. Takahashi didn't come yesterday evening.

Sono kotae wa yoku wakaranakatta n' desu. Mō ichido setsumei shite kudasai.
I didn't understand that answer very well. Could you explain it once more, please?

Kinō no asa Wada san ni denwa shita kedo, kaisha ni inakatta n' desu.
I called Ms. Wada yesterday morning, but she wasn't in the office.

Dō shite Shinkansen de ikanakatta n' desu ka.
Why didn't you go by Shinkansen (Bullet Train)?

The comparable forms for **desu** are **datta** ("was/were") and **ja nakatta** ("wasn't/weren't").

Senshū no tesuto de watashi wa ichiban datta ga, konshū wa mō dame da to omoimasu.
In last week's test, I was first, but this week I don't think I'll be any good.

San-nen-kan Nyū Yōku ni sunde ita kedo, amari suki ja nakatta n' desu.
I lived in New York for three years, but I didn't like it much.

6. PLAIN FORM + KARA – "BECAUSE"

When you want to explain the reason for something (in other words, where you might say "because" or "so" in English), the word you need is **kara**. It can come after the plain form of the verb or an -i adjective. Note that **kara** comes at the end of the first part of the sentence before the comma, so it's the first part of the sentence that is giving the reason, and the second part that gives the result.

Shinkansen de itta kara, jikan ga amari kakarimasen deshita.
We went by Shinkansen, so it didn't take very long. [Lit: Because we went by Shinkansen, ...]

Shitsumon ga mada ōi kara, mō ichido setsumei shimashō.
There are still a lot of questions, so let me explain it again. [Lit: Because there are still a lot of questions, ...]

Katō san wa hansamu de, shinsetsu-na hito da kara, gārufurendo ga ōi deshō.
Mr. Katō is handsome, and a kind man, so I'm sure he has many girlfriends!

Maiku san wa Nihon no koto ga yoku wakaru kara, Nihon no seikatsu wa mondai nai to omoimasu.
Mike understands well about Japan, so I don't think he'll have any problems with Japanese life.

Kono purintā wa amari tsukawanakatta kara, mada atarashi-sō desu.
Because we didn't use the printer much, it still looks new.

As in English, it is possible to say only the part of the sentence giving the reason (that part beginning with "because" in English, or ending in **kara** in Japanese).

A. **Saitō san wa sabishi-sō desu ne.**
   Ms. Saitō looks lonely, doesn't she?
B. **Ē, bōifurendo ga ima Igirisu ni iru kara.**
   Yes, because her boyfriend is in Britain at the moment.

7. TALKING ABOUT PERIODS OF TIME

To talk about something which has been going on for some time, simply use the **-te imasu** form. This corresponds to the "have/has been —ing" form in English.

Ni-nen-kan Nihongo o benkyō shite imasu.
I've been studying Japanese for two years.

Chōdo ichi-nen-kan kono uchi ni sunde imasu.
I've been living in this house for just a year.

San-ji han kara denwa de hanashite imasu yo.
She's been talking on the phone since 3:30!

Chichi wa jū-nen mae kara sono kaisha ni tsutomete imasu.
My father has been working at that company for ten years. [Lit: since ten years ago.]

Mō ichi-jikan-han matte imasu ga, mada kite imasen.
I've been waiting an hour and a half already, but he hasn't come yet.

VOCABULARY

Amerika de mo: in the US too
ban: evening
boku: I [informal, used by men and young boys]
chōdo: exactly, precisely
Chūka ryōri: Chinese cuisine
dansei: males, men
dochira: where? [formal]
Fuji san: Mount Fuji
gārufurendo: girlfriend
go-enryo naku: without standing on ceremony
hansamu: handsome
ichiban suki: like the most
ichiban: the first, number one, most
iroiro: all kinds of, various
jitsu wa: in fact
jōsei: females, women
kara: because
kekkon shite ita: was married [from kekkon suru]
kinō no ban: yesterday evening
kita: came [from kuru]
kodomotachi: children
mō ichido: once more
ni-nen mae ni: two years ago
ni-nen-kan: a two-year period
no naka de: among, within
o-hitori: single, unmarried
o-ikutsu: how old?
ōi: many, abundant, a lot of
oishi-sō: looks tasty
rikon: divorce
sabishii: lonely
-sai: – years old

san-jū-roku-sai: thirty-six years old
setsumei: explanation
Shinkansen: (high-speed train known as) Bullet Train
shita: did [from **suru**]
shitsumon: question
tenpura: tempura (deep fried food)
tsukaimasu: use [from **tsukau**]
tsukau n' desu ka: do you use?
ureshii: happy
yoku aru: frequently occurring

TEST YOURSELF

1. *Read through the dialog at the beginning of the lesson again, and then say if the following statements are true or false.*

   1. Maiku san wa hashi o tsukau koto ga dekimasu.   T/F

   2. Maiku san wa tenpura mo sushi mo dai-suki desu.   T/F

   3. Fumiko san no o-niisan wa gakkō de Eigo o benkyō shite imasu.   T/F

   4. Maiku san wa Nihon dake de Nihongo o benkyō shite imasu.   T/F

   5. Maiku san wa biiru o nonde imasu.   T/F

   6. Maiku san wa kekkon shite imasu.   T/F

2. *Complete the crossword by filling in the answers to the clues, and find out who is coming to visit Mike in Japan next month.*

1.	once more	7.	expensive-looking
2.	used (informal)	8.	question
3.	marriage	9.	explanation
4.	most, number one	10.	bought (informal)
5.	drank (informal)	11.	last week
6.	various		

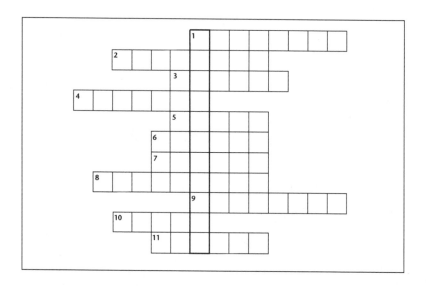

3. Make up questions and give answers about which of the choices given is the longest, shortest, biggest, etc., as in the example.

Example   kuruma, densha, Shinkansen - hayai
>   **Q. Kuruma to densha to Shinkansen no naka de, dore ga ichiban hayai desu ka.**
>   **A. Shinkansen wa ichiban hayai to omoimasu.**

1. Fuji san, Eberesuto, Makkinrii - takai

2. Tōkyō, Rondon, Manira - atsui

3. Eigo, Nihongo, Doitsugo - muzukashii

4. sake, biiru, wain - suki

5. eiga, supōtsu, kaimono - tanoshii

6. aka, shiro, kuro - suki

4. You've just come out of a long meeting, and your friend, who's been waiting for you, questions you too closely for comfort about it. Answer his questions, in each case predicting what his next question is going to be based on your answer, as in the example.

Example: **Q. Dō shite issho ni tenisu o shinakatta n' desu ka.**
>   **A.** (have a lot of study) **Benkyō ga takusan atta kara.**
>   **Q. Dō shite benkyō ga takusan atta n' desu ka.**

A. (had a test) **Tesuto ga atta kara.**

Q. **Dō shite** etc.

1. Dō shite kaigi ga san-ji ni owaranakatta n' desu ka.

   (there were lots of questions)

2. Why were there lots of questions?

   (because the explanation wasn't very good)

3. Why wasn't the ...?

   (because I hadn't studied the report much)

4. Why hadn't you ...?

   (because I had a headache)

5. Why ...?

   (because last night [**kinō no ban**] I drank a lot)

6. Why ...?

   (because it was my friend's birthday)

5. *How would you say the following sentences in Japanese?*

   1. Mr. Fukuda got married three years ago.

   2. Ms. Takahashi's boyfriend is handsome, and kind-looking, isn't he!

   3. What sport do you like best?

   4. I think that he phoned at 2:30.

   5. Ms. Tanaka has a headache this morning, so I don't think she'll go to work.

   6. I bought my car three years ago, but it still looks new.

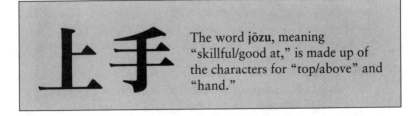

上手　The word jōzu, meaning "skillful/good at," is made up of the characters for "top/above" and "hand."

DAI NANA-KA KARA DAI JŪ-IK-KA MADE NO FUKUSHŪ

REVIEW OF LESSONS 7 TO 11

Read Dialogs 7 to 11 aloud, and try to understand the meaning without referring back to the English translations in previous lessons.

Dialog 7: Atama ga itai!

Okusan	Ohayō gozaimasu. Atama wa dō desu ka.
Watanabe	Itai yo! Atama ga itai! Ima nan-ji?
Okusan	Osoi desu yo. Mō jū-ni-ji jup-pun mae desu. Kōhii wa?
Watanabe	A, ii ne. Tomoko to Fumiko to Hiro wa doko ni iru?
Okusan	Tomoko wa tonari no uchi de, tomodachi to issho ni terebi o mite imasu. Fumiko wa ni-kai de gakkō no Eigo no shukudai o shite imasu.
Watanabe	Hiro wa?
Okusan	Hiro wa gakkō de yakyū no renshū o shite imasu. Mō sugu kaerimasu. Hai, kōhii. Atsui desu yo. Ki o tsukete.

Fumiko	(running downstairs) O-tōsan, ohayō!
Okusan	Fumiko, ki o tsukete. O-tōsan wa kōhii o nonde iru yo.
Watanabe	Fumiko, Eigo no shukudai wa dō? Muzukashii?
Fumiko	Iie, muzukashiku nai yo. Eigo ga suki desu.
Okusan	A, mō hiru-gohan no jikan desu ne. Fumiko, Tomoko o yonde. Mada tonari ni imasu.
Fumiko	Hai.
Okusan	(to her husband) Ne, kyō no gogo wa minna de Kawasaki ni ikimasu ne.
Watanabe	Ē? Kawasaki? Dō shite?
Okusan	Oboete imasen ka. Kyō wa haha no tanjōbi desu yo ne.
Watanabe	O-kāsan no tanjōbi? A, atama ga itai! Mata neru yo! Oyasumi nasai!

QUESTIONS:

1. Watanabe san wa kesa genki desu ka.

2. Mō jū-ni-ji desu ka.

3. Kodomotachi no naka de, dare ga uchi ni imasu ka.

4. Watanabe san no okusan wa dō shite kyō no gogo Kawasaki ni ikimasu ka.

Dialog 8: Iya desu ne!

Okusan	Sūtsu wa doko deshō ne. (to sales assistant) Anō, sumimasen, sūtsu wa doko desu ka.
Assistant	Sūtsu desu ka. Koko o mō sukoshi massugu itte kudasai. Migi-gawa ni gozaimasu.
Okusan	Arigatō. A, koko desu ne. Kono gurē no sūtsu wa ii desu ne.
Watanabe	Gurē wa dame. Suki ja nai yo.
Okusan	Sō desu ka. Ja, kono burū no wa dō desu ka. (looking inside at the label) A, kono dezainā wa yūmei desu yo. Ii desu ne.
Watanabe	Yūmei-na dezainā desu ka. Takai deshō. Motto yasui sūtsu ga ii desu. A, kore wa ii.
Okusan	Sore wa ii desu ga, saizu wa chotto chiisai desu ne. (to sales assistant) Sumimasen, motto ōkii saizu wa arimasu ka.

| Assistant | Gozaimasu. Kochira e dōzo. |

Mrs. Watanabe suddenly sees one of her old schoolfriends.

Okusan	A, Sachiko san, konnichiwa! O-hisashiburi desu ne.
Friend	A, Michiko san, konnichiwa. O-genki desu ka.
Okusan	Hai, genki desu. Arigatō. Sachiko san wa?
Friend	Hai, o-kage sama de.
Okusan	Kyō wa konde imasu ne.
Friend	Sō desu ne. Iya desu ne. Kaimono wa suki desu ga, Ginza no depāto wa itsumo konde imasu ne. Michiko san wa yoku Ginza e kimasu ka.
Okusan	Tokidoki kimasu. Watashi mo kaimono wa suki desu ga, kyō wa shujin no atarashii sūtsu o mite imasu ...
Friend	A, wakarimashita. Go-shujin to issho desu ka. Sore wa taihen deshō!
Okusan	Sō desu! (Mr Watanabe comes out of the room where he changed suits) A, shujin desu. Dō desu ka. Saizu wa daijōbu desu ka.
Watanabe	Saizu wa daijōbu desu ga, dezain wa chotto ...

QUESTIONS:

1. Watanabe san to okusan wa, doko de kaimono o shite imasu ka.

2. Ima nani o mite imasu ka.

3. Watanabe san wa dō shite burū no sūtsu wa dame da to omotte imasu ka.

4. Watanabe san wa kaimono ga suki da to omoimasu ka.

Dialog 9: Shūmatsu wa dō deshita ka.

Watanabe	A, Neruson san, ohayō gozaimasu.
Mike	Ohayō gozaimasu. Kyō wa, densha wa konde imasu ne.
Watanabe	Sō desu ne. Getsuyōbi wa itsumo sō desu ne. Tokorode, shūmatsu wa dō deshita ka. Dokoka e ikimashita ka.

Mike	Ē, totemo tanoshikatta desu. Tomodachi futari to issho ni, yama e ikimashita. Doyōbi no asa itte, kinō no yoru kaerimashita. Dakara kesa chotto tsukarete imasu.
Watanabe	Ii desu ne. Doko ni ikimashita ka.
Mike	Nihon Arupusu no onsen ni ikimashita. Machi no namae wa wasuremashita kedo, totemo kirei-na tokoro deshita.
Watanabe	Onsen! Ii ne. Soto no onsen mo arimashita ka.
Mike	Arimashita. Doyōbi no yoru mo, nichiyōbi no asa mo hairimashita. Tenki wa chotto samukatta kedo, onsen no yu wa taihen atsukatta desu.
Watanabe	Ryokan ni tomarimashita ka.
Mike	Hai, sō desu. Konde imashita ga, wakai onna no hitotachi ga takusan tomatte imashita yo.
Watanabe	Sō desu ka. Hanashi o shimashita ka.
Mike	Iie, chansu ga arimasen deshita. Watashitachi o mite, minna hazukashikatta deshō.
Watanabe	Sore wa zannen deshita ne.
Mike	Ē, sō desu ne. Tokorode, Watanabe san wa nani o shimashita ka. Dokoka e ikimashita ka.
Watanabe	Taihen deshita yo. Zenzen omoshiroku arimasen deshita. Kazoku to issho ni Tōkyō e itte, kaimono o shimashita ga, nichiyōbi no depāto wa, mō iya desu yo!
Mike	Nanika kaimashita ka.
Watanabe	Ē, atarashii sūtsu o kaimashita kedo, hontō ni jikan ga kakarimashita. Kyō wa, watashi mo taihen tsukarete imasu yo.

QUESTIONS:

1. Kyō wa nanyōbi desu ka.

2. Maiku san wa hitori de onsen e ikimashita ka.

3. Onna no hitotachi wa dō shite Maiku san-tachi ni hanasanakatta n' desu ka.

4. Maiku san wa onsen ga suki da to omoimasu ka.

Dialog 10: *Nihon no koto, dō omoimasu ka.*

Mike	Mina san, hajimemashite. Watashi wa Maiku Neruson to mōshimasu. Amerika no Ohaio-shu kara kimashita. Watashi wa san-shūkan mae ni Nihon e kimashita. Gakkō no shigoto wa omoshiroi to omoimasu. Ganbarimasu. Yoroshiku onegai shimasu.
Watanabe	Yoku dekimashita, arigatō. Nihongo ga jōzu desu ne.
Mike	Iie, mada mada dame desu. Hazukashikute, taihen deshita!
Watanabe	Daijōbu deshita yo. A, Katō sensei desu. Neruson san wa mada atte inai deshō. Atama ga yokute, omoshiroi hito desu yo. Shōkai shimashō.

Mr. Watanabe introduces Mike to Mr. Kato, and they chat.

Katō	Neruson sensei, Nihon wa mada san-shūkan desu ne. Nihon no koto, dō omoimasu ka.
Mike	Totemo omoshirokute, dai-suki desu! Nihon wa ii kuni da to omoimasu.
Katō	Sō desu ka. Ii kotae desu ne. Tabemono mo daijōbu desu ka.
Mike	Hai, Nihon ryōri wa totemo suki desu. Sashimi ya sushi ya soba wa zenbu taberu koto ga dekimasu.
Katō	Sō desu ka. Ja, Nihon no seikatsu wa, mondai nai deshō! Anō, shumi wa nan desu ka. Supōtsu wa suki desu ka.
Watanabe	(laughing) Neruson sensei, ki o tsukete kudasai yo. Kore kara gakkō no sensei no yakyū chiimu no hanashi da to omoimasu. Katō sensei wa yakyū chiimu no manejā de, itsumo chiimu no koto dake o kangaete imasu.
Katō	Sore wa uso desu yo! Neruson san, sensei no yakyū chiimu ga aru kedo, issho ni shimasen ka.
Mike	(hesitating) Watashi wa yakyū ga suki da kedo, hayaku hashiru koto ga dekimasen.
Katō	Daijōbu desu yo. Sa, tsugi no gēmu wa nichiyōbi no asa desu ga.
Mike	Nichiyōbi no asa?!
Watanabe	Ja, Neruson sensei, ganbatte kudasai!

QUESTIONS:

1. Maiku san wa itsu kara Nihon ni imasu ka.

2. Maiku san wa sashimi o taberu koto ga dekimasu ka.

3. Katō sensei wa nani o yoku kangaete imasu ka.

4. Maiku san wa sono tsugi no nichiyōbi no asa ni nani o suru to omoimasu ka.

Dialog 11: Mada o-hitori desu ka.

Mike	Oishi-sō desu ne.
Okusan	Dōzo, go-enryo naku tabete kudasai.
Mike	Ja, itadakimasu.
Okusan	O-hashi wa o-jōzu desu ne.
Mike	Arigatō. Demo hashi wa Amerika de mo tokidoki tsukaimasu yo.
Okusan	Ē? Amerikajin mo o-hashi o tsukau n' desu ka.
Mike	Ē, Nihon ryōri ya Chūka ryōri no resutoran ga takusan arimasu kara, tokidoki tsukaimasu.
Fumiko	Neruson san, Nihon ryōri no naka de, nani ga ichiban suki desu ka.
Mike	Iroiro suki da kara, muzukashii shitsumon desu ne. Hmmmm. Ichiban suki-na no wa tenpura desu. Sushi mo dai-suki desu.
Okusan	Kyō wa o-sushi ga takusan arimasu kara, dōzo tabete kudasai!
Fumiko	Neruson san wa yon-shūkan mae ni Nihon e kita n' deshō ne.
Mike	Hai, sō desu. Chōdo yon-shūkan mae desu.
Fumiko	Nihongo ga yoku dekiru ne! O-niisan wa ni-nen-kan Eigo o benkyō shite iru kedo, mada zenzen jōzu ja nai yo.
Hiro	Uso da! Boku wa kurasu no naka de ichiban da yo!
Mike	(laughing) Nihongo no benkyō wa kono yon-shūkan dake ja nai n' desu yo. Amerika no daigaku de mo, ni-nen-kan Nihongo o benkyō shita kara, ima sukoshi dekimasu.
Okusan	Sō desu ka. Ne, Neruson san, shitsurei desu ga, o-ikutsu desu ka.

144   LESSON 12

Mike	Yoku aru shitsumon desu ne. Watashi wa san-jū roku desu.
Okusan	San-jū-roku-sai desu ka. Mada o-hitori desu ka.
Mike	Ima hitori desu. Mae ni kekkon shite ita kedo, ni-nen mae ni rikon shita n' desu.
Okusan	Sō desu ka. Hen-na shitsumon o shite, gomen nasai.
Watanabe	Sa, Neruson san, biiru mo sukoshi dō desu ka.

QUESTIONS:

1. Amerikajin wa doko de tokidoki hashi o tsukaimasu ka.

2. Fumiko chan wa, o-niisan wa Eigo ga yoku dekiru to omotte imasu ka.

3. O-niisan wa itsu kara Eigo no benkyō o shite imasu ka.

4. Maiku san wa kekkon shite imasu ka.

TEST YOURSELF

1. *Pair each of the words or phrases in the left-hand column with a word or phrase of similar (though perhaps not exactly the same) meaning from the right-hand column. Be careful! There is one word too many in each column, so you should be left with two words that don't make a pair.*

ban	tsutomeru
buraun	omou
chotto	kurasu
dame	ōi
hataraku	yoru
heta	ikutsu
jūgyō	uso ja nai
kangaeru	hen
minna de	chairo
nan-sai	o-kāsan
haha	sukoshi
takusan	jōzu ja nai
zenzen	warui
hontō	issho ni

2. *Mr. Watanabe has been asking Mike about the baseball game yesterday. Their conversation is below, but the lines are mixed up. Unscramble the lines and label them A, B, C, etc., in the correct order.*

1. ___ Ā, dakara yakyū ga dekinakatta n' desu ka.

2. ___ Ā sō desu ka. Dō shite? Hayaku hashiru koto ga dekinakatta kara?

3. ___ Daijōbu desu yo. Sono chiimu wa minna heta deshō!

4. ___ Sore dake ja nai n' desu. Sono mae no ban, tomodachi no uchi ni itte, takusan nonda kara, nichiyōbi no asa atama ga taihen itakatta desu yo.

5. ___ Hai, shimashita ga, watashi wa zenzen dame deshita yo.

6. ___ Kinō, yakyū o shimashita ka.

7. ___ Ee, sō desu. Watashi wa chiimu no naka de ichiban heta datta kara, totemo hazukashikatta desu.

3. *Look at the clues below, and see if you can find the Japanese equivalents in the word square.*

1. hobby	9. because, and so	17. older brother
2. lie	10. morning	18. but
3. finish	11. was able to	19. well, healthy
4. face	12. not at all, never	20. think about
5. meet	13. painful	21. buy
6. met	14. when?	22. only
7. this morning	15. blue-green	23. expensive
8. sleep	16. red	

P	A	K	E	S	A	O	I	T
I	T	S	U	K	I	W	R	D
I	T	A	I	K	P	A	T	E
K	A	N	G	A	E	R	U	K
N	E	R	U	S	H	U	M	I
E	S	D	A	A	A	S	B	T
G	S	A	O	K	A	O	S	A
A	I	K	N	E	Z	N	E	Z
I	O	E	T	A	K	A	I	N

4. *Imagine you are in Japan on a short business trip – you arrived in the country last Tuesday, and you're leaving tomorrow – and now you're traveling down to Osaka on the Shinkansen. As often happens in Japan, the person sitting next to you starts up a conversation. Fill in your part with appropriate responses.*

Stranger	Shitsurei desu ga, kuni wa dochira desu ka.
You	
Stranger	Sō desu ka. Itsu Nihon e kita n' desu ka.
You	
Stranger	Itsu made desu ka.
You	
Stranger	Mijikai desu ne! Nihon o dō omoimasu ka
You	(in Tokyo, a lot of people!)
Stranger	Sō desu ne. Konde imasu ne. Shitsurei desu ga, o-ikutsu desu ka.
You	
Stranger	Sō desu ka. O-hitori desu ka.
You	
Stranger	Ii desu ne. Tokorode, Nihongo wa o-jōzu desu ne. Muzukashii desu ka.
You	
Stranger	Kanji o yomu koto mo dekimasu ka.
You	
Stranger	Kanji wa muzukashii deshō!

5. Answer the following questions about yourself.

1. Kyō wa nan-yōbi desu ka.

2. Tokidoki hashi o tsukaimasu ka.

3. Ichiban suki-na tabemono wa nan desu ka.

4. Kekkon shite imasu ka.

5. Doko ni sunde imasu ka.

6. Nihongo wa muzukashii to omoimasu ka.

7. Mainichi Nihongo no benkyō o shimasu ka.

8. Shumi wa nan desu ka.

9. Tenisu ga dekimasu ka.

10. Nihon no koto yoku wakarimasu ka.

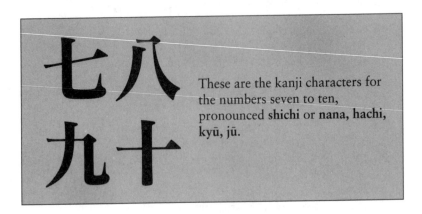

These are the kanji characters for the numbers seven to ten, pronounced **shichi** or **nana, hachi, kyū, jū.**

NI-JŪ-ICHI-NICHI WA YASUMI NO HI DESU.
THE TWENTY-FIRST IS A HOLIDAY.

Mike is still at the Watanabe's house, and Mrs. Watanabe is doing most of the talking now.

Okusan	**Neruson san wa sukii ga dekimasu ka.** Can you ski, Mr. Nelson?
Mike	**Hai, sukoshi dekimasu. Amari jōzu ja nai kedo.** Yes, a little. I'm not very good, though.
Okusan	**Sō desu ka. Jitsu wa, watashitachi wa san-gatsu ni sukii ni ikimasu ga, moshi yokattara, Neruson san mo issho ni ikimasen ka.** I see. The fact is, we're going skiing in March, and if it's all right (with you), won't you come with us?
Mike	**Dōmo arigatō, sore wa ii desu ne. Nan-nichi ni ikimasu ka.** Thank you, that'll be nice. What date are you going?

Okusan	Jū-hachi-nichi no yoru ni itte, ni-jū-ichi-nichi no gogo kaerimasu. Sore wa kinyōbi kara getsuyōbi made desu. Ni-jū-ichi-nichi wa yasumi no hi da kara, sukii-jō wa konde iru to omoimasu ga. We're going on the evening of the 18th, and coming back on the afternoon of the 21st. That's from Friday to Monday. The 21st is a holiday, so I think the ski resort will be crowded.
Mike	Yasumi no hi desu ka. Donna yasumi? A holiday? What kind of holiday?
Okusan	San-gatsu ni-jū-ichi-nichi wa shunbun no hi desu. March 21st is "shunbun no hi."
Mike	Shunbun no hi? "Shunbun" wa Eigo de nan to iimasu ka. "Shunbun no hi"? What do you say for "shunbun" in English?
Okusan	Sa, Eigo no kotoba ga wakarimasen ga, sono hi ni wa, yoru no jikan to hiruma no jikan ga onaji desu. Well, I don't know the English word, but on that day, the hours of night and day are the same.
Mike	Ā, hai, wakarimashita. Ah, yes, I understand.
Okusan	Neruson san, biiru ga nai n' desu ne. Gomen nasai. Dōzo. Mr. Nelson, you don't have any beer! Please excuse me – here you are.
Hiro	Boku mo biiru o nonde mo ii? Can I have some beer too?
Okusan	Hiro, dame desu yo. Mada jū-ni sai deshō. Biiru o nonde wa ikemasen. Sa, mō sorosoro neru jikan desu. Hiro, no you can't! You're still (only) twelve years old. You mustn't drink beer. Well, it's getting on to bedtime [Lit: sleep time].
Hiro	O-kāsan! Neruson san ga kuru kara, osoku made okite mo ii, to kinō itta deshō. Mom! Yesterday you said that because Mr. Nelson was coming, it would be all right to stay up late, didn't you?

Okusan	Hai, sō iimashita kedo, mō osoi desu yo.
	Yes, I said that, but it's already late.
Mike	Sa, watashi mo sorosoro kaerimasu.
	Well, I must be going shortly.
Okusan	E? Mō? Mada ii deshō.
	What? Already? You don't need to go yet, do you?
	[Lit: It's still okay, isn't it?]
Mike	Sumimasen ne. Demo, ashita no asa mata yakyū da kara.
	Thank you. But tomorrow morning it's baseball again, so ...
Okusan	Sō desu ka. Yakyū no gēmu desu ka. Ja, ganbatte kudasai ne!
	Ah, a baseball game. Well, have a good game [Lit: try hard].
Mike	Hai, ganbarimasu. Dewa, kore de shitsurei shimasu. Iroiro arigatō gozaimashita. Konban wa taihen tanoshikatta desu.
	Yes, I will. Well, please excuse me. Thank you for everything. This evening has been extremely enjoyable.
Okusan	Iie, kochira koso. Mata dōzo.
	The pleasure's ours. Please come again.

STRUCTURE AND USAGE NOTES

1. THE MONTHS

The names of the months are very straightforward in Japanese, as they are simply the equivalents of "month one, month two, month three," etc.

nan-gatsu	what month?		
ichi-gatsu	January	shichi-gatsu	July
ni-gatsu	February	hachi-gatsu	August
san-gatsu	March	ku-gatsu	September
shi-gatsu	April	jū-gatsu	October
go-gatsu	May	jū-ichi-gatsu	November
roku-gatsu	June	jū-ni-gatsu	December

Kodomo no hi wa nan-gatsu desu ka. Go-gatsu desu ka.
What month is Children's Day? Is it May?

Nihon de, ichiban atsui toki wa shichi-gatsu to hachi-gatsu desu.
In Japan, the hottest time is July and August.

Shi-gatsu ni Amerika e kaerimasu.
I'm returning to the USA in April.

Shujin no tanjōbi mo watashi no tanjōbi mo jū-ichi-gatsu desu.
My husband's birthday and my birthday are both in November.

Other associated words are **sengetsu** ("last month"), **kongetsu** ("this month"), and **raigetsu** ("next month").

Sengetsu wa shutchō ga ōkatta kedo, kongetsu wa amari nai n' desu.
I had a lot of business trips last month, but there aren't many this month.

Jitsu wa, raigetsu kekkon suru n' desu.
The truth is, I'm getting married next month.

2. THE DATES

The words for the dates are irregular up to the 10th, so it's probably best to learn them by heart.

nan-nichi	what date?		
tsuitachi	1st	muika	6th
futsuka	2nd	nanoka	7th
mikka	3rd	yōka	8th
yokka	4th	kokonoka	9th
itsuka	5th	tōka	10th

After the tenth, the numbers revert back to ones you are already familiar with, followed by -**nichi**, the word for "day." Note that there are three exceptions: the 14th, 20th and 24th.

jū-ichi-nichi	11th	ni-jū-ichi-nichi	21st
jū-ni-nichi	12th	ni-jū-ni-nichi	22nd
jū-san-nichi	13th	ni-jū-san-nichi	23rd
jū-yokka	14th	ni-jū-yokka	24th
jū-go-nichi	15th	ni-jū-go-nichi	25th
jū-roku-nichi	16th	ni-jū-roku-nichi	26th
jū-shichi-nichi	17th	ni-jū-shichi-nichi	27th
jū-hachi-nichi	18th	ni-jū-hachi-nichi	28th
jū-ku-nichi	19th	ni-jū-ku-nichi	29th
hatsuka	20th	san-jū-nichi	30th
		san-jū-ichi-nichi	31st

Watashi no tanjōbi wa hachi-gatsu tōka desu.
My birthday is August (the) 10th.

A. Saitō san no natsu-yasumi wa nan-nichi kara nan-nichi made desu ka.
   When is your summer vacation, Ms. Saitō? [Lit: From what date to what date ...?]
B: Mikka kara tōka made desu.
   From the 3rd to the 10th.

Jū-go-nichi ni Yōroppa no shutchō kara kaerimasu.
I return from my European business trip on the 15th.

Tsugi no gēmu wa kongetsu no jū-san-nichi desu.
The next game is on the 13th of this month.

Shi-gatsu tsuitachi ni atarashii konpyūtā kōsu ga hajimarimasu.
On April 1st the new computer course begins.

3. DONNA – "WHAT KIND OF?"

This word belongs to another group of ko-, so-, a and do- words. They are konna ("this kind of"), sonna ("that kind of"), anna ("that kind of," – not connected to either of us), and donna ("what kind of?").

Nihon no fuyu wa donna tenki desu ka.
What kind of weather is it in Japan in the winter?

Sonna shitsumon ni kotaeru koto ga dekimasen.
I can't answer that kind of question.

Donna supōtsu ga suki desu ka.
What kind of sports do you like?

Konna resutoran wa iya desu ne.
This kind of restaurant is horrible, isn't it?

Anna hito wa dai-kirai desu.
I loathe that sort of person.

These words can also be used in front of adjectives to mean "this much, to this extent," etc., in which case they need to be followed by ni.

Kongetsu, sonna ni isogashiku arimasen.
This month, we're not that busy.

Konna ni atsui hi wa amari nai'n' desu ne!
We don't have many days this hot, do we!

Sono Chūka ryōri no resutoran wa sonna ni takaku nai to omoimasu.
I don't think that Chinese restaurant is that expensive.

Konna ni muzukashii to omoimasen deshita.
I didn't think it would be this difficult.

4. - TO IIMASHITA – REPORTED SPEECH

The verb **iimasu** (plain form: **iu**) means "say," "speak," "report," so it is often used to relate what someone else has said. In such a case, it is preceded by the particle **to**, which signals a quotation.

Maiku san wa, "Hayaku hashiru koto ga dekimasen," to iimashita ga, jitsu wa totemo hayai desu.
Mike said, "I can't run fast," but in fact he's very fast.

Wada san wa, "Kore de shitsurei shimasu," to itte, kaerimashita.
Mr. Wada said, "Excuse me," and went home.

In reported speech, when you're talking about what someone else said rather than quoting their actual words, simply put everything that was said into the plain form.

Maiku san wa, ashita yakyū o suru to iimashita. [= Maiku san wa, "Ashita yakyū o shimasu," to iimashita.]
Mike said he's playing baseball tomorrow.

Watanabe san wa chotto isogashii kara, kaigi ni denai to iimashita. [= Watanabe san wa, "Chotto isogashii kara, kaigi ni demasen," to iimashita.]
Mr. Watanabe said he's busy, so he won't attend the meeting.

Fukuda san wa san-ji han ni kuru to iimashita ka. [= Fukuda san wa, "San-ji han ni kimasu," to iimashita ka.]
Did Ms. Fukuda say she would come at 3:30?

Takahashi san wa shi-gatsu tsuitachi ni kekkon suru to iimashita ga, hontō desu ka.
Ms. Takahashi said she's getting married on April 1st – is it true?

Saitō san wa nan to iimashita ka.
What did Ms. Saitō say?

Keiko chan wa kinō atama ga itakatta kara konakatta to iimashita.
Keiko said she didn't come yesterday because she had a headache.

The particle **to** is also used with other verbs which show some sort of quotation, such as **kiku** ("ask," "hear"), **omou** ("think"), **kaku** ("write"), and **kotaeru** ("reply").

Haha wa, Ohaio wa ima totemo atsui, to tegami ni kakimashita.
My mother wrote in her letter that it's very hot in Ohio now.

Watanabe san ni, itsu sukii ni iku ka, to kikimashita. Demo, mada wakaranai to kotaemashita.
I asked Mr. Watanabe when he was going skiing, but he replied that he didn't know yet.

Wada san to Ogawa san wa onaji kaisha ni tsutomete iru ka to kikimashita.
He asked if Mr. Wada and Mr. Ogawa were working in the same company.

It's common to miss out **da** when reporting on questions.

Watashi wa Amerikajin ka to kikimashita.
He asked if I was American.

Kyō wa jū-san-nichi ka to kikimashita ka.
He asked if it was the 13th today.

When you are talking about what someone else says in the present tense, then it's usual to use the **-te iru** form.

Takahashi san wa tsukareta to itte imasu.
Ms. Takahashi says she's tired.

Sūzan san wa itsumo wakaranai to itte imasu.
Susan is always saying she doesn't understand.

Tomodachi wa haru ni Nihon e kuru to itte imasu
My friend says she'll come to Japan in the spring.

5. EIGO DE NAN TO IIMASU KA – "WHAT DO YOU SAY IN ENGLISH?"

The verb **iimasu** is also useful for when you want to ask how to say something in English or Japanese.

A. **Sensei, sumimasen ga, "the fall" wa Nihongo de nan to iimasu ka.**
   Teacher, excuse me, but how do you say "the fall" in Japanese?
B. **"Aki" to iimasu.**
   It's "aki."

"Tegami" o Eigo de "letter" to iimasu ka.
For "tegami," do you say "letter" in English?

"Itadakimasu" wa Eigo de nan to iu deshō ka.
I wonder what you say for "Itadakimasu" in English.

6. ASKING PERMISSION

When you want to ask permission to do something, add **mo ii desu
ka** to the -te form, which is like saying "—ing, is it alright?" A
positive answer to such a request can simply be **Hai, ii desu** or **Hai,
-te mo ii desu.**

A. Sumimasen ga, koko ni suwatte mo ii desu ka.
Excuse me, but is it all right if I sit here?

B: Ii desu. Dōzo.
Yes, please go ahead.

A. Denwa o tsukatte mo ii desu ka.
Is it all right if I use the phone?

B. Hai, tsukatte mo ii desu yo. Dōzo.
Yes, it's all right to use it. Go ahead.

Nihongo de setsumei shite mo ii desu ka.
Is it okay to explain it in Japanese?

Kyō hayaku kaette mo ii desu ka.
Is it all right to go home early today?

Shitsumon o kiite mo ii desu ka.
May I ask a question?

Haha wa, itte mo ii to iimashita ga, chichi wa dame da to iimashita.
My mother said I could go, but my father said I couldn't. [Lit: ...
said it was no good.]

When you want to ask if it's all right *not* to do something, then find
the negative -nai form (e.g. **ikanai**, "don't go" or **tabenai**, "don't
eat"), and change it to -**nakute**. Then add the ending -**mo ii desu**.
This is the equivalent of "it's all right not to ..." or "you don't need
to ...".

A. Kore o zenbu tabenakute mo ii desu ka.
Is it all right if I don't eat all of this?

B. Hai, (tabenakute mo) ii desu yo.
Yes, it's all right (if you don't eat it).

Chotto isogashii kara, kyō no kaigi ni denakute mo ii desu ka.
I'm a bit busy, so is it okay if I don't attend today's meeting?

Hazukashii kara, Nihongo de no jiko shōkai o shinakute mo ii desu ka.
I'm embarrassed, so is it all right if I don't introduce myself in Japanese?

Issho ni ikanakute mo ii desu ka.
Is it all right if I don't go with you?

You can also use this pattern to give permission, as well as ask for it.

Namae to jūsho o kakanakute mo ii desu.
It's all right not to write your name and address.

Kongetsu wa taihen atsui kara, kaisha no naka de nekutai o shinakute mo ii desu.
As it's extremely hot this month, you don't need to wear neckties in the office.

7. REFUSING PERMISSION

To refuse permission, again find the -te form of the verb, and then add **wa ikemasen**. The word **ikemasen** means "mustn't," "forbidden," "bad," so this is a very strong refusal. (In the next lesson we will be learning a more indirect way of suggesting you shouldn't do something.)

Sono heya ni haitte wa ikemasen yo.
Hey, you mustn't go into that room.

Nihongo no jūgyō de wa, Eigo de hanashite wa ikemasen.
In the Japanese class, you mustn't speak in English.

Sonna shitsumon o kiite wa ikemasen yo.
You mustn't ask that kind of question.

Sono tegami o yonde wa ikemasen.
You mustn't read that letter.

Kono koto o denwa de hanashite wa ikemasen.
You musn't talk about this matter on the phone.

8. SHUNBUN NO HI – AND OTHER NATIONAL HOLIDAYS

The national holidays in Japan, when banks, government offices and business are closed, are as follows. (When a national holiday falls on a Sunday, the following Monday becomes a holiday.)

January 1	Ganjitsu	New Year's Day
January 15	Seijin no hi	Coming-of-Age Day
February 11	Kenkoku kinenbi	National Foundation Day
March 20 or 21	Shunbun no hi	Spring Equinox Day
April 29	Midori no hi	Greenery Day
May 3	Kenpō kinenbi	Constitution Day
May 5	Kodomo no hi	Children's Day
September 15	Keirō no hi	Respect for the Aged Day
September 23 or 24	Shūbun no hi	Autumnal Equinox Day
October 10	Taiiku no hi	Sports Health Day
November 3	Bunka no hi	Culture Day
November 23	Kinro kansha no hi	Labor Thanksgiving Day
December 23	Tennō tanjōbi	Emperor's Birthday

If May 3rd and May 5th both fall on weekdays, then the day in between also becomes a holiday. This period from the end of April to the beginning of May, when there are a number of holidays in a short period of time, is generally known as Golden Week, and is a popular time for taking a short vacation.

VOCABULARY

aki: fall/autumn
anna: that kind of
bunka no hi: Culture Day
denai: doesn't attend [from **deru**]
deru: go out, appear, attend
donna: what kind of?
fuyu: winter
ganjitsu: New Year's Day
go-gatsu: May
gomen nasai: excuse me, I beg your pardon
hachi-gatsu: August
haru: spring
heya: room
hi: day
hiruma: daytime
ichi-gatsu: January

iimasu: say [from iu]
iroiro arigatō gozaimashita: thank you for everything
isogashii: busy
jū-gatsu: October
jū-hachi-nichi: 18th (of the month)
jū-ichi-gatsu: November
jū-ni-gatsu: December
kaigi ni deru: attend a meeting
keirō no hi: Respect for the Aged Day
kenkoku kinenbi: National Foundation Day
kenpō kinenbi: Constitution Day
kinro kansha no hi: Labor Thanksgiving Day
kochira koso: the pleasure's mine
kodomo no hi: Children's Day
kongetsu: this month
konna: this kind of
kōsu: course (of study)
kotaeru: answer, respond
kotoba: word
ku-gatsu: September
mata dōzo: please come again
midori no hi: Greenery Day
moshi yokattara: if it's all right
nan-gatsu: which month?
nan-nichi: what date?
natsu-yasumi: summer vacation
natsu: summer
neru jikan: time to sleep
-nichi: [added to numbers to give the date]
ni-gatsu: February
ni-jū-ichi-nichi: 21st (of the month)
nonde mo ii: is it all right to drink?
nonde wa ikemasen: you mustn't drink
okite mo ii: all right to stay up [from okiru, to get up]
onaji: same
osoku made: until late
raigetsu: next month
roku-gatsu: June
san-gatsu: March
seijin no hi: Coming-of-Age Day
sengetsu: last month
shi-gatsu: April
shichi-gatsu: July
shūbun no hi: Autumnal Equinox Day

shunbun no hi: Spring Equinox Day
shutchō: business trip
sō iimashita: said so [from **iu**]
sonna: that kind of
sorosoro: slowly, gradually, soon
sukii ni ikimasu: go skiing
sukii-jō: ski resort
sukii: skiing
taiiku no hi: Sports Health Day
tegami: letter
tennō tanjōbi: Emperor's Birthday
toki: time, period
yasumi no hi: vacation, holiday
yasumi: vacation, rest, pause
Yōroppa: Europe

TEST YOURSELF

1. *Read through the dialog at the beginning of the lesson again, and then say if the following statements are true or false.*

   1. Sangatsu ni-jū-ichi-nichi wa shunbun no hi desu.   T/F

   2. Neruson san wa suki ga jōzu ja nai kedo, sukoshi dekimasu. T/F

   3. Okusan wa, "shunbun" no koto o Nihongo de setsumei dekimasen deshita.   T/F

   4. Hiro kun mo biiru o nonde imasu.   T/F

   5. Neruson san ga kite iru kara Hiro kun wa mada okite imasu. T/F

   6. Maiku san wa ashita mata yakyū gēmu o mimasu.   T/F

2. *Here are some of the events Mike has marked on his calendar over the next couple of months. Make sentences about what will be happening on the various days, as in the example.*

Example:

MARCH
18
Go skiing

San-gatsu jū-hachi-nichi ni sukii ni ikimasu.

1.

MARCH
28
tennis in Kawasaki

_____

2.

MARCH
31
Ms. Takahashi's party!!

_____

3.

APRIL
4
Sue coming to <u>Japan</u>!

_____

4.

APRIL
14
Japanese course finishes

_____

5.

APRIL
29
Golden Week begins

_____

3. *A new secretary, Ms. Obata, has joined the staff at Yokohama High School, and Mr. Watanabe is explaining some of the things it's all right for her to do and not do. How does he tell her that it's all right:*

1. to use both the red phone and the black phone?

2. not to attend the 2:00 meeting?

3. to go home at 4:30?

4. to drink coffee in this room?

5. to talk to Mr. Nelson in Japanese?

6. not to do a self-introduction in front of everyone?

4. *On this first morning at the school, Ms. Obata has a short, simple conversation with Mike in English, and she's so excited about it that she tells her mother all about it when she gets home. How does she relate the conversation? The first three lines have been done for you,*

Mike	Are you Ms. Obata?	Neruson san wa, Obata san ka to kikimashita.
Obata	Yes, I am.	Watashi wa, hai, sō da to kotaemashita
Mike	How do you do?	Neruson san wa, hajimemashite to iimashita.

Mike   Excuse me, but what time does today's meeting begin? (**kiku**)
Obata   At 2:00. (**kotaeru**)
Mike   Which room is it in? (**kiku**)
Obata   I'm sorry, but I don't know. (**kotaeru**)
Mike   Ah, time for lunch. (**iu**) Are you also going now, Ms. Obata? (**kiku**)
Obata   No, I'm not going yet. (**iu**)

5. *How would you say these sentences in Japanese?*

1. How do you say "kochira koso" in English?

2. Mr. Tanaka said he'd be at the office until 6:00.

3. You mustn't use that kind of word.

4. Next month's business trip is from the 3rd to the 7th.

5. Is it all right if I use this desk?

6. Thank you for everything. It's been very enjoyable.

3 月21日

The names of the months use a combination of the number of the month plus the character for "moon/month," which is pronounced **gatsu**. The dates combine numbers with the character for "day," which is pronounced **ka** or **nichi**. Arabic numbers are often used instead of kanji numbers.

KARE TO HANASANAI HŌ GA II DESU YO.
IT'S BEST NOT TO TALK TO HIM!

A group of the staff at Yokohama High School are going to see a movie together tonight. Mike and Ms. Takahashi agree to meet in a coffee shop for something to eat before going to meet the others. Ms. Takahashi is already waiting when Mike goes in.

Mike	**A, Takahashi san, konbanwa. Mō chūmon shita n' desu ka.** Ah, Ms. Takahashi, evening. Have you already ordered?
Takahashi	**Iie, mada desu. Menyū o dōzo.** No, not yet. Here's the menu.
Mike	**Arigatō. Sa, nani ni shimashō ka.** (reading the menu) **Hamu sando … tsuna sarada … supagetti … piza tōsuto … ā, watashi wa piza tōsuto ni shimasu. Piza tōsuto to hotto kōhii. Takahashi san wa?** Thank you. Let's see, what shall I have? Ham sandwiches … tuna salad … spaghetti … pizza toast …

	I'll have pizza toast … Pizza toast and a hot coffee. How about you?
Takahashi	O-naka ga suita kara, watashi mo piza tōsuto desu. Sore kara, remon tii. (to waitress) **Sumimasen! Piza tōsuto futatsu to, hotto hitotsu to remon tii o hitotsu kudasai.** I'm hungry, so I'll have pizza toast too. And a lemon tea. Excuse me! Two pizza toasts, one coffee and one lemon tea, please.
Waitress	**Piza tōsuto futatsu, hotto hitotsu, remon tii o hitotsu desu ne. Kashikomarimashita.** Two pizza toasts, one coffee and one lemon tea. Certainly.
Takahashi	(looking out of the window) **Ara, Kenji san! Are wa Kenji san desu!** Ah, Kenji! That's Kenji!
Mike	**Bōifurendo desu ka. Doko? Dono hito ga Kenji san desu ka.** Your boyfriend? Where? Which one is Kenji?
Takahashi	**Yūbinkyoku no mae ni imasu. Kōshū denwa no tonari desu.** He's in front of the post office. Next to the public telephone.
Mike	**Hai, hai. Ā, ima Takahashi san o mita deshō! Ee? Dō shite mukō e aruite iku n' desu ka. Hen desu ne.** Yes, yes. Ah, he just saw you, didn't he! Eh? Why is he walking the other way? That's odd, isn't it?
Takahashi	**Jitsu wa, kinō no yoru denwa de kenka shita n' desu. Watashi wa konban gakkō no sutaffu to issho ni, eiga o mi ni iku to itta n' desu ne. Sore de, Kenji san wa okotte, dame da to iimashita. Dakara watashi mo okotte, kore kara mō awanai hō ga ii, to itta n' desu. Sore de, kaiwa ga owarimashita.** The truth is, we had an argument on the phone last night. I said I was going to see a movie with the staff at the school tonight, right? So Kenji got angry, and said I couldn't go. That's why I got angry, and said it would be better if we didn't meet any more. And with that, the conversation ended.
Mike	**Sō desu ka. Dō shimasu ka. Ima Kenji san o yonda hō ga ii deshō.**

	I see. What will you do? You'd better call out to him now, hadn't you?
Takahashi	**Iie, kyō wa kare to hanasanai hō ga ii to omoimasu.** No, I think it's better if I don't talk to him today.
Mike	**Sō desu ka. A, piza tōsuto ga kimashita.** I see. Ah, here comes the pizza toast.
Waitress	**Hai, hotto no o-kyaku sama wa?** The customer who ordered coffee?
Mike	**Watashi desu. Dōmo.** That's me. Thank you.
Takahashi	**Sa, jikan ga amari nai kara, hayaku tabeta hō ga ii desu ne. Itadakimasu.** Well, we don't have much time, so we'd better eat quickly. Bon appetit.

STRUCTURE AND USAGE NOTES

1. PIZA TŌSUTO – AND OTHER WORDS BORROWED FROM ENGLISH

There are many foreign words which have entered the Japanese language, most of them from English, to describe things not native to Japan, such as Western-style food, clothes (see Lesson 8, Structure and Usage Note 2), and furnishings. Younger people also consider it fashionable to use borrowed foreign words, and you are likely to come across lots of them in the worlds of advertising, fashion and music. These imported words are known as **gairaigo**, or "words from abroad." Here are a few examples.

In the home	Technology	Food and drink
tēburu table	**shii dii** CD	**piza** pizza
kāten curtain	**konpyūtā** computer	**hanbāgā** hamburger
ranpu lamp	**bideo** video	**sutēki** steak
kāpetto carpet	**furoppi** floppy disk	**sarada** salad
beddo bed	**fakkusu** fax	**kēki** cake
kusshon cushion	**kopii** photocopy	**kōra** cola
airon iron	**monitā** monitor	**chokorēto** chocolate
taoru towel	**kiibōdo** keyboard	**appurupai** apple pie

In some cases, the borrowed words are not immediately recognizable because they have been abbreviated.

word processor=	wā(do) puro(sessa) =	wāpuro
television =	terebi(jon) =	terebi
sandwich =	sando(itchi) =	sando
air conditioner =	ea kon(dishonā) =	eakon
family computer =	fami(ri) kon(pyūtā) =	famikon
apartment =	apāto(mento) =	apāto

2. HITOTSU, FUTATSU – "ONE, TWO" – ANOTHER WAY OF COUNTING

You already know the numbers **ichi, ni, san,** etc., to which you can add endings such as **-nin** (to count people), **-nichi** (to give the date), **-ji** (to give the time) and **-sai** (to give your age). As mentioned earlier (Lesson 9, Structure and Usage Note 4) there are also special ways of counting things which are flat, or long and thin, etc., and this too involves attaching special endings to **ichi, ni, san.**

However, there is also another set of numbers, for counting *things*. The word **ichi** by itself simply means the number "one," but **hitotsu** means "one thing/one object." This counting system which begins with **hitotsu** is the one you need when shopping, or ordering several dishes in a restaurant, or otherwise talking about a number of objects. Note that the number usually comes *after* the item to which it is referring.

ikutsu	how many?		
hitotsu	one	muttsu	six
futatsu	two	nanatsu	seven
mittsu	three	yattsu	eight
yottsu	four	kokonotsu	nine
itsutsu	five	tō	ten

Otōto wa, o-naka ga taihen suita kara, chokorēto kēki o mittsu tabeta to iimashita.
My little brother said he was really hungry, so he ate three chocolate cakes!

Maiku san no atarashii apāto ni wa, heya ga ikutsu arimasu ka.
In Mike's new apartment, how many rooms are there?

Sumimasen, kōra o mō futatsu kudasai.
Excuse me, could we have two more colas, please?

Ōkii mondai wa hitotsu dake arimasu.
There's only one major problem.

Kono yottsu no machi no naka de, dore ga ichiban ōkii desu ka.
Which of these four towns is the biggest?

These numbers only go up to ten, and then revert back to the system of **ichi, ni, san,** etc.

Watashi no kaisha ni, shisha ga jū-san arimasu.
My company has thirteen branch offices.

3. YŪBINKYOKU NO MAE NI – "IN FRONT OF THE POST OFFICE" – AND OTHER PREPOSITIONS

When you are talking about the location of something in Japanese, instead of saying, for example, "underneath the table" or "inside the building," you say the equivalent of "the table's underneath" (**tēburu no shita**) or "the building's inside" (**tatemono no naka**). Here are some of the most commonly-used words for describing the location of something or someone.

ue	on, on top, above	soba	nearby, by the side
shita	below, under	mae	in front of
naka	in, inside	ushiro	behind
tonari	next to	soto	outside
aida	between	chikaku	near

Kissaten wa ginkō to yūbinkyoku no aida ni arimasu.
The coffee shop is between the bank and the post office.

Eki no mae de aimashō.
Let's meet in front of the station.

Depāto no naka ni, kissaten ga mittsu to resutoran ga itsutsu arimasu.
Inside the department store there are three coffee shops and five restaurants.

Maiku san no apāto no naka wa totemo kirei da kedo, tatemono no soto wa kitanai desu.
The inside of Mike's apartment is really nice, but the outside of the building is dirty.

Tanaka san kara no tegami wa wāpuro no ue ni atta kedo, ima doko deshō ka.
The letter from Mr. Tanaka was on top of the word processor, but where is it now?

Kōshū denwa wa mukō no mise no ushiro ni arimasu.
There's a public telephone behind that shop over there.

Saitō san no apāto wa ichiban ue ni arimasu.
Ms. Saitō's apartment is right at the top.

4. MI NI IKU – "GO TO SEE"

Just as in English we can say "go to see, go to buy, go to eat," etc.,
so in Japanese it is possible to create phrases with the same kind of
meaning. Just remove -masu from the -masu form of the verb, and
add ni iku. Here are some examples.

shi ni iku	go to do
tabe ni iku	go to eat
nomi ni iku	go to have a drink
kai ni iku	go to buy
ai ni iku	go to meet
mi ni iku	go to see

Nomi ni ikimashō.
Let's go for a drink.

Ashita no asa tomodachi to issho ni tenisu o shi ni ikimasu.
I'm going to play tennis with some friends tomorrow morning.

Kinō Yokohama e atarashii sūtsu o kai ni itta kedo, taihen takakute,
kaimasen deshita.
Yesterday I went to Yokohama to buy a new suit, but they were
really expensive, so I didn't buy one.

Senshū no doyōbi wa tanjōbi datta kara, gārufurendo to issho ni
sono atarashii Indo ryōri no resutoran e tabe ni itta n' desu.
Last Saturday it was my birthday, so I went to eat at that new Indian
restaurant together with my girlfriend.

5. YONDA HŌ GA II – "YOU'D BETTER CALL TO HIM" AND OTHER ADVICE

To make a strong suggestion or recommendation that someone do
something, add hō ga ii to the plain past form of the verb, that is, the
-ta form. This is the equivalent of the English "you'd better ..." or
"you ought to ..." or "it would be best if you ...".

Kaigi no repōto o wāpuro de kaita hō ga ii to omoimasu.
I think it would be best to write up the report of the meeting on the
word processor.

Tsukareta n' desu ka. Ja, konban hayaku neta hō ga ii desu ne.
You're tired? Well, you'd better go to bed early tonight.

Jikan ga amari nai kara, mō sugu chūmon shita hō ga ii desu ne.
We don't have much time, so we should order soon, right?

Osoi kara, takushii de kaetta hō ga ii to omoimasu yo.
It's late, so I think it would be better if you went home by taxi.

Atsui toki ni, eakon o tsukatta hō ga ii deshō.
It's probably best to use an air conditioner when it's hot.

If you want to suggest that someone *shouldn't* do something, then add **hō ga ii** to the -nai form of the verb (that is, the plain negative of the present tense).

Mada wakai kara, sonna ni takusan nomanai hō ga ii desu yo.
You're still young, so you shouldn't drink so much.

Ano hito wa o-kyaku san da kara, kare to kenka shinai hō ga ii desu yo!
He's a customer, so it would be best if you don't argue with him!

Konban soto e denai hō ga ii desu yo. Samui kara.
It's best not to go out tonight, because it's cold.

Yoru, hitori de machi o arukanai hō ga ii desu.
It's best not to walk in the city alone at night.

Sonna ni hayaku okoranai hō ga ii desu yo.
You shouldn't get angry so quickly.

Sore wa Wada san no wāpuro da kara, tsukawanai hō ga ii to omoimasu.
That's Mr. Wada's word processor, so I think it would be better not to use it.

VOCABULARY

aida: between
airon: iron
apāto: apartment
appurupai: apple pie
ara: oh! [used mostly by women]
aruite iku: walk away [from **aruku**]
awanai hō ga ii: best not to meet [from **au**]
beddo: bed
chikaku: near, close

chokorēto: chocolate
chūmon: an order, request
eakon: air conditioner
fakkusu: fax
famikon: family computer
furoppi: floppy disk
futatsu: two (objects)
gairaigo: words imported from abroad
hamu: ham
hanasanai hō ga ii: best not to talk
hanbāgā: hamburger
hitotsu: one (object)
hotto (kōhii): hot coffee
ikutsu: how many?
Indo ryōri: Indian cuisine
itsutsu: five (objects)
kaiwa: conversation
kāpetto: carpet
kare: him, he
kashikomarimashita: certainly [formal]
kāten: curtain
kēki: cake
kenka: argument
kiibōdo: keyboard
kitanai: dirty
kokonotsu: nine (objects)
kopii: photocopy
kōra: cola
kōshū denwa: public telephone
kusshon: cushion
menyū: menu
mi ni iku: go to see
mise: shop
mittsu: three (objects)
monitā: a monitor
mukō: the other direction, over there
muttsu: six (objects)
naka: inside
nanatsu: seven (objects)
o-kyaku sama: guest, customer
o-naka ga suita: I'm hungry [from suku, become empty]
o-naka: stomach
okotte: got angry, and ... [from okoru]
piza: pizza

ranpu: lamp
remon tii: lemon tea
sando: sandwich
sarada: salad
shii dii: CD
shisha: branch office
shita: below, under
soba: near, next to
sore de: so, therefore, and then
supagetti: spaghetti
sutaffu: staff
sutēki: steak
tabeta hō ga ii: had better eat
tēburu: table
tō: ten (objects)
tōsuto: toast
tsuna: tuna
ue: above, on top
ushiro: behind, in back of
wāpuro: word processor
yattsu: eight (objects)
yonda hō ga ii: best to call [from **yobu**]
yottsu: four (objects)
yūbinkyoku: post office

TEST YOURSELF

1. *Read through the dialog at the beginning of the lesson again, and then say if the following statements are true or false.*

   1. Maiku san mo Takahashi san mo piza tōsuto o chūmon shimashita. T/F

   2. Kenji san no soba ni kōshū denwa ga arimashita. T/F

   3. Kenji san ga yūbinkyoku no mae kara kissaten e aruite kimashita. T/F

   4. Kenji san wa, Takahashi san ga gakkō no sutaffu to issho ni eiga o mi ni iku kara, okorimashita. T/F

   5. Maiku san wa, Kenji san to hanasanai hō ga ii to omoimashita. T/F

   6. Futari wa yukkuri tabete mo ii desu. T/F

2. Look at the **gairaigo** words below, and try to guess what English words they come from.

Sports:
bōringu
gorufu
basukettobōru
aisu skēto
haikingu
sāfingu
uindo sāfingu

Countries:
Airurando
Ōsutoraria
Indo
Nyū Jiirando
Burajiru
Itaria
Ōsutoria

3. After the movie, Mike and the other staff from school go for a coffee. In the coffee shop, everyone talks at once, and everyone wants to give advice to the others. What do they say in response to the comments below? Use **hō ga ii** in your answers, as in the example.

Example:

A. [angrily] **Dame da! Sore wa uso da!**
   (best not to argue in a coffee shop)
B. **Kissaten no naka de kenka shinai hō ga ii desu yo.**

1. Mina san, shitsurei shimasu. Watashi wa aruite kaerimasu.
   (late, so better to go home by taxi)

2. Tsukareta!
   (should go home soon)

3. O-naka ga suita ne!
   (should eat spaghetti or pizza toast)

4. Kono jaketto wa kitanai desu ne!
   (should buy a new one)

5. Sono futari wa mainichi mainichi kenka shite imasu ne.
   (better if they got divorced)

6. Watashi wa chokorēto kēki o mō hitotsu chūmon shimasu yo.
   (shouldn't eat so much chocolate)

4. *Mike has tidied his room a little today. Look at the before and after
   pictures below, and see if you can spot the differences. Make
   sentences like the one in the example, using the cues provided.*

Example: (denwa – ue – naka) **Kinō, denwa ga wāpuro no ue ni
atta kedo, ima tsukue no naka ni arimasu.**

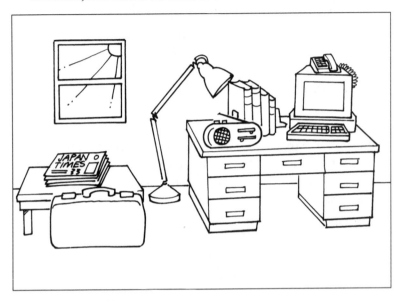

1. shinbun – ue – shita

2. ranpu – tonari – shita

3. rajio – aida – ue

4. sūtsukēsu – mae – ushiro

5. tenki – ii – warui

6. kāten – nai – aru

5. How would you say these sentences in Japanese?

1. Two hot coffees, one hamburger and one spaghetti, please.

2. I have a headache, so I think it would be best to stay (**iru**) at home and watch TV.

3. This movie looks interesting, doesn't it? Shall we go to see it tonight?

4. Who lives in that big house next to the post office?

5. Do you think it would be better not to call Mr. Wada?

6. Mr. Watanabe asked how many desks we had altogether in the school.

The word **denwa** is made up of the kanji characters for "electricity" and "speak," and means "telephone."

DAI JŪ-GO-KA

WATASHI NO KEIYAKU NI TSUITE DESU GA.
IT'S ABOUT MY CONTRACT.

Mike is talking to Mr. Watanabe in the staff room at school.

Mike	**Watanabe san, chotto shitsumon ga arimasu ga, ii desu ka.** Mr. Watanabe, is it all right to ask a question? [Lit: I have a question – is it allright (to ask you)?]
Watanabe	**Ii desu yo. Dōzo. Nan deshō ka.** Of course. Go ahead. What is it?
Mike	**Watashi no keiyaku ni tsuite desu ga.** It's concerning my contract.
Watanabe	**Keiyaku ni tsuite no shitsumon desu ka. Demo watashi wa keiyaku no koto ga yoku wakaranai n' desu yo. Kōchō sensei to hanashita hō ga ii to omoimasu. Nanika, mondai ga dekimashita ka.** A question concerning your contract? But I don't really know about contract matters. I think it would be better to talk to the principal. Has there been some kind of problem?

Mike	Iie, iie, mondai ja nai n' desu. Jitsu wa, raigetsu watashi no tomodachi ga Nihon e kuru yotei desu. Kanojo wa, gaikoku wa hajimete da kara, kūkō made mukae ni ikitai to omotte iru n' desu ga. No, no, it's not a problem. The fact is, my friend plans to come to Japan next month. It's her first time abroad, so I think I'd like to go to the airport to meet her.
Watanabe	A, wakarimashita. Yasumi no koto desu ka. Ah, I see. It's about a day off.
Mike	Ee, moshi yokattara, ichi-nichi yasumi o toritai n' desu. Yes, if it's all right, I'd like to take one day off.
Watanabe	Sore wa mondai nai to omoimasu. Tada, sono koto ni tsuite memo o kaite, watashi ni dashite kudasai. Saitō san ga sono tokubetsu no yōshi o motte imasu kara, kanojo ni kiite kudasai. I don't think that's a problem. Just write a memo concerning the details, and submit it to me. Ms. Saitō has the special forms, so ask her.

Just then, Ms. Saitō comes into the teachers' room to talk to Mike.

Saitō	Neruson san, chotto ii desu ka. Kōchō sensei kara no messēji desu ga, moshi yokattara, kyō ka ashita Neruson san to uchiawase o shitai to itte imashita ga. Mr. Nelson, do you have a moment? There's a message from the principal – he said that, if it's all right with you, he'd like to meet with you today or tomorrow.
Mike	Kōchō sensei to no uchiawase desu ka. Nanika ... Meet with the principal? Is there something ...?
Saitō	Shinpai shinaide kudasai! Tada kore kara no keikaku ni tsuite sōdan suru tsumori da to omoimasu. Don't worry! I think it's just that he intends to consult you about upcoming projects.
Mike	Sō desu ka. Jikan o ima kimemasu ka. I see. Shall we decide the time now?
Saitō	Hai, onegai shimasu. Kōchō sensei no sukejūru o motte imasu kara, ima kimemashō. Yes, please do. I have the principal's schedule, so we can decide now.
Mike	Watashi wa, ashita no asa jū-ji made aite imasu ga. I'm free tomorrow morning until 10:00.

Saitō	Ashita no asa wa chotto muzukashii desu ne. Kōchō sensei wa kyōiku iinkai ni yoru tsumori da to itte imashita ga. Gogo wa?
	Tomorrow morning's a bit difficult. I think the principal intends to call in on the education committee. How about the afternoon?
Mike	Gogo wa, san-ji han made jūgyō ga arimasu ga, sono ato wa aite imasu.
	I have classes until 3:30, but I'm free after that.
Saitō	Ja, yo-ji ni shimashō.
	Right, let's make it 4:00.

STRUCTURE AND USAGE NOTES

1. NI TSUITE – "REGARDING" OR "CONCERNING"

The phrase **ni tsuite** means "regarding," "concerning," "about" and comes after the thing to which it refers.

Kachō kara no memo ni tsuite shitsumon ga arimasu ga.
I have a question concerning the memo from the section chief.

Takahashi san wa mō ichi-jikan gurai bōifurendo ni tsuite hanashite ita n' desu yo. Tsukaremashita!
Ms. Takahashi was talking about her boyfriend for an hour. I'm exhausted!

Sumimasen ga, kyūryō no koto ni tsuite kiite mo ii desu ka.
Excuse me, but is it all right if I ask about a salary matter?

Moshi moshi, Saitō san? Ashita no kaigi ni tsuite desu ga.
Hello, Mr. Saitō? (I'm calling) about tomorrow's meeting.

Kyōiku iinkai no kaigi ni tsuite repōto o kaite kudasai.
Please write a report on the meeting of the education committee.

Kyō no kaigi wa nan ni tsuite desu ka.
What's today's meeting about?

Buchō wa, kyonen no keikaku to kotoshi no keikaku ni tsuite iroiro kikimashita.
The department manager asked all sorts of questions concerning last year's projects and this year's projects.

2. YOTEI – MAKING PLANS

The word **yotei** is very useful for when you are discussing plans and schedules. When it comes after the plain form of a verb, it is the equivalent of "I plan to (do)."

Shachō no ashita no yotei wa nan desu ka.
What's the president's schedule for tomorrow?

Kotoshi no natsu yasumi ni wa, gaikoku e iku yotei desu.
For my summer vacation this year, my plan is to go abroad.

A. **Ashita no asa wa aite imasu ka.**
   Are you free tomorrow?

B. **Sumimasen ga, ashita wa Yokohama no shisha ni yoru yotei desu kara, chotto muzukashii desu.**
   I'm sorry, but tomorrow I'm scheduled to drop by at the Yokohama branch office, so it's a bit difficult.

Jū-ji ni kachō to uchiawase o suru yotei deshita ga, mada kite imasen ne. Dō shita n' deshō ka.
I was supposed to have a consultation with the section manager at 10:00, but he's not here yet. I wonder what's happened?

Kaigi wa go-ji made ni owaru yotei desu.
The meeting is scheduled to finish at 5:00.

Kōchō sensei wa, sono koto o ashita made ni kimeru yotei da to iimashita.
The principal said that he plans to decide on that matter by tomorrow.

Keiyaku ni tsuite kanojo to sōdan suru yotei desu.
I plan to talk over the contract with her.

3. IKITAI – "I WANT TO GO" AND OTHER DESIRES

To express a wish or desire to do something, replace **-masu** with **-tai**.

Plain form	-masu form	-tai form	Meaning
iku	iki-masu	iki-tai	want to go
taberu	tabe-masu	tabe-tai	want to eat
hanasu	hanashi-masu	hanashi-tai	want to talk
kimeru	kime-masu	kime-tai	want to decide
toru	tori-masu	tori-tai	want to take
kau	kai-masu	kai-tai	want to buy
uru	uri-masu	uri-tai	want to sell
suru	shi-masu	shi-tai	want to do

The -tai form is generally used to talk about your own wishes and wants, or to ask someone else about their feelings. It is not generally used to describe what someone else wants, because in Japanese it is considered that you can never *really* know what another person wants to do. To get around this, you can use the equivalents of "I think that he wants to ...," "He said that he wants to ...," "I heard that he wants to ...," etc.

Maiku san wa, keiyaku ni tsuite hanashitai to iimashita.
Mike said he wants to talk about the contract.

Sukoshi dake tabetai n' desu.
I only want to eat a little.

Wada san wa kotoshi gaikoku e ikitai to itte imasu.
Mr. Wada says that he wants to go abroad this year.

Piitā san wa chotto sabishikute, kuni e kaeritai to itte imasu yo.
Peter is a little lonely, and says he wants to go back to his own country.

Shachō kara no memo ni tsuite kikitai n' desu ga.
I'd like to ask you about the memo from the president.

Buchō wa minna de atarashii keikaku no koto o sōdan shitai to iimashita.
The department manager said he wants us all to confer about the new project.

Takahashi san wa, o-kane ga nai kara, kuruma o uritai to iimashita.
Ms. Takahashi said that she doesn't have any money, so she wants to sell her car.

The -tai ending acts in the same way as -i adjectives, so it has a negative form which ends in -taku arimasen, for talking about things you *don't* want to do, and a past form which ends in -takatta desu, for talking about what you wanted to do previously.

Sono koto ni tsuite kenka o shitaku nai n' desu yo.
Hey, I don't want to argue about that!

Ichi-nichi yasumi o toritakatta kedo, taihen isogashikute, toru koto ga dekimasen deshita.
I wanted to take a day off, but I couldn't because I was extremely busy.

Kyō wa ii tenki da kara, benkyō o shitaku nai ne!
It's such nice weather today, I don't want to study!

Kenji san wa, kinō kanojo ni denwa shitakatta kedo, kyō wa mō shitaku nai, to iimashita.
Kenji said that yesterday he wanted to call her, but today he doesn't any more.

Tsukarete ita kara, pātii e amari ikitaku nakatta kedo, totemo tanoshikatta desu.
I was tired, so I didn't really want to go to the party, but it was very enjoyable.

The -tai form is a verb ending showing that you want to *do* something. If, however, you want a *thing*, then you need the -i adjective hoshii. As with -tai, you need to use phrases like "I think that ...," "He said that ...," etc., if you are describing what someone else wants. (Note that wa marks the person who wants the object, and ga marks whatever it is they want.)

Watashi wa atarashii wāpuro ga hoshii desu ga, o-kane ga nai kara, dame desu.
I want a new word processor, but I don't have any money, so it's impossible.

Kanojo wa, bōifurendo ga hoshii to iimashita.
She said she wants a boyfriend.

Tanjōbi ni wa, nani ga hoshii desu ka.
For your birthday, what would you like?

Mae ni o-kane dake hoshikatta kedo, ima wa o-kane ja nakute, jikan mo hoshii n' desu.
Before I just wanted money, but now it's not money, I want time, too.

Saitō san wa motto nagai yasumi ga hoshii to iimashita.
Ms. Saitō said she wants a longer vacation.

4. MARKING ALTERNATIVES

The particle ka is used to mark alternatives, so it is similar to the English "or" when it comes between nouns.

Buchō ka kachō ga sore o kimeta hō ga ii to omoimasu.
I think it's best if the department chief or the section chief decides that.

Doyōbi ka nichiyōbi ni ikimasu.
I'll go on Saturday or Sunday.

Sono koto ni tsuite, Wada san ka Tanaka san to sōdan shite kudasai.
With regard to that matter, please consult Mr. Wada or Mr. Tanaka.

Rainen no natsu yasumi ni wa, Yōroppa ka Amerika ni ikitai to
omoimasu.
Next (year's) summer vacation, I think I'd like to go to Europe or the
USA.

Kōra ka kōhii ga hoshii desu.
I want some cola or coffee.

5. SHINAIDE KUDASAI – "PLEASE DON'T"

You have already come across the -te kudasai form, used when you
want to ask someone to do something (e.g. **Kore o tsukatte kudasai**,
"Please use this."). However, you might want to ask them *not* to do
something. In this case, start with the negative -nai form, and then
add -de kudasai (e.g. **Kore o tsukawanaide kudasai**, "Please don't use
this.").

Sō shinaide kudasai.
Please don't do that.

Uchiawase no jikan o mada kimenaide kudasai. Sono mae ni kachō
to sōdan shitai kara.
Please don't set the time of the meeting yet. Before that, I want to
consult the chief section head.

Fukuda san ni keiyaku no koto o hanasanaide kudasai.
Please don't talk to Ms. Fukuda about the contract matters.

Sō iwanaide kudasai.
Don't say that.

Sono repōto o mada buchō ni dasanaide kudasai.
Don't give that report to the (department) chief yet, please.

Kūkō made mukae ni konaide kudasai. Hajimete ja nai kara, watashi
wa hitori de daijōbu desu.
Please don't come to meet me at the airport. It's not the first time, so
I'll be all right by myself.

Watashi no koto o wasurenaide kudasai!
Please don't forget about me!

6. TSUMORI – TALKING ABOUT INTENTIONS

The word **tsumori** means "intention," so the sentence-ending **tsumori desu** after the plain form of a verb can usually be translated as "intend to do," or "mean to do."

Sore wa mondai desu ne. Dō suru tsumori desu ka.
That's a problem, isn't it? What do you intend to do?

Sono keikaku ni tsuite Watanabe san to hanasu tsumori datta ga, wasuremashita.
I meant to talk to Mr. Watanabe about that project, but I forgot.

Rainen no san-gatsu ni kuni e kaeru tsumori desu.
I intend to return home next March [Lit: next year's March].

Sonna ni takusan tabenai tsumori deshita ga, totemo oishii kara, zenbu tabemashita!
I didn't mean to eat so much, but it was really delicious, so I ate all of it!

Donna kuruma o kau tsumori desu ka.
Which car do you intend to buy?

Katō san wa kyūryō ni tsuite buchō to hanasu tsumori da to iimashita.
Ms. Kato said she means to talk to the department manager about her salary.

Takahashi san wa rainen no natsu made ni kekkon suru tsumori da to iimashita.
Ms. Takahashi said she intends to get married by next summer.

7. ARIMASU VS. MOTTE IMASU – HAVING AND HOLDING

The verb **motsu** means "hold," but you will usually come across it in the **-te iru** form, when it means "possess, hold, have."

A. **Takahashi san wa kuruma o motte imasu ka.**
   Do you have a car, Ms. Takahashi?
B. **Kyōnen made motte imashita ga, o-kane ga kakatta kara, urimashita.**
   I had one until last year, but it cost (so much) money, so I sold it.

Dare no sūtsukēsu o motte imasu ka.
Whose suitcase are you carrying?

Sono shachō kara no memo o motte imasu ka.
Do you have that memo from the president?

O-kane o motte imasen!
I don't have any money!

Ima eakon o motte imasen ga, rainen no natsu made ni kau tsumori desu.
I don't have an air conditioner at the moment, but I intend to buy one by next summer.

Both **aru** and **motsu** can be translated into English as "have," but **aru** is used when something exists, whereas **motsu** includes the nuance of possession.

Denwa ga arimasu ka.	**Denwa o motte imasu ka.**
Do you have a phone?	Do you possess a phone?
[Lit: Is there a phone?]	

A. **Atarashii sukejūru ga arimasu ka.**
   Do you have the new schedule?
B. **Hai, arimasu.**
   Yes, I do.
A. **Ima motte imasu ka.**
   Do you have it (with you) now?
B. **Iie, motte imasen. Tsukue no naka ni arimasu.**
   No, I don't. It's in my desk.

VOCABULARY
aite imasu: be free, have no engagements [from **aku**]
buchō: department head, manager
dashite kudasai: please submit [from **dasu**, to put out, send, show]
dekimashita: happened, be completed
gaikoku: foreign country, abroad
hajimete: first time
hoshii: want
ichi-nichi: one day
iinkai: committee
ikitai: want to go [from **iku**]
kachō: section head, assistant manager
kanojo: she, her
keikaku: plan, project, scheme
keiyaku: contract
kimemasu: decide [from **kimeru**]
kōchō: principal, head teacher
kotoshi: this year
kūkō: airport

kyō ka ashita: today or tomorrow
kyōiku: education
kyonen: last year
kyūryō: salary, wages
made ni: by [date or time]
memo: memo
messēji: message
motte imasu: have, hold [from **motsu**]
mukae ni ikitai: want to go to meet
ni tsuite: concerning, regarding
o-kane: money
onegai shimasu: please (do that)
rainen: next year
shachō: president
shinpai shinaide: don't worry
shinpai: worry, anxiety
sōdan suru: consult, confer with, talk over
sono ato: after that
sukejūru: schedule
tada: just, only, simply
tokubetsu no: special, particular
toritai: want to take [from **toru**]
tsumori: intention
uchiawase: meeting, consultation
urimasu: sell [from **uru**]
yoru: call in, drop by
yōshi: a form, a blank
yotei: plan, program, schedule

TEST YOURSELF

1. *Read through the dialog at the beginning of the lesson again, and then say if the following statements are true or false.*

    1. Maiku san wa, keiyaku ni tsuite chotto mondai ga arimasu.
    T/F

    2. Maiku san no tomodachi wa onna no hito desu. T/F

    3. Maiku san wa, kūkō made tomodachi o mukae ni iku tsumori desu. T/F

    4. Kare wa keiyaku ni tsuite kōchō sensei to hanashitai no desu.
    T/F

5. Kōchō sensei wa, ashita no asa wa aite imasu. T/F

6. Kōchō sensei to no uchiawase wa ashita desu. T/F

2. *Ms. Takahashi and her boyfriend Kenji are back on speaking terms again. However, they're always arguing about what they want to do, as they have very different tastes, and rarely want to do the same thing. Look at the chart below, and make up sentences like the ones in the example about what they do and don't want to do. (Don't forget that in Japan, a circle is often used instead of a check mark to mean "yes/correct/positive.")*

Example: **Takahashi san wa doyōbi no asa Tōkyō de kaimono o shitai n' desu ga, Kenji san wa shitaku arimasen. Takahashi san mo, Kenji san mo, doyōbi no gogo yakyū o mi ni ikitai n' desu.**

	Ms Takahashi	Kenji
do some shopping in Tokyo on Saturday morning	O	X
go to see baseball on Saturday afternoon	O	O
1. talk about the summer vacation	O	X
2. eat in an Italian restaurant	O	O
3. go to the beach on Sunday	O	X
4. join an English (language) class	O	X
5. see a movie tonight	X	O
6. get married next year	O	X

3. *The new secretary at Yokohama High School, Ms. Obata, is not doing too well. In fact, Mr. Watanabe has to tell her repeatedly not to do certain things. How does he ask her not to:*

1. eat sandwiches in this room?

2. talk to her boyfriend on the phone?

3. use that printer?

4. write reports on the teachers' word processor?

5. read the paper at her desk?

6. listen to her Walkman in the school?

4. *Below is Mike's diary, showing some of the things he'll be doing during the next two weeks. Make sentences about his schedule like the one in the example, using* **yotei desu.**

Example: (6th, evening, go for a drink with Mr. Watanabe)
Muika no yoru, Watanabe san to nomi ni iku yotei desu.

M **6**	evening: go for drink with Mr. Watanabe	M **13**	
T **7**	p.m.: meeting with Principal	T **14**	a.m.: submit report to Principal
W **8**		W **15**	p.m.: call Sue. Consult re summer vacation
T **9**	a.m.: attend meeting of education committee	T **16**	
F **10**		F **17**	
S **11**	evening: bowling with staff from school	S **18**	a.m.: go to Tokyo, buy new suit!
S **12**		S **19**	

5. *How would you say these sentences in Japanese?*

1. Is it all right if I ask a question about my salary?

2. Are you free on Tuesday afternoon?

3. This summer, I intend to buy a new car.

4. There's a meeting in the next room, so please don't go in.

5. I'm hungry, so I want to eat a lot!

6. Next spring, I plan to go to America with my family.

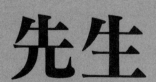

The **sen** part of **sensei** means "prior/previous" and the **sei** part means "be alive, born." The whole word **sensei** means "teacher/ professor," and is also used to refer to doctors and dentists.

DAI JŪ-SAN-KA KARA DAI JŪ-GO-KA MADE NO FUKUSHŪ

REVIEW OF LESSONS 13 TO 15

Read Dialogs 13 to 15 aloud, and try to understand the meaning without referring back to the translations in previous lessons.

Dialog 13: Ni-jū-ichi-nichi wa yasumi no hi desu.

Okusan	Neruson san wa sukii ga dekimasu ka.
Mike	Hai, sukoshi dekimasu. Amari jōzu ja nai kedo.
Okusan	Sō desu ka. Jitsu wa, watashitachi wa san-gatsu ni sukii ni ikimasu ga, moshi yokattara, Neruson san mo issho ni ikimasen ka.
Mike	Dōmo arigatō, sore wa ii desu ne. Nan-nichi ni ikimasu ka.
Okusan	Jū-hachi-nichi no yoru ni itte, ni-jū-ichi-nichi no gogo kaerimasu. Sore wa kinyōbi kara getsuyōbi made desu. Ni-jū-ichi-nichi wa yasumi no hi da kara, sukii-jō wa konde iru to omoimasu ga.

Mike	Yasumi no hi desu ka. Donna yasumi?
Okusan	San-gatsu ni-jū-ichi-nichi wa shunbun no hi desu.
Mike	Shunbun no hi? "Shunbun" wa Eigo de nan to iimasu ka.
Okusan	Sa, Eigo no kotoba ga wakarimasen ga, sono hi ni wa, yoru no jikan to hiruma no jikan ga onaji desu.
Mike	Ā, hai, wakarimashita.
Okusan	Neruson san, biiru ga nai n' desu ne. Gomen nasai. Dōzo.
Hiro	Boku mo biiru o nonde mo ii?
Okusan	Hiro, dame desu yo. Mada jū-ni sai deshō. Biiru o nonde wa ikemasen. Sa, mō sorosoro neru jikan desu.
Hiro	O-kāsan! Neruson san ga kuru kara, osoku made okite mo ii, to kinō itta deshō.
Okusan	Hai, sō iimashita kedo, mō osoi desu yo.
Mike	Sa, watashi mo sorosoro kaerimasu.
Okusan	E? Mō? Mada ii deshō.
Mike	Sumimasen. Demo, ashita no asa mata yakyū da kara.
Okusan	Sō desu ka. Yakyū no gēmu desu ka. Ja, ganbatte kudasai ne!
Mike	Hai, ganbarimasu. Dewa, kore de shitsurei shimasu. Iroiro arigatō gozaimashita. Konban wa taihen tanoshikatta desu.
Okusan	Iie, kochira koso. Mata dōzo.

QUESTIONS:

1. Maiku san wa Watanabe san-tachi to issho ni sukii ni ikitai to omotte imasu ka.

2. "Shunbun no hi" wa Eigo de nan to iimasu ka.

3. O-kāsan wa dō shite Hiro kun ga biiru o nonde wa ikenai to iimashita ka.

4. Jikan ga osoi kedo, Hiro kun wa mada okite imasu ne. Dō shite desu ka.

LESSON 16

189

Dialog 14: *Kare to hanasanai hō ga ii desu yo.*

Mike	A, Takahashi san, konbanwa. Mō chūmon shita n' desu ka.
Takahashi	Iie, mada desu. Menyū o dōzo.
Mike	Arigatō. Sa, nani ni shimashō ka. (reading the menu) Hamu sando ... tsuna sarada ... supagetti ... piza tōsuto ... ā, watashi wa piza tōsuto ni shimasu. Piza tōsuto to hotto kōhii. Takahashi san wa?
Takahashi	O-naka ga suita kara, watashi mo piza tōsuto desu. Sore kara, remon tii. (to waitress) Sumimasen! Piza tōsuto futatsu to, hotto hitotsu to remon tii o hitotsu kudasai.
Waitress	Piza tōsuto futatsu, hotto hitotsu, remon tii o hitotsu desu ne. Kashikomarimashita.
Takahashi	(looking out of the window) Ara, Kenji san! Are wa Kenji san desu!
Mike	Bōifurendo desu ka. Doko? Dono hito ga Kenji san desu ka.
Takahashi	Yūbinkyoku no mae ni imasu. Kōshū denwa no tonari desu.
Mike	Hai, hai. Ā, ima Takahashi san o mita deshō! Ee? Dō shite mukō e aruite iku n' desu ka. Hen desu ne.
Takahashi	Jitsu wa, kinō no yoru denwa de kenka shita n' desu. Watashi wa konban gakkō no sutaffu to issho ni, eiga o mi ni iku to itta n' desu ne. Sore de, Kenji san wa okotte, dame da to iimashita. Dakara watashi mo okotte, kore kara mō awanai hō ga ii, to itta n' desu. Sore de, kaiwa ga owarimashita.
Mike	Sō desu ka. Dō shimasu ka. Ima Kenji san o yonda hō ga ii deshō.
Takahashi	Iie, kyō wa kare to hanasanai hō ga ii to omoimasu.
Mike	Sō desu ka. A, piza tōsuto ga kimashita.
Waitress	Hai, hotto no o-kyaku sama wa?
Mike	Watashi desu. Dōmo.
Takahashi	Sa, jikan ga amari nai kara, hayaku tabeta hō ga ii desu ne. Itadakimasu.

QUESTIONS:

1. Dare ga chūmon o shimasu ka.

2. Kenji san no tonari ni nani ga arimasu ka.

3. Takahashi san wa, kyō Kenji san to hanashitai n' desu ka.

4. Maiku san to Takahashi san wa konban nani o shi ni ikimasu ka.

Dialog 15: *Watashi no keiyaku ni tsuite desu ga.*

Mike	Watanabe san, chotto shitsumon ga arimasu ga, ii desu ka.
Watanabe	Ii desu yo. Dōzo. Nan deshō ka.
Mike	Watashi no keiyaku ni tsuite desu ga.
Watanabe	Keiyaku ni tsuite no shitsumon desu ka. Demo watashi wa keiyaku no koto ga yoku wakaranai n' desu yo. Kōchō sensei to hanashita hō ga ii to omoimasu. Nanika, mondai ga dekimashita ka.
Mike	Iie, iie, mondai ja nai n' desu. Jitsu wa, raigetsu watashi no tomodachi ga Nihon e kuru yotei desu. Kanojo wa, gaikoku wa hajimete da kara, watashi wa kūkō made mukae ni ikitai to omotte iru n' desu ga.
Watanabe	A, wakarimashita. Yasumi no koto desu ka.
Mike	Ee, moshi yokattara, ichi-nichi yasumi o toritai n' desu.
Watanabe	Sore wa mondai nai to omoimasu. Tada, sono koto ni tsuite memo o kaite, watashi ni dashite kudasai. Saitō san ga sono tokubetsu no yōshi o motte imasu kara, kanojo ni kiite kudasai.

Just then, Ms. Saitō comes into the teachers' room to talk to Mike.

Saitō	Neruson san, chotto ii desu ka. Kōchō sensei kara no messēji desu ga, moshi yokattara, kyō ka ashita Neruson san to uchiawase o shitai to itte imashita ga.
Mike	Kōchō sensei to no uchiawase desu ka. Nanika ...
Saitō	Shinpai shinaide kudasai! Tada kore kara no keikaku ni tsuite sōdan suru tsumori da to omoimasu.
Mike	Sō desu ka. Jikan o ima kimemasu ka.
Saitō	Hai, onegai shimasu. Kōchō sensei no sukejūru o motte imasu kara, ima kimemashō.
Mike	Watashi wa, ashita no asa jū-ji made aite imasu ga.
Saitō	Ashita no asa wa chotto muzukashii desu ne. Kōchō sensei wa kyōiku iinkai ni yoru tsumori da to itte imashita ga. Gogo wa?
Mike	Gogo wa, san-ji han made jūgyō ga arimasu ga, sono ato wa aite imasu.
Saitō	Ja, yo-ji ni shimashō.

QUESTIONS:

1. Dare ga keiyaku no koto ga yoku wakarimasu ka.

2. Maiku san wa nagai yasumi o toritai n' desu ka.

3. Maiku san wa ashita nani ni tsuite kōchō sensei to hanasu yotei desu ka.

4. Dō shite ima Saitō san to uchiawase no jikan o kimeru koto ga dekimasu ka.

TEST YOURSELF

1. Which is the odd man out in the following? Underline the word in each group which doesn't fit with the others.

1.	mittsu	itsu	kokonotsu	futatsu
2.	aki	fuyu	natsu	shunbun
3.	hamu	piza	sando	wain
4.	toki	hiruma	yoru	asa
5.	ushiro	shisha	shita	mae
6.	watashi	kare	onna	kanojo
7.	ikutsu	donna	dore	anna
8.	shutchō	buchō	kachō	kōchō

2. Put these words into the correct order to make sentences. Be careful – there is one extra word in each group.

1. wa ashita asa desu rainen no yakyū suru o Maiku yotei san

2. takusan dekiru nomanai ga ii konban omoimasu to hō

3. no tsuite natsu gaikoku omoimasu ikitai e to kotoshi

4. kiite desu shitsumon ka dare ii o mo

5. muzukashii nakatta omoimasen to konna deshita ni

6. tsumori tsuite hanasanaide kyūryō san ni ni koto no Takahashi kudasai

3. *Imagine you have to call Mr. Wada at Takada Company to arrange an appointment, and fill in the missing lines.*

Wada Moshi moshi, Wada desu ga.
You [give your name]
Wada Ā, dōmo!
You [say you're calling about the contract]
Wada Hai, hai. Sore ni tsuite, sugu hanashita hō ga ii desu ne.
You [ask him if he's free this afternoon]
Wada Kyō wa chotto muzukashii desu ne. Iroiro-na uchiawase ga arimasu kara. Ashita wa dō desu ka.
You [tell him you're scheduled to attend a meeting from 10:00 tomorrow morning]
Wada Ja, ashita no gogo wa dō desu ka.
You [tell him yes, the afternoon is free]
Wada Ni-ji ni shimashō ka.
You [agree with him]
Wada Ja, ashita no ni-ji desu ne. Dewa, shitsurei shimasu.

4. *Complete the crossword puzzle by finding words which fill the blanks in the sentences below.*

Across

1. Neruson san no apāto no _____ ni dare ga sunde imasu ka.

5. Sumimasen, kono denwa o tsukatte _____ ii desu ka.

7. Sono keikaku ni _____ hanashitai n' desu ga.

9. Kissaten wa yūbinkyoku no _____ ni arimasu.

10. Nihongo no tesuto wa _____ ni muzukashii to omoimasen deshita.

12. Tanjōbi wa nan-_____ desu ka.

13. Tesuto wa hajimarimasu kara, kore kara hanashite wa _____

Down

2. Kotoshi no natsu yasumi ni doko e _____ n' desu ka.

3. "Autumn" wa Nihongo de ___ to iimasu.

4. Kanojo wa _____ takai kyūryō ga hoshii to iimashita.

6. Hotto o _____ kudasai.

8. Takahashi san to Saitō san no _____ ni dare ga suwarimasu ka.

9. Sono _____ o yonde wa ikemasen yo!

11. Nihon no _____ wa atsui desu ka.

5. *Answer these questions about yourself.*

1. Sukii wa dekimasu ka. O-jōzu desu ka.

2. Tanjōbi wa nan-gatsu, nan-nichi desu ka.

3. Anata no kuni ni wa, yasumi no hi ga takusan arimasu ka.

4. Donna supōtsu ga suki desu ka.

5. Anata wa ashita yasumi o totte mo ii desu ka.

6. Ima ikutsu desu ka.

7. Kinō, nan-ji made okite imashita ka.

8. Anata no kuni de wa, ichiban atsui toki wa nan-gatsu desu ka.

9. Anata wa kekkon shite imasu ka. Bōifurendo ka gārufurendo ga imasu ka.

10. Yoku okorimasu ka.

11. Anata no uchi ka apāto ni wa, heya ga ikutsu arimasu ka.

12. Gaikoku e iku yotei ga arimasu ka.

 Fukushū, meaning "review," combines characters for "repeat" and "learn."

KAMAKURA E ITTA KOTO GA ARIMASU KA.

HAVE YOU EVER BEEN TO KAMAKURA?

It's Friday, and Mike is chatting to Ms. Takahashi during the lunch break.

Takahashi **Neruson san wa Kamakura e itta koto ga arimasu ka.**
Have you ever been to Kamakura, Mr. Nelson?

Mike **Iie, arimasen. Ikitai kedo.**
No, I haven't. I'd like to go though.

Takahashi **Ja, nichiyōbi ni watashitachi to issho ni Kamakura e ikimasen ka. Saitō san mo Wada san mo issho ni iku to itte imasu ga. Tenki ga yokattara, pikkunikku o suru tsumori desu.**
Well, would you like to go to Kamakura with us on Sunday? Ms. Saitō and Ms. Wada say they're coming too. If the weather's nice, we plan to have a picnic.

Mike	Ii desu ne. Demo, tenki ga yoku nakattara, dō shimasu ka. Konban ame ga furu to kikimashita ga.
	Sounds good. But what will we do if the weather's not good? I heard that it's going to rain tonight.
Takahashi	Sonna koto o kangaenaide kudasai. Nichiyōbi wa kitto ii tenki desu yo.
	Don't even think about that! It'll definitely be nice weather on Sunday.
Mike	Wakarimashita! Densha de iku n' desu ka.
	I see! Will we go by train?
Takahashi	Sō desu. Densha no hō ga hayai to omoimasu. Sore dake ja nakute, dare mo kuruma o motte imasen kara, shikata ga arimasen yo.
	Yes. I think the train's quicker. And not only that, no one owns a car, so we have no choice.

The four are now in Kamakura, standing in front of the **daibutsu**, or great statue of Buddha, for which Kamakura is famous.

Mike	Konna ni ōkii daibutsu wa mita koto ga arimasen ne.
	I've never seen such a big statue of Buddha.
Takahashi	Naka ni haitte, atama no naka made noboru koto mo dekimasu yo. Watashi wa haitta koto ga nai kedo.
	You can go inside, and climb up inside the head too. I've never been in it though.
Mike	Sa, hairimashō ka.
	Well, shall we go in?
Takahashi	Chotto matte. Sono mae ni, minna no shashin o toritai kara. Hai, mina san, soko ni tatte kudasai yo. Ā, dame desu. Soko ni tattara, daibutsu ga shashin ni hairimasen.
	Hold on. Before that, I want to take a picture of everyone. Okay, everybody, stand over there. No, that's no good. If you stand there, the Buddha isn't in the picture.
Mike	Sono kaidan no ue ni suwattara, dō desu ka.
	How about if we sit at the top of those steps?
Takahashi	Sō ne. Sono hō ga ii. Hai, mina san, soko ni suwatte kudasai. Ii desu ka. Hai, chiizu! Dōmo arigatō. Sa, daibutsu ni hairimashō.

Yes, that'd be better. Right, everyone, sit over there. Okay? Cheese! Thanks. Right, let's go into the statue of the Buddha.

Mike   Mite yo. Daibutsu no ushiro ni sugoi hito ga narande imasu ne. Jikan ga kakaru deshō.
Hey, look. There's an incredible number of people lining up behind the statue. It'll take ages.

Takahashi   Saki ni hiru-gohan o tabetara, dō desu ka.
How about if we have lunch first?

Mike   Sō desu ne. Demo ne, chotto samuku natte, sora mo kuraku natte imasu ne. Pikkunikku wa chotto ... Are!? Ame ja nai n' desu ka.
Yes, okay. But, it's got a little cold, and the sky is getting dark, isn't it? About this picnic ... Hey, isn't that rain?

Takahashi   Sō desu yo. Ara, sugoi ame da! Dareka kasa o motte imasu ka. Dare mo kasa o motte inai n' desu ka. Sa, ichiban chikai resutoran made hashirimashō yo. Hayaku!
Yes, it is. Aagh, incredible rain! Does anyone have an umbrella? No one has an umbrella? Right, let's run to the nearest restaurant. Quickly!

STRUCTURE AND USAGE NOTES

1. -TA KOTO GA ARIMASU KA – "HAVE YOU EVER ...?"

This phrase using the plain past form of the verb (e.g. **tabeta**, "ate," **itta**, "went") followed by **koto ga arimasu ka** is used when you are asking someone about their experiences, so it is the equivalent of the English "Have you ever ...?" You have already come across the word **koto** to mean "thing/event," and coupled with the past form of a verb you can think of it as "experience," so **tabeta koto** is "experience of eating," and **itta koto** is "experience of going." A literal translation of **Sushi o tabeta koto ga arimasu ka** would therefore be "Do you have experience of eating sushi?" or more colloquially, "Have you ever eaten sushi?"

Fuji san ni nobotta koto ga arimasu ka.
Have you ever climbed Mt. Fuji?

Kamakura no daibutsu o mita koto ga aru kedo, Nara no daibutsu o mita koto wa arimasen.
I've seen the great statue of Buddha at Kamakura, but I haven't seen the one at Nara.

Sonna koto o kangaeta koto ga nai n' desu yo!
I've never considered such a thing!

Sugoi hito da to kikimashita ga, atta koto ga nai kara, yoku wakarimasen.
I hear that he's an amazing person, but I've never met (him), so I don't really know.

Sashimi o tabeta koto ga arimasu ka.
Have you ever eaten raw fish?

A positive answer to the last question would be **Hai, arimasu,** "Yes, I have" (or **Hai, tabeta koto ga arimasu,** "Yes, I have eaten it"), and a negative answer would be **Iie, arimasen,** "No, I haven't" (or **Iie, tabeta koto ga arimasen,** "No, I haven't eaten it").

A. **Amerika e itta koto ga arimasu ka.**
    Have you ever been to the USA?
B. **Iie, arimasen. Kyonen Kanada e itta kedo, Amerika wa mada desu.**
    No, I haven't. I went to Canada last year, but I haven't been to the USA yet [Lit: ... but the USA is not yet].

A. **Onsen ni haitta koto ga arimasu ka.**
    Have you ever been in a hot spring bath?
B. **Arimasu yo. Dai-suki desu.**
    I certainly have. I love them.

A. **Densha no naka ni kasa o wasureta koto ga arimasu ka.**
    Have you ever forgotten your umbrella on the train?
B. **Mochiron arimasu yo!**
    Of course I have!

2. -TARA – "IF ..."

To make this kind of "if" sentence in Japanese, just add **-ra** to the plain past tense of the verb (e.g. **tabeta, itta,** etc.). Hence **tabetara** means "if you eat," **ittara** means "if you go," and **denwa shitara** means "if you call." In practice this is often called the **-tara** form, as all verbs end in **-tara** (or occasionally **-dara**).

Plain form	Plain past	-tara form	Meaning
taberu	tabeta	tabetara	if I/you, etc., eat
iku	itta	ittara	if you go
kuru	kita	kitara	if you come
suru	shita	shitara	if you do
aru	atta	attara	if there is
naru	natta	nattara	if it becomes
hanasu	hanashita	hanashitara	if you speak
nomu	nonda	nondara	if you drink
da	datta	dattara	if it is

Ame ga futtara, uchi ni ite, bideo o mimashō.
If it rains, let's stay home and watch a video.

O-kanemochi dattara, doko e ikitai to omoimasu ka.
If you were rich, where do you think you'd like to go?

Yukkuri hanashitara, wakaru to omoimasu.
If you speak slowly, I think I'll understand.

Soko o migi ni magattara, eki ni demasu.
If you turn right there, you'll come out at the station.

Kaigi ga san-ji made ni owattara, shisha no Nagai san ni denwa shite kudasai.
If the meeting finishes by 3:00, please call Mr. Nagai at the branch office.

Sono kaidan ni nobottara, o-tearai wa migi-gawa ni arimasu.
If you go up the stairs, you'll find the restrooms on your right.

Do the same thing with the negative when you want to talk about if something *doesn't* happen, that is, add -ra to the negative of the plain past tense (the one that ends in -nakatta). The ending then becomes -nakattara.

Plain form	Negative	Negative past	-tara form	Meaning
kuru	konai	konakatta	konakattara	if you don't come
iku	ikanai	ikanakatta	ikanakattara	if you don't go
suru	shinai	shinakatta	shinakattara	if you don't do
nomu	nomanai	nomanakatta	nomanakattara	if you don't drink
toru	toranai	toranakatta	toranakattara	if you don't take
aru	nai	nakatta	nakattara	if there isn't

Wada san ga sugu konakattara, dō shimasu ka.
If Ms. Wada doesn't come soon, what will we do?

Watashi wa shashin o takusan toranakattara, yasumi no koto o sugu wasuremasu.
If I don't take lots of photos, I soon forget vacations.

Jikan ga nakattara, shinakute mo ii desu yo.
If you don't have time, it's all right if you don't do it.

Hayaku nenakattara, hayaku okiru koto mo dekimasen yo.
If you don't go to sleep early, you won't be able to get up early either.

Ashita no asa jikan ga attara, iinkai no kaigi ni dete kudasai.
If you have time tomorrow morning, please attend the committee meeting.

The word **moshi,** or "if," can be added to the beginning of a sentence to alert the listener early on that this is going to be an "if" sentence, and it also adds emphasis. However, it is still necessary to have the -tara verb ending.

Moshi Wada san kara denwa ga attara, atarashii yotei o oshiete kudasai.
If there's a call from Ms. Wada, please tell her about the new plan.

Moshi mondai ga attara, oshiete kudasai.
If there are any problems, please let me know.

The -**tara** ending can also be added to -i adjectives. Once again, find the past tense -**katta** ending, and add -ra.

Takakattara, mochiron kaimasen.
If it's expensive, of course I won't buy it.

Kibun ga warukattara, konakute mo ii desu yo.
If you're feeling bad, you don't need to come.

Chikakattara, aruku koto ga dekiru deshō.
If it's close, we can walk, right?

Moshi yokattara, kore o tsukatte kudasai.
If you'd like to [Lit: If it's all right], please use this.

You can use the -**tara** form for making suggestions, in which case it can be translated as "How about —ing?" or "Why don't we ...?"

Konshū no nichiyōbi ni pikkunikku o shitara dō desu ka.
How about a picnic this Sunday? [Lit: If we have a picnic this Sunday, how about it?]

Soko de mattara dō desu ka.
Why don't we wait over there?

Kotoshi no natsu yasumi ni, gaikoku e ittara dō desu ka.
How about going abroad this summer vacation? [Lit: This summer vacation, if we go abroad, how about it?]

Sometimes the **dō desu ka** ending is left off, and the meaning merely implied.

Koko de suwattara?
How about if we sit here?

Saki ni ittara?
How about if you go on ahead?

The -**tara** form can only be used for sentences where the two events mentioned take place one after the other. Therefore, you can use it for the equivalent of "If we go to Tokyo, let's visit Michiko," but not for "If we go to Tokyo, we should call Michiko beforehand." Another way of making "if" sentences is with the verb ending -**eba**, which will be explained in the next lesson.

3. DARE MO, DOKO MO, NANI MO – "NOBODY," "NOWHERE," "NOTHING"

When question words like **dare**, **nani**, or **doko** are followed by **mo** and a negative verb, the meanings change from "who," "what," "where" to "not anyone," "not anything" and "not anywhere."

A. **Tonari no heya ni dare ga imasu ka.**
   Who's in the next room?
B. **Dare mo imasen.**
   No one.

O-kane ga nakattara, nani mo dekimasen.
If you don't have money, you can't do anything.

Kyō wa kibun ga amari yoku nai kara, doko e mo ikitaku nai n' desu.
I don't really feel well today, so I don't want to go anywhere.

Hoka ni nani mo nakattara, kore de kaigi o owarimashō.
If there isn't anything else, let's finish the meeting here.

Dare mo konakattara, dō shimashō ka.
If no one comes, what shall we do?

Kōshū denwa wa, doko ni mo arimasen ne.
There isn't a public telephone anywhere, is there?

4. DENSHA NO HŌ GA HAYAI – "THE TRAIN'S FASTER" AND OTHER COMPARATIVES

When making a comparison between two things, imagine they're on two sides (hō) of a pair of scales, being measured against each other. Then you just need to ask the equivalent of "Which side is fast/slow/expensive?": **Dotchi no hō ga hayai/osoi/takai desu ka.** The word **dotchi** is a common short form of **dochira**, in this case meaning "which one."

If you want to answer that "this one" or "that one" is the faster (or slower, or whatever), then use **kotchi (kochira)** or **sotchi (sochira)**: **Kotchi no hō ga hayai/osoi/takai desu.**

A. Takushii to densha to, dochira no hō ga hayai desu ka.
   Which is faster, a taxi or the train? [Lit: Which is fast ...?]
B. Konna toki ni, densha no hō ga hayai to omoimasu.
   At this time, I think the train is faster.

A. Kamakura to Yokohama to, koko kara dotchi no hō ga tōi desu ka.
   Which is further from here, Kamakura or Yokohama?
B. Sō desu ne. Kamakura no hō ga tōi to omoimasu.
   Hmmm. I think Kamakura is further.

A. Kore to kore to, dochira no hō ga ii desu ka.
   Which is the better of these two?
B. Yasui hō o kaimashō.
   Let's buy the cheaper one.

A. Ōsaka to Nagoya to, dochira no hō ga hiroi desu ka.
   Which is bigger (in area), Osaka or Nagoya?
B. Mochiron Ōsaka no hō ga hiroi desu yo.
   Of course Osaka is bigger!

You might also hear this pattern without **no hō.**

O-sake to biiru to, dochira ga suki desu ka.
Which do you like, sake or beer?

Doyōbi to nichiyōbi to, dotchi ga ii desu ka.
Which is better, Saturday or Sunday?

5. SAMUKU NATTE – "IT'S GETTING COLD"

The verb **naru** means "become/get" so it can be used with adjectives to make phrases such as "get late," "get more expensive," "grow old," "become dark," and with nouns for phrases like "become a teacher," "become president," "become an adult." With -ii adjectives, first drop the final -i and add -ku.

Samuku narimashita ne! Mō sugu fuyu desu yo.
It's got cold, hasn't it! It'll soon be winter!

Natsu yasumi ga dandan chikaku natte imasu.
The summer vacation is gradually getting closer.

Wada san wa, kibun ga waruku natta to itte imasu ga, mō kaetta hō ga ii deshō.
Ms. Wada says she's feeling bad – it would be better if she went home, wouldn't it?

Osoku natte, sumimasen.
I'm sorry I'm late. [Lit: It has become late, and I'm sorry.]

With -na adjectives and with nouns, add **ni**.

Nihongo ga taihen o-jōzu ni narimashita ne.
You've got really good at Japanese, haven't you!

Kare wa kitto yūmei ni narimasu yo.
He's definitely going to become famous.

Ōkiku nattara, nani ni naritai n' desu ka.
When you grow up, what do you want to be?

Sonna ni takusan tabetara, byōki ni narimasu yo!
If you eat that much, you'll get sick!

Keiyaku ga kinyōbi made ni dekinakattara, ōki-na mondai ni naru to omoimasu.
If the contract isn't done by Friday, I think there'll be big problems.

6. DAREKA – "SOMEONE"

Adding -ka to the end of questions words such as **dare, itsu, nani** and **doko** is a bit like putting "some" in front of equivalent words in English (or in the case of questions and negatives, "any").

A. **Shūmatsu ni, dokoka e ikimashita ka.**
   Did you go anywhere on the weekend?
B. **Iie, o-kane ga nai kara, doko e mo ikimasen deshita.**
   No, I don't have any money, so I didn't go anywhere!

Gomen kudasai! Dareka imasu ka.
Excuse me! Is there anyone there?

Nanika tabemashita ka.
Have you eaten anything?

Itsuka nomi ni ikimashō.
Let's go drinking sometime.

Kasa wa doko ni aru deshō ka. Dokoka de wasureta to omou yo.
I wonder where my umbrella is? I think I left it somewhere.

Dareka saki ni itte, narandara dō desu ka.
How about if someone goes on ahead and lines up?

Itsuka Hokkaidō e ikitai ne.
I want to go to Hokkaido sometime.

Daijōbu desu ka. Nanika atta n' desu ka.
Are you okay? Did something happen? [Lit: Was there something?]

Note that the particles o and ga are usually dropped after these
words.

7. THE WEATHER

The Japanese are very conscious of nature and the seasons, and so
the weather is a common topic of conversation. Comments on the
weather are used as greetings, as small talk, and frequently as
opening paragraphs in letters. Here are some of the phrases you are
most likely to hear.

Dandan samuku natte imasu ne.
It's gradually getting colder, isn't it?

Kinō, sugoi ame deshita ne.
That was incredible rain yesterday, wasn't it?

Kyō wa atatakai desu ne.
It's warm today, isn't it?

Mushiatsukute, iya desu ne.
It's horrible and humid, isn't it?

Kaze ga tsuyoi desu ne. Ki o tsuketa hō ga ii desu yo.
The wind is strong, isn't it? You'd better take care.

Suzushiku narimashita ne. Mō sorosoro aki deshō.
It's got cooler, hasn't it? It'll soon be fall.

Sora o mite kudasai yo. Kitto yuki ga furimasu.
Just look at the sky. It's definitely going to snow.

VOCABULARY

ame ga furu: it rains [Lit: the rain falls]
ame: rain
are: look! listen!
atatakai: warm
byōki: ill
chiizu: cheese
chikai: close, nearby
daibutsu: large statue of Buddha
dandan: gradually, little by little
dare mo: no one
dareka: someone
dochira/dotchi: which one? [of two]
furu: fall, drop
hiroi: large (in area), spacious, extensive
hō: direction, side
hoka ni: other, another, else
Hokkaidō: the northernmost of the four main islands of Japan
kaidan: steps, stairs
Kamakura: city close to Yokohama, famous for its large statue of Buddha
kasa: umbrella
kaze: wind
kibun ga ii: feel good
kibun ga warui: feel bad
kitto: definitely, without fail
kochira/kotchi: this side, this one (of two)
koto ga arimasu ka: have you ever …?
kuraku: dark [from **kurai**]
mita koto wa arimasen: I've never seen [from **miru**]
mochiron: of course, naturally
moshi: if
mushiatsui: hot and humid
narande imasu: are lined up, lining up [from **narabu**]
naru: become, get
noboru: climb, go up
o-kanemochi: rich person
okiru: get up, get out of bed
o-tearai: restroom

pikkunikku: picnic
saki ni: in advance, ahead, before
samuku natte: getting cold
shashin: photograph
shikata ga arimasen: it can't be helped
sochira/sotchi: that side, that one [of two]
sono hō ga ii: that would be best
sore dake ja nakute: not only that
sugoi: amazing, incredible
suwattara: if you sit [from **suwaru**]
suzushii: cool
tabetara: if we eat [from **taberu**]
tattara: if you stand [from **tatsu**]
tatte kudasai: please stand [from **tatsu**]
tōi: far, distant
tsuyoi: strong
yokattara: if it's all right
yoku nakattara: if it's not all right
yuki: snow

TEST YOURSELF

1. *Read through the dialog at the beginning of the lesson again, and then say if the following statements are true or false.*

   1. Takahashi san mo, Saitō san mo, Wada san mo, nichiyōbi ni Kamakura e iku tsumori desu. T/F

   2. Takahashi san wa, nichiyōbi wa ii tenki da to omotte imasu. T/F

   3. Takahashi san wa kuruma o motte imasu. T/F

   4. Daibutsu no naka ni hairu koto ga dekimasu ga, atama made hairu koto ga dekimasen. T/F

   5. Minna kaidan no ue ni suwattara, daibutsu mo shashin ni hairimasu. T/F

   6. Tenki ga dandan waruku natte imasu. T/F

2. *While waiting in the restaurant for the rain to stop, Mike chats to the others about various things they've done in their past. In the table below you can see some of the things that Ms. Wada and Ms. Saitō have and haven't done. Make up sentences like the ones in the example, using* **koto ga arimasu.**

Examples: Wada san wa gaikoku e itta koto ga arimasu ga,
Saitō san wa arimasen.
Wada san mo Saitō san mo Eigo o benkyō shita koto ga arimasu.

-ta koto ga arimasu ka.	Ms Wada	Ms Saito
travelled abroad?	O	X
studied English?	O	O
1. owned a car?	O	X
2. climbed Mt. Fuji?	O	O
3. lived in Tokyo?	X	O
4. been to Hokkaido?	X	X
5. met Mr. Watanabe's wife?	O	X
6. taken a video?	O	O

3. *Choose which of the two alternatives in each case is most appropriate to finish the sentence.*

1. Wada san wa kaigi ni denakattara,
   a. hiru-gohan o tabemasen.
   b. keiyaku no koto o sōdan suru koto wa dekimasen.

2. Kibun ga warukattara,
   a. hayaku neta hō ga ii deshō.
   b. hayaku okita hō ga ii deshō.

3. Wada san ga konakattara,
   a. dō shimashō ka.
   b. watashi mo ikimasen.

4. Tōkattara,
   a. denwa shimasen.
   b. arukimasen.

5. Moshi yokattara,
   a. mita koto ga nai to omoimasu.
   b. shashin o toritai n' desu ga.

6. Kore o takusan nondara,
   a. byōki ni naru to omoimasu yo.
   b. wakaku naru to omoimasu yo.

4. *How's your general knowledge? Using the cues below, make up questions and then see if you know the answers, as in the example.*

Example:　Children's Day, Respect for the Aged Day – first?
Q. Kodomo no hi to Keirō no hi to, dochira (no hō) ga saki desu ka.
A. Kodomo no hi no hō ga saki desu.

1. Amazon, Nile – longer?
2. Mt. Fuji, Mt. McKinley – higher?
3. Hong Kong, Taiwan – further from Japan?
4. Japan, Philippines – big?
5. Tokyo, New York – has most people?

And now some questions about you:

6. mountains, sea – like?
7. telephone, fax – often use?
8. Mexican food, Chinese food – often eat?
9. study, work – like?
10. newspapers, books – often read?

5. *How would you say these sentences in Japanese?*

1. If it doesn't rain, shall we go somewhere on Sunday?

2. Have you ever eaten in that restaurant?

3. Which do you like better, the summer or the winter?

4. My stomach hurts, so I don't want anything to eat.

5. It's gradually getting warmer, isn't it? It'll soon be spring.

6. If you have time, could you call Mr. Fukuda and tell him about the meeting time?

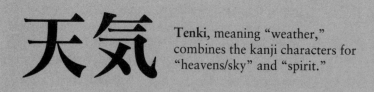

天気　Tenki, meaning "weather," combines the kanji characters for "heavens/sky" and "spirit."

SŌ SUREBA ...

IF YOU DO THAT ...

Mike is going to the theater this afternoon to see Kabuki with Mr. Kato, a teacher from his school. He's just talking to him on the phone now.

Mike   **Sa, nan-ji ni, doko de aimashō ka.**
So what time and where shall we meet?

Katō   **Watashi ga saki ni Maiku san no apāto ni ikimashō ka. Sō sureba, issho ni eki made aruku koto ga dekimasu ne.**
Shall I come to your apartment first? If I do that, we can walk to the station together, can't we?

Mike   **Jitsu wa, watashi wa iroiro-na yōji ga aru n' desu. Dakara sugu uchi o dete, Katō san ni au mae ni yōji o sureba ii to omotte ita n' desu ga.**
The fact is, I have various things to do. So I was thinking it would be better if I went out soon and did the errands before we met up.

Katō	Watashi mo issho ni iku yo. Sō sureba, yōji ga owatte kara, dokoka de ranchi o taberu koto mo dekimasu ne. Kabuki wa nagai kara, hairu mae ni nanika tabeta hō ga ii to omoimasu. Ii desu ka.
	I'll come with you. If I do that, then after the errands are done we can have some lunch somewhere, can't we? Kabuki is long, so I think it's better if we have something to eat before we go in. Is that okay?
Mike	Mochiron ii n' da kedo, Katō san ni wa zenzen omoshiroku nai to omoimasu yo. Mazu, haha no tanjōbi ni purezento o okuru tame ni yūbinkyoku e ikimasu. Sore kara, gasu-dai to denki-dai o harau tame ni ginkō e ikimasu. Sono ato ...
	Of course it's okay, but I think it'll be completely uninteresting for you. First I'm going to the post office to mail a present for my mother's birthday. Then I'm going to the bank to pay the gas and electricity bills. After that ...
Katō	Daijōbu desu yo. Ja, jū-ji-han goro Maiku san no tokoro ni ikeba, jikan ga jūbun arimasu ka.
	It's okay. So if I come to your place at 10:30, will there be enough time?
Mike	Hai hai, ii desu. Ja, matte imasu yo.
	Yes, it's fine. I'll be waiting.

Later, at the post office.

Mike	Kono kozutsumi o Amerika made okuritai n' desu ga, ikura deshō ka.
	I'd like to send this parcel to the USA. How much is it, please?
Clerk	Kōkūbin desu ne. (he weighs the parcel) Hai, yon-sen hyaku en desu. Kono yōshi ni kakikonde kudasai.
	Airmail, right? That's 4,100 yen. Please fill in this form.
Mike	Sore kara, hyaku-jū en kitte o yon-mai kudasai.
	And four 110-yen stamps, please.
Clerk	Hyaku-jū en kitte o yon-mai desu ne. Zenbu de yon-sen go-hyaku yon-jū en desu. Hai, go-sen-en o-azukari shimasu. O-tsuri wa yon-hyaku roku-jū en desu. Dōzo.
	Four 110-yen stamps. That's 4,540 yen altogether. Thank you, 5,000 yen. Here's 460 yen change.

Mike	Arigatō. (to Mr. Katō) **Sugoi hito ga ushiro ni narande imasu ne. Ginkō mo konna ni konde ireba, yamemashō.**
	Thank you. There's an incredible number of people lining up behind us, aren't there? If the bank is this crowded, let's not bother.
Katō	**Demo, gasu-dai to denki-dai o harawanakereba ...**
	But if you don't pay your gas and electricity ...
Mike	**Ii n' desu yo. Shinpai shinaide. Jikan wa mada jūbun arimasu.**
	It's okay. Don't worry. There's still enough time.

STRUCTURE AND USAGE NOTES

1. AU MAE NI – "BEFORE MEETING"

In order to talk about one event happening before another, use **mae ni** ("before") after the plain form of the verb. You can use the present tense of the plain form (**iku, taberu, suru**, etc.), whether you're talking about two events in the past, present or future.

Sono fakkusu o Nagoya shisha ni okuru mae ni, misete kudasai.
Before you send that fax to the Nagoya branch, please show it to me.

Watashi wa neru mae ni, itsumo hon o yomimasu.
Before I go to sleep, I always read a book.

Kissaten ni hairu mae ni, watashi wa ginkō ni yoru kara, dōzo saki ni itte kudasai.
Before we go into the coffee shop, I have to drop in at the bank, so please go on ahead.

Harau mae ni, kono yōshi ni kakikonde kudasai.
Before you pay, please fill in this form.

Sono repōto o buchō ni dasu mae ni, kopii o torimashita ka.
Before you gave that report to the department head, did you take a copy?

2. YŌJI GA OWATTE KARA – "AFTER THE ERRANDS ARE FINISHED"

When you want to talk about one event happening *after* another, use the -te form of the verb with **kara**. This is the equivalent of the English "after —ing," and can be used whether the second part of the sentence is in the past, present or future. (Be careful not to confuse this with **kara** after the plain form of the verb, when it means "because." See Lesson 11, Structure and Usage Note 6.)

Gasu-dai to denwa-dai to denki-dai o haratte kara, o-kane wa nani mo nai to omoimasu.
After I pay the gas bill, the telephone bill and the electricity bill, I don't think I'll have any money.

Kabuki o mite kara, dokoka e nomi ni ikimashō ka.
After we've seen Kabuki, shall we go for a drink somewhere?

Kaigi ga owatte kara, watashi wa kaette mo ii desu ka. Kibun ga chotto warui kara.
After the meeting finishes, is it all right if I go home? Because I don't feel very well.

Sono shukudai o owatte kara, sugu neta hō ga ii to omoimasu.
After you finish your homework, I think you should go straight to bed.

Shashin ga dekite kara, misete kudasai ne.
When the photographs are done, please let me see them [Lit: please show me].

Nihon e kite kara Nihongo no benkyō o hajimemashita.
I started to learn Japanese after I came to Japan.

3. SŌ SUREBA – "IF WE DO SO"

The verb ending -eba shows another way of making "if" sentences. To form it, start with the plain form of the verb, drop the final -u and replace it with -eba.

Plain form	-eba form	Meaning
sur-u	sur-eba	if I (you, etc.) do
kur-u	kur-eba	if I come
kak-u	kak-eba	if I write
hara-u	hara-eba	if I pay
okur-u	okur-eba	if I send
ar-u	ar-eba	if I have
tsukur-u	tsukur-eba	if I make
dekir-u	dekir-eba	if I can

O-kane ga jūbun areba, Amerika dake ja nakute, Kanada e mo ikitai desu.
If I have enough money, I want to go to Canada, as well as the USA [Lit: I want to go not only to the USA, but also to Canada].

Moshi dekireba, kotoshi gaikoku e ikitai n' desu.
If I can, I want to go abroad this year.

Ame ga fureba, dekakeru yotei o yamemashō.
If it rains, let's drop the plan to go out.

Minna de sōdan sureba ii to omoimasu.
I think it's best if we discuss it altogether.

Ranchi ni wa, sando dake o tsukureba ii desu ka.
Is it all right if I just make sandwiches for lunch?

When you want to talk about a situation if something *doesn't* happen, then find the negative plain form (ending in **-nai**), drop the final **-i** and add **-kereba**.

Plain negative	-kereba form	Meaning
tsukawana-i	tsukawana-kereba	if I (you, etc.) don't use
ikana-i	ikana-kereba	if I don't go
wakarana-i	wakarana-kereba	if I don't understand
na-i	na-kereba	if there isn't
dekakena-i	dekakena-kereba	if we don't go out
kawana-i	kawana-kereba	if I don't buy
matte ina-i	matte ina-kereba	if he isn't waiting

Jisho o tsukawanakereba, kono Nihongo no shukudai ga dekimasen.
If I don't use a dictionary, I can't do this Japanese homework.

Shinkansen no kippu o kyō kawanakereba, mō toru koto ga dekinai to omoimasu.
If we don't buy the Shinkansen tickets today, I don't think we'll be able to get any.

Kare ga eki no mae de matte inakereba, koko made denwa shite kudasai.
If he's not waiting in front of the station, please give us a call here.

Hoka ni shitsumon ga nakereba, kore de owarimashō.
If there aren't any more questions, let's finish here.

Jikan ga nakereba, shikata ga arimasen.
If you don't have time, it can't be helped.

O-sake o yamenakereba, byōki ni narimasu yo.
If you don't quit drinking, you'll get sick.

With -i adjectives, drop the final -i and add -kereba. With negatives (atsuku nai, yoku nai, omoshiroku nai, etc.), do the same thing, that is, drop the final -i from the nai, and add -kereba.

-i adjective	-kereba form	Meaning
atsu-i	atsu-kereba	if it's hot
ii/yo-i	yo-kereba	if it's good
isogashi-i	isogashi-kereba	if you're busy
hoshi-i	hoshi-kereba	if you want
taka-i	taka-kereba	if it's expensive
samuku na-i	samuku na-kereba	if it's not cold
yasuku na-i	yasuku na-kereba	if it's not cheap
yoku na-i	yoku na-kereba	if it's not good
tōku na-i	tōku na-kereba	if it's not far

Ashita tenki ga yokereba, dokoka e ikimashō ka.
If the weather's nice tomorrow, shall we go somewhere?

Hazukashikereba, jiko shōkai o Eigo de shite mo ii desu.
If you're shy, it's okay to introduce yourself in English.

Hontō ni hoshikereba, dōzo katte kudasai.
If you really want it, go on and buy it.

Kozutsumi ga sonna ni omoku nakereba, kōkūbin de okutte mo ii desu.
If the parcel isn't too heavy, it's okay to send it by airmail.

Tōku nakereba, aruite ikimashō ka.
If it's not far, shall we walk?

Takaku nakereba, kaimasu.
If it's not too expensive, I'll buy it.

The -ba forms for **desu** are de areba ("if it is") and de nakereba ("if it isn't"). However, **de areba** is fairly formal, and **nara** is used more often in everyday speech.

Kirai nara, tabenakute mo ii desu.
If you don't like it, you don't have to eat it.

Kaigi ga jū-ji nara, daijōbu desu.
If the meeting is at 10:00, it's okay.

Sensei nara, kore ga wakaru deshō.
If he's a teacher, he'll probably understand this.

Kōkūbin de nakereba, dame da to omoimasu.
If it's not airmail, I think it's impossible (for it to get there on time).

Nichiyōbi de nakereba, iku koto ga dekimasen.
If it's not a Sunday, I can't go.

4. MAZU – "FIRST OF ALL"

Use the word **mazu** ("first of all/to begin with") when you are
beginning to describe a sequence of events, instructions, or
directions. Other useful words to continue with are **sore kara** ("and
then/after that"), **soshite** ("then"), **sono ato** ("after that"), **sono tsugi
ni** ("next"), and **saigo ni** ("finally/at the end").

**Mazu Igirisu ni itte, sore kara Furansu ni itte, saigo ni Itaria ni
ikimashita. Totemo tanoshikatta desu yo.**
First we went to Britain, then we went to France, and finally we went
to Italy. It was really enjoyable!

**Ashita isogashii desu yo. Mazu Ginza no depāto e itte, chichi no
tanjōbi no purezento o kaimasu. Sore kara ginkō to yūbinkyoku e
ikimasu. Sono ato, tomodachi ni atte, ranchi o tabemasu. Sono tsugi
ni Tōkyō eki ni itte, Ōsaka made no kippu o kaimasu. Sono ato,
hoka no tomodachi no atarashii apāto ni yorimasu. Saigo ni,
Yokohama e kaette, ane to eiga o mi ni ikimasu.**
I'm busy tomorrow! First of all I'm going to a department store in
Ginza and buying a birthday present for my father. Then I'm going
to the bank and the post office. After that, I'll meet a friend and have
lunch. Next I'm going to Tokyo station to buy a ticket to Osaka.
After that I'll drop in at the new apartment of another friend. Finally,
I'll go back to Yokohama and go to see a movie with my older sister.

5. TAME NI – "IN ORDER TO"

The phrase **tame ni** after a noun means "for the benefit of" or "for
the sake of," showing purpose. The English equivalent is often
simply "for."

Kono jisho wa gaijin no tame desu.
This dictionary is for (the benefit of) foreigners.

Kare wa shigoto no tame ni raigetsu Yōroppa ni ikimasu.
He's going to Europe next month on business [Lit: for the sake of
work].

Nihongo no benkyō no tame ni totemo isogashii desu.
I'm very busy with my Japanese studies.

Nan no tame ni Nihon e kita n' desu ka.
Why [Lit: for what purpose] did you come to Japan?

It can also come after the plain form of the verb, in which case it is very often expressing a reason, meaning "for the purpose of" or "in order to." Note that in Japanese, the reason is given in the first part of the sentence, whereas in English it is usually in the last part.

Kēki o tsukuru tame ni, tamago o kaimasu.
I'm going to buy some eggs to make a cake.

Kitte o kau tame ni yūbinkyoku e ikimasu.
I'm going to the post office (in order) to buy some stamps.

Takahashi san wa, Eigo o benkyō suru tame ni, Eikaiwa no kurasu ni hairimashita.
Ms. Takahashi has joined an English conversation class in order to study English.

Taberu tame ni, shigoto o shimasu.
I work in order to eat.

Kono kaigi wa rainen no yasumi no hi o kimeru tame desu.
This meeting is for the purpose of deciding next year's vacation days.

Watashi no keiyaku no koto o sōdan suru tame ni, buchō to hanashitai n' desu.
I want to talk to the department manager in order to discuss my contract.

Kore o miseru tame ni kimashita.
I came to show you this.

6. YON-MAI – "FOUR (FLAT THINGS)"

Here is another way of counting, this time for flat things such as stamps, records, compact discs, pizzas, pieces of paper, envelopes and tickets. Use **ichi, ni, san,** etc. followed by -mai.

Kyōto made ni-mai kudasai.
Two (tickets) to Kyoto, please.

Kono hagaki wa, ichi-mai ikura desu ka.
How much is one of these postcards?

Sumimasen, hyaku-jū en kitte san-mai to, hyaku nana-jū en kitte o yon-mai kudasai.
Excuse me, could I have three 110-yen stamps and four 170-yen stamps, please?

Shii dii o takusan motte imasu ne! Nan-mai deshō ka.
You have such a lot of CDs! However many are there?

Ōkii fūtō san-mai to chiisai fūtō jū-mai kudasai.
Three large envelopes and ten small envelopes, please.

VOCABULARY

au mae ni: before meeting
dekakeru: go out
denki-dai electricity charges
denki: electricity
denwa-dai: telephone charges
Eikaiwa: English conversation
fūtō: envelope
gasu-dai: gas charges
gasu: gas
hagaki: postcard
harau: pay
ikeba: if we go
jisho: dictionary
jūbun: enough, sufficient
kabuki: Japanese classical play
kakikonde: please fill in/out [from kakikomu]
kippu: ticket
kitte: stamp
kōkūbin: airmail
kozutsumi: parcel
-mai: [counter for flat objects]
mazu: first of all, to begin with
miseru: show
o-azukari shimasu: receive, be entrusted with [from azukaru]
okuru: send
purezento: present
ranchi: lunch
saigo ni: finally, at the end
sono ato: after that
soshite: then
sureba: if I do
tamago: egg
tame ni: for the purpose of, benefit of
-te kara: after —ing
tsukuru: make
yameru: quit, stop, cease, drop (idea or plan)

yōji: errand, chore, something to do
yon-mai: four [flat objects]

TEST YOURSELF

1. Read through the dialog at the beginning of the lesson again, and then say if the following statements are true or false.

1. Futari wa eki no mae de aimasu. T/F
2. Katō san wa Maiku san to issho ni yūbinkyoku made ikimasu. T/F
3. Maiku san wa ginkō e iku mae ni, yūbinkyoku e iku yotei desu. T/F
4. Maiku san wa jū-ji han mae ni uchi o demasu. T/F
5. Kare wa kozutsumi o kōkūbin de okurimasu. T/F
6. Ginkō wa konde imasu ga, yūbinkyoku wa amari konde imasen. T/F

2. It's a school holiday tomorrow, but it'll be a busy day for Mike, as he has lots of things to do. Look at the list he's made, and make sentences about the things he's going to do, using -te kara, as in the example.

Example: **Ku-ji han ni Kawasaki de tenisu o shimasu.**
Tenisu o shite kara, denki-dai o harau tame ni ginkō e ikimasu.
Denki-dai o haratte kara, ...

9:30	play tennis in Kawasaki
	go to bank to pay electricity bill
	go to department store to buy father's birthday present
12.00	meet Mr. Itō in coffee shop
1.30	go to see movie
	buy Shinkansen tickets to Kyoto
4.30	go back home
	write letter to Susan
	study Japanese
9.00	go for a drink with Mr. Kato

Now imagine it's the next day, and you're talking about what Mike did in the daytime yesterday. Beginning with his return home, describe his day but this time working backwards, using **mae ni**, as in the example.

Example: **Uchi e kaeru mae ni, Kyōto made no Shinkansen no kippu o kaimashita.**
Shinkansen no kippu o kau mae ni, ...

3. *Imagine you're at the post office, and complete your part of the conversation below.*

You (I'd like to send this parcel to Britain – how much is it, please? By airmail.)

Clerk Igirisu desu ka. Sore wa ni-sen yon-hyaku en desu. Kono yōshi ni kakikonde kudasai.

You (And, how much is a postcard to Australia?)

Clerk Hyaku-go-jū en desu.

You (Three 150-yen stamps, please.)

Clerk Hai, dōzo. Sore de ii desu ka.

You (How much is this letter?)

Clerk Doko desu ka.

You (The USA.)

Clerk Hyaku-kyū-jū en desu. Hai, zenbu de san-zen yon-jū en desu.

4. *Match up the questions or statements from the column on the left with the most appropriate responses from the list on the right. Be careful – there are two responses too many.*

1. Dō shite Nihon e kita . n' desu ka
2. Amerika e iku to kikimashita ga, yasumi desu ka.
3. Kore wa ii jisho desu ne.
4. Isogashii desu ka.
5. Kaimono ni iku n' desu ka.

a. Ē, Nihongo no tesuto no tame desu.
b. Iie, shigoto no tame desu.
c. Tomodachi ni shashin o miseru tame desu.
d. Rainen no keikaku o sōdan suru tame desu.
e. Uchi o dekakeru tame desu.
f. Iie, kekkon suru tame desu.

6. Nan no tame ni shigoto o yameta n' desu ka. Kuni e kaeru n' desu ka.

g. Nihongo o benkyō suru tame desu.

7. Nan no tame no kaigi desu ka.

h. Hai, atarashii kutsu o kau tame ni ikimasu.

i. Ē, gaijin no tame no desu.

5. *How would you say these sentences in Japanese?*

1. Tomorrow I'm going to Tokyo to buy tickets for Kabuki.

2. If you don't understand, please ask Ms. Saitō.

3. Let's have lunch before we go out.

4. If you don't have enough time, you don't need to come.

5. Are you going to send this parcel airmail?

6. Mr. Takeda said he'd like to quit his job.

 These two characters mean "silver" and "go," but when combined into one compound word they mean "a bank," and the word is pronounced ginkō.

KI O TSUKENAKEREBA NARIMASEN YO
YOU MUST TAKE CARE!

Mike and the Watanabe family are just settling themselves down on the train as they set off for their skiing weekend. The train is packed full with people, luggage and skis.

Mike	**Sugoi nimotsu desu ne!** What a lot of luggage!
Watanabe	**Sō desu ne. Demo san-nin no kodomo mo iru deshō? Dakara zenbu de go-nin-bun no yōfuku, go-nin-bun no sukii-uea nado o motte konakereba narimasen ne. Taihen desu yo.** Yes, but we have three children! So altogether we have to bring clothes for five people, ski-wear for five people, and so on. It's tough!
Mike	**Ā, wakarimashita! Densha no naka wa sugoku konde imasu ne. Shiteiseki no kippu o katte, yokatta.** Ah, I see! The train's incredibly crowded inside, isn't it? I'm glad we bought tickets for reserved seats.

Watanabe	Sō desu ne. Kodomo ga suwaru koto ga dekinakereba, motto urusaku narimasu yo.
	Yes, if the children can't sit down, they get even noisier!
Mike	Densha no kippu to ieba, watashi wa mada haratte inai n' desu ne. Ikura deshita ka.
	Talking of train tickets, I haven't paid yet, have I? How much were they?
Watanabe	Ichi-man ni-sen en. (Mike gives him the money.) Arigatō. Kodomo wa urusai desu ne. (to the children) Ii kagen ni shi nasai!
	11,000 yen. Thank you. The children are noisy, aren't they? Behave yourselves properly!
Mike	Kōfun shite iru n' deshō. Watashi mo totemo tanoshimi ni shite imasu yo. Ashita no asa hayaku okite, ichi-nichi-jū sukii shitai n' desu.
	They must be excited. I'm really looking forward to it too. I want to get up early tomorrow morning and ski all day long.
Okusan	Sō desu ka. Ja, minna konban hayaku nenakereba narimasen ne. Tokorode, Neruson san wa sukii ga yoku dekiru to kikimashita ga.
	I see. Well, everyone must go to bed early tonight, right? By the way, I heard that you can ski well, Mr. Nelson.
Mike	Daigakusei no toki yoku yatte, sore kara Kanada ni sunde ita toki mo, ik-kagetsu ni ni-kai gurai yarimashita. Demo saikin wa amari yatte inai kara, abunai to omoimasu. Toshi o totta kara, ki o tsukenakereba narimasen yo!
	When I was a university student I often did, and when I was living in Canada I went about twice a month. But I haven't done much recently, so I think it'll be risky. I'm getting old, so I'll have to take care!
Okusan	Sonna koto nai n' deshō.
	No, that's not so, not at all!
Watanabe	A, shanai hanbai no hito ga kimashita. Neruson san, biiru demo nomimashō. (to the woman with the trolley) Ja, kōra o yon-hon to biiru o ni-hon kudasai. Sa, mina san, tanoshii ryokō ni, kanpai!

Ah, here comes someone selling (food and drink). Mr. Nelson, let's have a beer or something. Four colas and two beers, please. Right everyone, here's to an enjoyable trip.

All	**Kanpai!**
	Cheers!
Mike	**Chotto shitsurei shimasu. Watashi wa tearai e ikimasu.**
	Please excuse me. I'm just going to the bathroom.
Okusan	**Kotchi da to omoimasu. A, Neruson san, abunai! Sono sukii ni ki o tsukete!**
	I think it's this way. Oh, Mr. Nelson, look out! Be careful of those skis!
Mike	(There is the sound of a crash.) **Itai! Ashi ga itai!**
	Ouch! My leg hurts!
Okusan	**Neruson san, daijōbu desu ka.**
	Mr. Nelson, are you all right?
Mike	**Iie, dame desu. Tatsu koto ga dekimasen. Itai!**
	No, it's no good. I can't stand up! Ouch!

STRUCTURE AND USAGE NOTES

1. -NAKEREBA NARIMASEN – "MUST" OR "HAVE TO"

In the previous lesson, you learned that the verb ending **-eba** is the equivalent of "if," and that the negative **-nakereba** is the equivalent of "if not." Another use of this **-nakereba** form is to make a pattern which means "must/have to." To do this, add **narimasen**, which means "it's no good/it won't do." You then have **-nakereba narimasen**, a pretty cumbersome pattern which literally means "if you don't …, it's no good," or in other words "you must/you have to."

Ashita wa o-kyaku ga takusan kuru kara, kyō ichi-nichi-jū ryōri o tsukuranakereba narimasen.
Tomorrow we have a lot of guests coming, so I have to spend all day today making food.

Jiko shōkai wa Nihongo de nakereba narimasen.
Your self-introduction must be in Japanese.

Ashita Narita kūkō made tomodachi o mukae ni iku kara, densha no jikan o shirabenakereba narimasen.
I have to go to Narita Airport tomorrow to meet a friend, so I have to check up on the train times.

Chichi wa shigoto no tame ni Yōroppa e ikanakereba narimasen.
My father has to go to Europe on business.

Kimeru mae ni, buchō to sōdan shinakereba narimasen.
Before I decide, I have to consult the department manager.

Kyō wa kaigi no repōto o kakanakereba naranai kara, osoku made kaisha ni iru to omoimasu.
Today I have to write up the meeting report, so I think I'll be at the office until late.

Heya ga kitanai desu ne. Sōji shinakereba narimasen.
The room's dirty, isn't it. I must clean it.

The negative "don't have to ..." is expressed with -nakute mo ii desu (see Lesson 13, Structure and Usage Note 6).

Kyō owaranakute mo ii desu.
You don't have to finish it today.

Ashita wa nichiyōbi dakara, konban hayaku nenakute mo ii desu.
Tomorrow's Sunday, so you don't have to go to bed early tonight.

You may also come across the verb endings -nakereba ikemasen and -nakereba dame desu, which can also be translated as "must/have to."

Sono shukudai o jibun de shinakereba ikemasen yo.
You must do your homework by yourself.

Sore o Ogawa san ni misenakereba dame desu yo.
You must show that to Mr. Ogawa.

2. FORMING ADVERBS FROM ADJECTIVES

To make an adverb (describing how something is done, such as "incredibly," "cheaply," "quickly") from an -i adjective, drop the final -i and add -ku.

-i adjective	Meaning	Adverb	Meaning
sugoi	incredible	**sugoku**	incredibly
yasui	cheap	**yasuku**	cheaply
hayai	quick, early	**hayaku**	quickly, early
ii/yoi	good, fine	**yoku**	well, often
isogashii	busy	**isogashiku**	busily

Kōra o sonna ni hayaku nomanaide kudasai.
Don't drink your cola so quickly.

Mō natsu dakara, ima sukii-uea o totemo yasuku kau koto ga dekimasu.
It's summer now, so you can buy ski-wear really cheaply.

Watanabe san wa Eigo ga yoku dekinai to itte imasu ga, waruku nai to omoimasu.
Mr. Watanabe says he can't speak English well, but I don't think he's bad.

Shinkansen ni hayaku notte kudasai. Ip-pun dake eki ni tomarimasu kara.
Get aboard the Bullet Train quickly. It only stops in the station for a minute.

With -na adjectives, you don't need the -na, but follow the word up with **ni** instead.

jōzu	skillful	jōzu ni	skillfully
shinsetsu	kind	shinsetsu ni	kindly, gently
genki	energetic	genki ni	energetically
kantan	simple	kantan ni	simply
kirei	pretty, neat	kirei ni	prettily, neatly

Nihongo no jiko shōkai o totemo jōzu ni shimashita.
He introduced himself very well in Japanese.

Kantan ni setsumei shite kudasai.
Please explain it simply.

Kanji o mada kirei ni kaku koto ga dekimasen.
I can't write kanji characters neatly yet.

3. KATTE, YOKATTA – "I'M GLAD WE BOUGHT ..."

The phrase **katte, yokatta** actually means "we bought, and it was good," but this -te yokatta ending can usually be thought of as "I'm glad that/it's lucky that/it's good that."

Densha no jikan o yoku shirabete, yokatta ne.
It's lucky that we checked up on the train times carefully, isn't it!

Sono kozutsumi o kōkūbin de okutte, yokatta desu.
It's good that you sent that parcel by airmail.

Kasa o wasurenakute, yokatta desu.
I'm glad I didn't forget my umbrella.

Saikin tenki ga yoku natte, yokatta desu ne.
I'm glad that the weather has got better recently.

The opposite meaning can be expressed with -te, zannen desu, or
"it's a shame/pity that ..."

Shiteiseki o toru koto ga dekinakute, zannen desu ne.
It's a shame we couldn't get reserved seats, isn't it?

Tanaka san wa issho ni konakute, zannen desu ne.
It's a pity that Ms. Tanaka didn't come with us, isn't it?

Tōkyō mo dandan abunaku natte, zannen desu.
It's a shame that Tokyo is gradually getting dangerous too.

4. TO IEBA – "TALKING OF ..."

The word **ieba** comes from **iu**, "to talk," and so **to ieba** means "if
you're talking about ...". This phrase is used at the beginning of a
sentence when you've just been reminded of something you want to
talk about.

A. Saitō san no tanjōbi no pātii ni ikimasu ka.
   Are you going to Ms. Saitō's birthday party?
B. Hai, ikimasu yo. A, tanjōbi to ieba, raishū wa haha no tanjōbi
   desu. Purezento o kawanakereba narimasen.
   Yes, I am. And talking of birthdays, next week it's my mother's
   birthday. I must buy her a present.

A. Ano kuruma wa taka-sō desu ne. Ikeda san no deshō.
   That car looks really expensive, doesn't it. It's Mr. Ikeda's, isn't it?
B. Hai, sō da to omoimasu. Ikeda san to ieba, saikin atte inai n' desu
   yo. Genki desu ka.
   Yes, I think so. Talking of Mr. Ikeda, I haven't seen him for a long
   time. Is he well?

5. ICHI-MAN – "TEN THOUSAND"

Japanese has a unit in counting which doesn't exist in English, and
that is **man**, or "ten thousand." **Ni-man** is therefore "twenty
thousand," and **go-man** is "fifty thousand." When you get up into
the hundreds of thousands (which is very likely when talking about
the price of airline tickets, or a few nights in a large hotel), things can
get pretty confusing, so it's usually advisable to write such numbers
down to double-check them. Here are some examples of large
numbers.

30,000	san-man
37,000	san-man nana-sen
83,500	hachi-man san-zen go-hyaku
100,000	jū-man
500,000	go-jū man
1,000,000	hyaku-man
1,200,000	hyaku-ni-jū-man
10,000,000	sen-man
100,000,000	ichi-oku

When reading large numbers, it might help to separate the digits into groups of four, instead of groups of three. Then if you temporarily ignore the right-hand group, what remains is the number of **man**. For example:

170,000 =	17,0000 =	17 man =	jū-nana-man
3,500,000 =	350,0000 =	350 man =	san-byaku go-jū-man

6. TOKI – "THE TIME WHEN ..."

The word **toki** by itself means "time/occasion" but it also often occurs in cases where English uses "when/whenever" to talk about what is or was happening during a certain period (for example, "whenever it rains ...," "when I was a student ...").

Ame no toki, kibun ga waruku narimasu.
Whenever it rains, I feel miserable.

Gakusei no toki, yoku Eigo no benkyō o shimashita.
When I was a student, I studied English a lot.

Nimotsu ga ōi toki, itsumo takushii ni norimasu.
Whenever I have a lot of luggage, I always take a taxi.

Tesuto no toki, atama ga itsumo itaku narimasu.
When I have a test, I always get a headache.

It can also be used after a verb or verb phrase. Remember that the verb should be in the plain form.

Densha ga konde iru toki, yoku takushii ni norimasu.
When the trains are crowded, I often take a taxi.

Amerika ni ryokō shite ita toki, hagaki o san-jū-mai gurai okurimashita.
When I was travelling in the USA, I sent about thirty postcards.

Kōfun shite iru toki, kao ga akaku narimasu.
When I get excited, my face goes red.

Shiteiseki no kippu o kau koto ga dekinai toki, itsumo shinpai shimasu.
When I can't get a reserved seat ticket, I always worry.

Apāto o sōji suru toki, itsumo ongaku o kikimasu.
Whenever I clean the apartment, I always listen to music.

Asa-gohan o tabete ita toki, ani kara denwa ga arimashita.
When I was eating breakfast, there was a call from my older brother.

Sukii ni iku toki, minna jibun no nimotsu o motanakereba narimasen.
When we go skiing, we all have to carry our own luggage.

7. PHRASES OF FREQUENCY

This is the pattern you need when you want to talk about the frequency with which something happens, as ik-kai means "once," ni-kai means "twice," and san-kai means "three times," etc. Here are some more examples of phrases you can use to indicate frequency.

ichi-nichi ni yon-kai	four times a day
ni-shūkan ni ik-kai	once every two weeks
ik-kagetsu ni ni-kai	twice a month
san-kagetsu ni ik-kai	once in three months
ichi-nen ni san-kai	three times a year
go-nen ni ik-kai	once in five years

Is-shūkan ni ik-kai gurai Ōsaka shiten ni ikanakereba naranai kara, itsumo shiteiseki no kippu o kaimasu.
I go to the Osaka branch about once a week, so I always buy a reserved seat ticket.

Wakai toki ni yoku ryokō shimashita ga, ima toshi o totta kara, ichi-nen ni ik-kai gurai dake desu.
When I was young I often used to go on trips, but now I'm old, so I only go about once a year.

Nihongo no kurasu wa is-shūkan ni nan-kai desu ka.
How many times a week is the Japanese class?

Atarashii kaisha de wa, rok-kagetsu ni ik-kai Yōroppa e shutchō ni ikimasu.
At my new company, I'll be going on a business trip to Europe once every six months.

8. YON-HON – "FOUR (LONG, THIN THINGS)"

Here's another counter, this time for counting long, thin objects such as pens, rolled umbrellas, bottles and cans of drink, rolls of film, flowers and bananas. The numbers up to ten are:

ip-pon	rop-pon
ni-hon	nana-hon/shichi-hon
san-bon	hap-pon/hachi-hon
yon-hon	kyū-hon
go-hon	jup-pon

Biiru o mō ip-pon kudasai.
Another (bottle of) beer, please.

Tako wa ashi ga nan-bon arimasu ka.
How many legs does an octopus have?

Kotoshi kasa o yon-hon mo densha no naka de wasuremashita yo.
This year I've forgotten four umbrellas on the train!

Sono akai hana o go-hon kudasai.
Five of those red flowers, please.

VOCABULARY

abunai: dangerous, look out!
ashi: leg, foot
biiru demo: beer or something
-bun: quantity, share, portion
daigakusei no toki: when I was a university student
gurai: about, approximately
hanbai: sales, selling
-hon: [counter for long, thin objects]
ichi-man: ten thousand
ichi-nichi-jū: all day long
ii kagen ni shi nasai: please behave yourselves
ik-kagetsu: one month
ik-kai: once, one time
jibun no: one's own, my own, your own
jibun: self, oneself
kōfun shite imasu: is/are excited
-man: [unit of ten thousand]
motte konakereba narimasen: have to bring [from **motte kuru**]
nenakereba narimasen: have to sleep [from **neru**]
nimotsu: luggage

noru: to get on/in (transportation)
oku: hundred million
ongaku: music
ryokō: trip, journey
saikin: recently
shanai: inside the train
shiraberu: investigate, look into
shiteiseki: reserved seat
sōji suru: do the cleaning
sukii-uea: ski-wear
sunde ita toki: when I was living [from **sumu**]
tako: octopus
tanoshimi ni shite imasu: I'm looking forward to
to ieba: talking of …
toshi o totta: old [from **toshi o toru**, to get older]
toshi: age
urusai: noisy
urusaku narimasu: get noisy
yarimashita: did, tried [from **yaru**]
yōfuku: clothes
yoku dekiru: can do well
yon-hon: four [long, thin objects]

TEST YOURSELF

1. Read the dialog at the beginning of the lesson again, and then say if the following statements are true or false.

1. Watanabe san no kazoku wa go-nin desu. T/F

2. Watanabe san to okusan to Maiku san wa suwaru koto ga dekimasu ga, san-nin no kodomo ga tatanakereba narimasen. T/F

3. Maiku san wa densha ni noru mae ni, kippu no o-kane o haraimashita. T/F

4. Maiku san wa ashita no asa hayaku okiru tsumori desu. T/F

5. Maiku san wa Kanada ni sunda koto ga arimasu. T/F

6. Minna kōra o nomimasu. T/F

2. *It's only a few weeks now before Sue arrives on her visit to Japan, and although Mike is still finding it hard to get around with a sprained ankle, he has lots of things to do in preparation. Look at the list he's made, and make sentences about what he has to do, using* **-nakereba narimasen.**

Example: - ask Watanabe about vacation days
Yasumi no hi ni tsuite Watanabe san ni kikanakereba narimasen.

Things to do:

– ask Watanabe about vacation days

– clean the apartment

– pay telephone bill

– buy 2 tickets for Kabuki

– buy new clothes

– call Shirazawa ryōkan

– check up on train times to Narita airport

---

3. *Answer these questions about how often you do certain things, using phrases such as* **is-shūkan ni ni-kai, ichi-nen ni ik-kai,** *etc.*

Example: **Tenisu o yoku shimasu ka.**
Hai, is-shūkan ni san-kai gurai shimasu.
or
Iie, ichi-nen ni ni-kai gurai dake shimasu.
or
Iie, zenzen shimasen.

1. Nihongo no benkyō o yoku shimasu ka.

2. Yoku kaimono ni ikimasu ka.

3. Resutoran de yoku tabemasu ka.

4. Tokidoki gaikoku e ikimasu ka.

5. Jibun no heya o yoku sōji shimasu ka.

6. Atarashii yōfuku o yoku kaimasu ka.

7. Shashin o yoku torimasu ka.

8. Umi e tokidoki ikimasu ka.

9. Yoku densha ni norimasu ka.

10. Tokidoki kēki o tsukurimasu ka.

4. *Read the questions below, and then use the pictures to help you answer them. Use* **toki** *in your answers, as in the example.*

Example: **Q. Itsu Nihongo no benkyō o hajimemashita ka.**

A. Nihon ni sunde ita toki, Nihongo no benkyō o hajimemashita.

1. Itsu sono nyūsu o kikimashita ka.

2. Atama wa itsu itaku narimashita ka.

3. Itsu okusan ni hajimete atta n' desu ka.

4. Itsu takushii ni norimasu ka.

5. Watanabe san wa itsu uchi ni yorimashita ka.

6. Itsu kare to sono koto ni tsuite hanashimashita ka.

5. *How would you say these sentences in Japanese?*

   1. You all have to buy your own tickets.

   2. A ticket from Tokyo to Osaka is about 13,500 yen.

   3. He speaks quickly, so I don't understand him very well.

   4. I'm glad we took the Shinkansen.

   5. Talking of London, have you ever been there, Mr. Wada?

   6. When I was in Japan last year, I climbed Mt. Fuji.

The characters for "cut" and "tally/sign" together make up the word **kippu,** meaning "ticket."

DAI JŪ-NANA-KA KARA DAI JŪ-KYŪ-KA MADE NO FUKUSHŪ

REVIEW OF LESSONS 17 TO 19

Read Dialogs 17 to 19 aloud, and try to understand the meaning without referring back to the translations in previous lessons.

Dialog 17: Kamakura e itta koto ga arimasu ka.

Takahashi	Neruson san wa Kamakura e itta koto ga arimasu ka.
Mike	Iie, arimasen. Ikitai kedo.
Takahashi	Ja, nichiyōbi ni watashitachi to issho ni Kamakura e ikimasen ka. Saitō san mo Wada san mo issho ni iku to itte imasu ga. Tenki ga yokattara, pikkunikku o suru tsumori desu.
Mike	Ii desu ne. Demo, tenki ga yoku nakattara, dō shimasu ka. Konban ame ga furu to kikimashita ga.
Takahashi	Sonna koto o kangaenaide kudasai. Nichiyōbi wa kitto ii tenki desu yo.
Mike	Wakarimashita! Densha de iku n' desu ka.

| Takahashi | Sō desu. Densha no hō ga hayai to omoimasu. Sore dake ja nakute, dare mo kuruma o motte imasen kara, shikata ga arimasen yo. |

In Kamakura, in front of the daibutsu.

Mike	Konna ni ōkii daibutsu wa mita koto ga arimasen ne.
Takahashi	Naka ni haitte, atama no naka made noboru koto mo dekimasu yo. Watashi wa haitta koto ga nai kedo.
Mike	Sa, hairimashō ka.
Takahashi	Chotto matte. Sono mae ni, minna no shashin o toritai kara. Hai, mina san, soko ni tatte kudasai yo. Ā, dame desu. Soko ni tattara, daibutsu ga shashin ni hairimasen.
Mike	Sono kaidan no ue ni suwattara, dō desu ka.
Takahashi	Sō ne. Sono hō ga ii. Hai, mina san, soko ni suwatte kudasai. Ii desu ka. Hai, chiizu! Dōmo arigatō. Sa, daibutsu ni hairimashō.
Mike	Mite yo. Daibutsu no ushiro ni sugoi hito ga narande imasu ne. Jikan ga kakaru deshō.
Takahashi	Saki ni hiru-gohan o tabetara, dō desu ka.
Mike	Sō desu ne. Demo ne, chotto samuku natte, sora mo kuraku natte imasu ne. Pikkunikku wa chotto ... Are!? Ame ja nai n' desu ka.
Takahashi	Sō desu yo. Ara, sugoi ame da! Dareka kasa o motte imasu ka. Dare mo kasa o motte inai n' desu ka. Sa, ichiban chikai resutoran made hashirimashō yo. Hayaku!

QUESTIONS:

1. Zenbu de nan-nin ga Kamakura e ikimasu ka.

2. Nan de ikimasu ka.

3. Shashin o toru tame, minna doko ni suwarimasu ka.

4. Hiru-gohan o tabete kara, minna nani o suru tsumori desu ka.

Dialog 18: Sō sureba ...

Mike   Sa, nan-ji ni, doko de aimashō ka.
Katō   Watashi ga saki ni Maiku san no apāto ni ikimashō ka.
        Sō sureba, issho ni eki made aruku koto ga dekimasu ne.
Mike   Jitsu wa, watashi wa iroiro-na yōji ga aru n' desu.
        Dakara sugu uchi o dete, Katō san ni au mae ni yōji o
        sureba ii to omotte ita n' desu ga.
Katō   Watashi mo issho ni iku yo. Sō sureba, yōji ga owatte
        kara, dokoka de ranchi o taberu koto mo dekimasu ne.
        Kabuki wa nagai kara, hairu mae ni nanika tabeta hō
        ga ii to omoimasu. Ii desu ka.
Mike   Mochiron ii n' da kedo, Katō san ni wa zenzen
        omoshiroku nai to omoimasu yo. Mazu, haha no
        tanjōbi ni purezento o okuru tame ni yūbinkyoku e
        ikimasu. Sore kara, gasu-dai to denki-dai o harau tame
        ni ginkō e ikimasu. Sono ato ...
Katō   Daijōbu desu yo. Ja, jū-ji-han goro Maiku san no
        tokoro ni ikeba, jikan ga jūbun arimasu ka.
Mike   Hai hai, ii desu. Ja, matte imasu yo.

Later, at the post office.

Mike   Kono kozutsumi o Amerika made okuritai n' desu ga,
        ikura deshō ka.
Clerk   Kōkūbin desu ne. (he weighs the parcel) Hai, yon-sen
        hyaku en desu. Kono yōshi ni kakikonde kudasai.
Mike   Sore kara, hyaku-jū en kitte o yon-mai kudasai.
Clerk   Hyaku-jū en kitte o yon-mai desu ne. Zenbu de yon-
        sen go-hyaku yon-jū en desu. Hai, go-sen-en o-azukari
        shimasu. O-tsuri wa yon-hyaku roku-jū en desu. Dōzo.
Mike   Arigatō. (to Mr Katō) Sugoi hito ga ushiro ni narande
        imasu ne. Ginkō mo konna ni konde ireba,
        yamemashō.
Katō   Demo, gasu-dai to denki-dai o harawanakereba ...
Mike   Ii n' desu yo. Shinpai shinaide. Jikan wa mada jūbun
        arimasu.

QUESTIONS:

1. Maiku san wa dō shite uchi o hayaku demasu ka.

2. Maiku san wa dō shite ginkō e iku tsumori desu ka.

3. Yūbinkyoku de, Maiku san wa nani o kakanakereba narimasen ka.

4. Yūbinkyoku wa konde imasu ka.

Dialog 19: *Ki o tsukenakereba narimasen yo.*

Mike	Sugoi nimotsu desu ne!
Watanabe	Sō desu ne. Demo san-nin no kodomo mo iru deshō? Dakara zenbu de go-nin-bun no yōfuku, go-nin-bun no sukii-uea nado o motte konakereba narimasen ne. Taihen desu yo.
Mike	Ā, wakarimashita! Densha no naka wa sugoku konde imasu ne. Shiteiseki no kippu o katte, yokatta.
Watanabe	Sō desu ne. Kodomo ga suwaru koto ga dekinakereba, motto urusaku narimasu yo.
Mike	Densha no kippu to ieba, watashi wa mada haratte inai n' desu ne. Ikura deshita ka.
Watanabe	Ichi-man ni-sen en. (Mike gives him the money.) Arigatō. Kodomo wa urusai desu ne. (to the children) Ii kagen ni shi nasai!
Mike	Kōfun shite iru n' deshō. Watashi mo totemo tanoshimi ni shite imasu yo. Ashita no asa hayaku okite, ichi-nichi-jū sukii shitai n' desu.
Okusan	Sō desu ka. Ja, minna konban hayaku nenakereba narimasen ne. Tokorode, Neruson san wa sukii ga yoku dekiru to kikimashita ga.
Mike	Daigakusei no toki yoku yatte, sore kara Kanada ni sunde ita toki mo, ik-kagetsu ni ni-kai gurai yarimashita. Demo saikin wa amari yatte inai kara, abunai to omoimasu. Toshi o totta kara, ki o tsukenakereba narimasen yo!
Okusan	Sonna koto nai n' deshō.
Watanabe	A, shanai hanbai no hito ga kimashita. Neruson san, biiru demo nomimashō. (to the woman with the trolley) Ja, kōra o yon-hon to biiru o ni-hon kudasai. Sa, mina san, tanoshii ryokō ni, kanpai!
All	Kanpai!
Mike	Chotto shitsurei shimasu. Watashi wa tearai e ikimasu.
Okusan	Kotchi da to omoimasu. A, Neruson san, abunai! Sono sukii ni ki o tsukete!
Mike	(There is the sound of a crash.) Itai! Ashi ga itai!
Okusan	Neruson san, daijōbu desu ka.
Mike	Iie, dame desu. Tatsu koto ga dekimasen. Itai!

QUESTIONS:

1. Maiku san to Watanabe san-tachi wa ima doko ni imasu ka.

2. Watanabe san wa dō shite nimotsu ga ōi desu ka.

3. Watanabe san wa donna kippu o kaimashita ka.

4. Densha no naka de nani o kaimashita ka.

TEST YOURSELF

1. Which is the odd man out in the following groups of words?

1. ik-kagetsu, ichi-mai, ichi-nichi, is-shūkan

2. hyaku, man, sen, hayaku

3. kozutsumi, denki-dai, tegami, hagaki

4. dō shite, mazu, saigo ni, soshite

5. yuki, kaze, tōi, ame

6. samuku, ōkiku, waruku, keiyaku

2. How would you say the following in Japanese?

1. 36,500 yen

2. 5 stamps

3. 7 bottles of beer

4. 6 months

5. 12:45

6. August 10th

3. *Test yourself on these common phrases or sayings – what are they in Japanese?*

   1. It can't be helped.

   2. Behave yourself!

   3. How do you do?

   4. Bon appetit.

   5. Cheers!

   6. Excuse me for disturbing you.

   7. Goodnight.

   8. Watch out!

   9. Please take care.

   10. That's a pity.

4. *Using the clues below, fill in the grid to find out where Mike is planning to go with Sue when she comes to Japan.*

   1. Biiru o ni-___ kudasai.

   2. Fuji san ni _____ koto ga arimasu ka.

   3. Watashi wa hazukashii toki, kao ga _____ narimasu.

   4. Kabuki no _____ o ni-mai motte imasu ga, issho ni ikimasen ka.

   5. Raishū shigoto de Amerika e ikanakereba _____.

   6. _____ ga warui kara, sugu uchi e kaeru to omoimasu.

   7. Kyōto _____ ja nakute, Nara e mo ikitai n' desu.

   8. O-sake o sonna ni takusan nomeba, _____ ni narimasu yo.

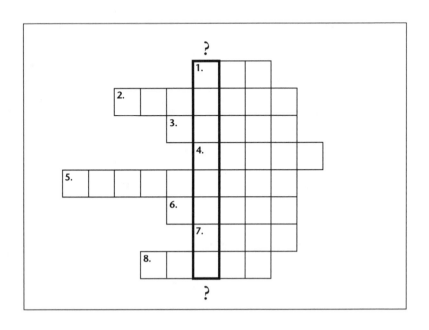

5. *Mike is chatting to Ms. Takahashi at school. Put the lines of their dialog in the correct order by writing the numbers 1-8 next to the appropriate line.*

___ a. *Mike*   Hai, mokuyōbi ni Hokkaidō e iku yotei desu.

___ b. *Mike*   Hai, ikimasu. Demo asa totemo hayaku okinakereba narimasen ne.

___ c. *Takahashi*   Sūzan san wa ashita kuru deshō.

___ d. *Mike*   Hontō? Ja, e-hagaki o okurimasu yo.

___ e. *Takahashi*   Ii desu ne. Watashi wa itta koto ga nai n' desu.

___ f. *Mike*   Sō desu. Ashita no asa jū-ji han ni.

___ g. *Takahashi*   Tanoshimi ni shite iru deshō. Kūkō made mukae ni ikimasu ka.

___ h. *Takahashi*   Ryōko wa? Dokoka e ikimasu ka.

6. *Answer these questions about yourself.*

1. Nihon e itta koto ga arimasu ka.

2. Kodomo no toki, doko ni sunde imashita ka.

3. O-kane ga takusan attara, nani o kaitai n' desu ka.

4. Nihongo to Furansugo to, dochira no hō ga muzukashii to omoimasu ka.

5. Anata no kuni de wa, nan-gatsu ni samuku narimasu ka.

6. Ashita nani o shinakereba narimasen ka.

7. Shii dii o nan-mai motte imasu ka.

8. Is-shūkan ni nan-kai gurai Nihongo no benkyō o shimasu ka.

These are the characters for **saigo,** meaning "last/final," as this is the last lesson of the book. The word combines the characters for "most" and "after/behind."

ANSWER KEY

LESSON 1:

1. 1-T, 2-T, 3-T

2. Free answers

3. 1. Hajimemashite.
   2. Amerikajin desu.
   3. Nihon no kuruma desu ka.
   4. Hai, sō desu.
   5. Iie, chigaimasu.

4. 1. A. Maiku san no sūtsukēsu desu ka.
      B. Hai, sō desu.
   2. A. Gakusei desu ka.
      B. Hai, sō desu.
   3. A. Sensei desu ka.
      B. Iie, chigaimasu.
   4. A. Watanabe san no kuruma desu ka.
      B. Hai, sō desu.
   5. A. Enjinia desu ka.
      B. Iie, chigaimasu.
   6. A. Amerikajin desu ka.
      B. Hai, sō desu.

5.   *You*   Shitsurei desu ga, Tanaka san desu ka.
     Tanaka   Hai, sō desu.
      You   Hajimemashite, [your company or school name] no [your name] desu.
     Tanaka   Hajimemashite, Fujimura no Tanaka desu.
      You   Watashi no meishi desu. Dōzo.

LESSON 2:

1. 1-T, 2-T, 3-F

2. 1. Hai, arimasu. OR Iie, arimasen.
   2. [Place name] ni arimasu (e.g. Nyū Yōku ni arimasu).
   3. Hai, ōkii uchi desu. OR Iie, ōkii uchi ja arimasen.
   4. Hai, arimasu. OR Iie, arimasen.
   5. [Country name or city name] kara desu (e.g. Nyū Yōku kara desu).

3. 1-hito 2-meishi 3-tsukue 4-denwa 5-pāto 6-purintā 7-konpyūtā (JIMU NO HITO)

4. 1. Tōkyō kara desu ka.
   2. (Watashi no) kaisha wa Nyū Yōku ni arimasu.
   3. Sumimasen ga, ginkō wa doko desu ka. OR ... doko ni arimasu ka.
   4. Denwa wa asoko ni arimasu. Dōzo. OR ... asoko desu.
   5. Sore wa watashi no uchi ja arimasen.

5. 1-ni 2-arimasen 3-asoko 4-ja 5-no 6-namae 7-wa 8-kara

LESSON 3:

1. 1-T, 2-F, 3-F, 4-T, 5-F

2. 1. Mizu o kudasai.
   2. O-cha o kudasai.
   3. Yaki-zakana teishoku o kudasai.
   4. Wain o kudasai.
   5. Sashimi o kudasai.
   6. Sore o kudasai.

3. 1. Q: Ashita eiga o mimasu ka.
      A: Iie, ashita (eiga o) mimasen.
   2. Q: Mainichi o-cha o nomimasu ka.
      A: Hai, mainichi (o-cha o) nomimasu.
   3. Q: Kyō kaisha e ikimasu ka.
      A: Iie, kyō (kaisha e) ikimasen.
   4. Q: Tokidoki sakana o tabemasu ka.
      A: Hai, tokidoki (sakana o) tabemasu.
   5. Q: Mainichi rajio o kikimasu ka.
      A: Iie, mainichi (rajio o) kikimasen.

4. 1. wa, o
   2. wa, ga
   3. no, o
   4. ga
   5. wa, e
   6. wa, no

5. 1. Eigo ga wakarimasu ka.
   2. Konban nani o shimasu ka.
   3. (Watashi wa) sashimi ga amari suki ja arimasen.
   4. Tanaka san wa nani o oshiemasu ka.
   5. Konban dono eiga o mimasu ka.
   6. Kono daigaku wa ōkii desu ne.

LESSON 4:

1. 1-F, 2-F, 3-T, 4-T, 5-T, 6-T

2. 1. yo-ji
   2. ni-ji han
   3. ku-ji yon-jū-go-fun
   4. jū-ichi-ji yon-jup-pun
   5. ichi-ji han
   6. roku-ji jū-go-fun

3. 1. Shichi-ji jū-go-fun ni kōhii o nomimasu.
   2. Shichi-ji han kara shichi-ji yon-jū-go-fun made rajio no nyūsu o kikimasu.
   3. Hachi-ji ni eki e ikimasu.
   4. Hachi-ji yon-jū-go-fun kara yo-ji yon-jū-go-fun made shigoto o shimasu.
   5. Roku-ji ni shinbun o yomimasu.
   6. Shichi-ji kara hachi-ji han made Nihongo o benkyō shimasu.
      OR ... Nihongo no benkyō o shimasu.
   7. Kū-ji han kara jū-ichi-ji made terebi o mimasu.

4. 1. Shichi-ji han ni aimashō.
   2. Ashita kara Nihongo o benkyō shimasu. OR ... Nihongo no benkyō o shimasu.
   3. Terebi de nyūsu o mimashō ka. OR Terebi no nyūsu o mimashō ka.
   4. Ashita no kaigi wa nan-ji kara desu ka.

5. Takushii de eki e ikimashō.
6. Wain wa mada arimasu ka.

5. Moshi moshi
   Moshi moshi
   konbanwa
   konbanwa
   eiga ga suki desu ne
   Hai, suki desu
   jikan ga arimasu ka
   Sore wa ii eiga desu ne
   Hai, sō desu
   nan-ji ni aimashō ka
   Eiga wa roku-ji han ni hajimarimasu
   aimashō
   mata ashita
   mata ashita

LESSON 5:

1. 1-T, 2-T, 3-T, 4-F, 5-F, 6-T

2. Gomen kudasai.
   Shitsurei shimasu.   OR   O-jama shimasu.
   Shitsurei shimasu.
   Itadakimasu.   OR   Onegai shimasu.

3. 1. Sumimasen ga, Yokohama Gakuin Kōkō wa doko desu ka.
      Tsugi no shingō de migi ni magatte kudasai. Hidari-gawa ni
      arimasu.
   2. Sumimasen ga, Ōsaka Daigaku wa doko desu ka.
      Massugu itte kudasai. Hidari-gawa ni arimasu.
   3. Sumimasen ga, Yamate eki wa doko desu ka.
      Tsugi no kado de hidari ni magatte kudasai. Migi-gawa ni
      arimasu.

4. 1. Sumimasen ga, kono hon wa ikura desu ka.
      Ni-sen go-hyaku roku-jū en desu.
   2. Sumimasen ga, kono surippa wa ikura desu ka.
      San-zen san-byaku nana-jū-go en desu.

3. Sumimasen ga, kono rajio wa ikura desu ka.
   Kyū-sen go-hyaku ni-jū en desu.
4. Sumimasen ga, kono terebi wa ikura desu ka.
   Rop-pyaku yon-jū go doru desu.
5. 8,255
6. 1,120
7. 5,093
8. 7,303

5. 1. Tsugi no shingō de hidari ni magatte kudasai.
2. Ashita uchi de terebi o mimasu.
3. Mondai ga arimasu ka.
4. Koko de namae to jūsho o kaite kudasai.
5. Sumimasen ga, sono hon wa ikura desu ka.
6. Hidari-gawa ni ōkii gakkō ga arimasu ne.
7. Tokorode, ashita nani o shimasu ka.
8. Kōhii wa ikaga desu ka.

LESSON 6:

Dialogue 1
1. Watanabe san wa sensei desu.
2. Gakkō wa Yokohama desu/ni arimasu.
3. Maiku san wa Amerikajin desu.

Dialogue 2
1. Jimu no hito desu.
2. Hai, arimasu.
3. Atarashii pāto no namae wa Saitō desu.

Dialogue 3
1. Iie, sakana ga suki desu.
2. Hai, sashimi teishoku ni shimasu.
3. "Kiku" wa hana desu.
4. Mizu o nomimasu.

Dialogue 4
1. Uchi kara denwa shimasu.
2. Eiga ga roku-ji han ni hajimarimasu.
3. Iie, aimasen.
4. Takushii de ikimasu.

Dialogue 5
1. Hidari-gawa ni arimasu.
2. Sen ni-hyaku en desu.
3. Hai, sō desu.
4. Kōhii o nomimasu.

1. migi – hidari, kono – sono, kirai – suki, e – kara, itadakimasu – go-chisō sama, koko – soko, iie – hai, ikimasu – kimasu, konbanwa – ohayō gozaimasu, oshiemasu – benkyō shimasu, sensei – gakusei, takusan – sukoshi, anata – watashi

2. 1. go-sen rop-pyaku go-jū en
   2. san-byaku jū doru
   3. jū-ni-ji ni-jū-go-fun
   4. san-zen kyū-hyaku kyū-jū go en
   5. yon-sen go-hyaku doru
   6. jū-ji yon-jup-pun

3. 1. koko (the only one that isn't a question word)
   2. ano (the only one that isn't a number)
   3. inu (the only one that isn't a time word)
   4. hashi (the only one that isn't a kind of food)
   5. daigaku (the only one that isn't a person)

4. 1. hanashimasu
   2. eki made ikimasu
   3. arimasu ka/takusan arimasu
   4. aimashō ka
   5. takusan arimasu/arimasu ka
   6. e ikimashō ka
   7. suwatte kudasai
   8. ni shimasu
   9. desu ka
   10. suki desu ne

5. 1. Watashi no namae wa ___ desu.
   2. Hai, suki desu./Iie, amari suki ja arimasen./Iie, kirai desu.
   3. Hai, ikimasu./Iie, ikimasen.
   4. Hai, tokidoki shimasu/Iie, tenisu o shimasen.
   5. ___ desu./___ ni arimasu.
   6. Hai, sukoshi wakarimasu./Iie, wakarimasen.
   7. Hai, imasu./Iie, imasen.
   8. Hai, mainichi mimasu./Tokidoki mimasu./Iie, mimasen.

1. 1-T, 2-F, 3-F, 4-T, 5-T, 6-T

2. sushi-takai/oishii, shukudai-muzukashii,
   densha-hayai, kaisha-ōkii/chiisai, inu-ōkii/chiisai,
   tatemono-takai

3. 1. Iie, amari muzukashiku arimasen yo.
   2. Iie, amari atarashiku arimasen yo.
   3. Iie, amari oishiku arimasen yo.
   4. Iie, amari yoku arimasen yo.
   5. Iie, amari samuku arimasen yo.

4. Itō san wa hiru-gohan o tabete imasu.
   Sakai san wa gakusei no shukudai o yonde imasu.
   Neruson san wa Eigo o oshiete imasu.
   Takahashi san wa Eigo o benkyō shite imasu.
   Ogawa san wa yakyū no renshū o shite imasu.

5. 1. Kyō no Nihongo no shukudai wa muzukashii desu ne.
   2. Haha no tanjōbi wa ashita desu. OR Ashita wa haha no
      tanjōbi desu.
   3. Jū-ni-ji mae ni kaerimasu.
   4. O-niisan wa doko ni sunde imasu ka.
   5. Maiku san wa kyō Kawasaki de Eigo o oshiete imasu.
   6. Sumimasen ga, Keiko wa ima imasen. Tonari no uchi de,
      terebi de eiga o mite imasu. Yobimashō ka.

1. 1-T, 2-T, 3-F, 4-F, 5-F, 6-T

2. akai, no, iya, dō shite, kaimasu, mimasu, ga, aimasu, kono,
   deshō, takaku

3. 1. Kirei-na hana desu ne.
   2. Genki-na kodomo desu ne.
   3. Takai tatemono desu ne.
   4. Yūmei-na hon desu ne.
   5. Hen-na eiga desu ne.

4. 1. a+c   2. c+b   3. a+b   4. c+a   5. b+a

5. 1. Asoko no hito wa Saitō san deshō ka.
    2. Motto kantan-na repōto o kaite kudasai.
    3. Kuroi jaketto wa chotto chiisai deshō.
    4. Kyō (no) densha wa totemo konde imasu ne.
    5. Tōkyō wa amari suki ja arimasen ga, Yokohama wa ii desu.
    6. Haha wa Tōkyō no yūmei-na depāto de hataraite imasu.

LESSON 9:

1. 1-T, 2-T, 3-F, 4-F, 5-T, 6-F

2. 1. Kayōbi no yoru nani o shimashita ka.
       Roku-ji han kara shichi-ji han made tenisu no renshū o
       shimashita.
    2. Suiyōbi no yoru nani o shimashita ka.
       Haha ni denwa o shimashita.
    3. Mokuyōbi no yoru nani o shimashita ka.
       Roku-ji kara hachi-ji made Nihongo no kurasu ga
       arimashita.
    4. Kinyōbi no yoru nani o shimashita ka.
       Takahashi san to issho ni resutoran ni ikimashita.
    5. Doyōbi to nichiyōbi (OR shūmatsu) ni nani o shimashita ka.
       Umi ni/e ikimashita.

3. 1. Kayōbi no yoru, roku-ji han kara shichi-ji han made tenisu
       no renshū o shimashita kedo, heta deshita. OR ... jōzu ja
       arimasen deshita.
    2. Suiyōbi no yoru, haha ni denwa shimashita kedo, imasen
       deshita.
    3. Mokuyōbi no yoru, roku-ji kara hachi-ji made Nihongo no
       kurasu ga arimashita kedo, watashi dake deshita.
    4. Kinyōbi no yoru, Takahashi san to issho ni resutoran ni
       ikimashita kedo, oishiku arimasen deshita.
    5. Shūmatsu ni umi e ikimashita kedo, taihen samukatta desu.

4. 1. Maiku san ni atte, Ginza e itte, eiga o mimashita.
    2. Sono eiga wa SF de, omoshiroku arimasen deshita.
    3. Kissaten ni haitte, kōhii o nomimashita.
    4. Eigo de hanashite ite, muzukashikatta desu.
    5. Watashi wa Eigo ga heta de, hazukashikatta desu.
    6. Takushi de kaette, takakatta desu.

5. 1. Itsu Amerika kara kaerimashita ka.
   2. Nan-nin ga yama no onsen e ikimashita ka.
   3. Hontō ni iya-na tenki deshita.
   4. Kinō no yoru sushi o takusan tabete, sake mo takusan nomimashita.
   5. Kesa shinbun o yomimashita kedo, mō nyūsu o wasuremashita.
   6. Shūmatsu ni, dokoka e ikimashita ka.

LESSON 10:

1. 1-T, 2-F, 3-T, 4-F, 5-T, 6-T

2. mōshimasu
   kara kimashita
   o oshiete imasu
   Furansugo o benkyō shimashita OR Furansugo no benkyō o shimashita
   itte
   no daigaku de
   Furansugo o benkyō shimashita OR Furansugo no benkyō o shimashita
   eiga to supōtsu desu

3. 1. Wada san wa, bōifurendo wa eki no mae de matte iru to omotte imasu.
   2. Fukuda san wa, sore wa hen-na gakkō da to omotte imasu.
   3. Itō san wa, sono kōhii wa amari oishiku nai to omotte imasu.
   4. Maiku san wa, Ogawa san no Nihongo wa yoku wakaranai to omotte imasu.
   5. Katō san wa, Watanabe san wa nete iru to omotte imasu.
   6. Nakayama san wa, konban Kenji san ni au koto ga dekinai to omotte imasu.

4. 1. Nagakute, omoshiroku arimasen ne.
   2. Yasukute, oishii desu ne.
   3. Muzukashikute, suki ja arimasen ne.
   4. Atama ga yokute, kirei desu ne.
   5. Atsukute, ii tenki desu ne.
   6. Hayakute, yasui desu ne.

5. 1. Tanaka san wa itsumo shigoto no koto o kangaete imasu.
   2. Tsugi no jūgyō wa ni-ji han ni hajimatte, san-ji ni-jup-pun ni owaru to omoimasu.
   3. Sakana ga oishikute, takusan tabemashita.
   4. Sūgaku wa suki ja nai kedo, kagaku wa suki desu.
   5. Densha wa sugu kuru deshō.
   6. Nihon no shinbun o yomu koto ga dekimasu ka.

LESSON 11:

1. 1-T, 2-T, 3-T, 4-F, 5-T, 6-F

2. 1. mō ichido
   2. tsukatta
   3. kekkon
   4. ichiban
   5. nonda
   6. iroiro
   7. taka-sō
   8. shitsumon
   9. setsumei
   10. katta
   11. senshū
      = MAE NO OKUSAN ("ex-wife")

3. 1. Fuji san to Eberesuto to Makkinrii no naka de, dore ga ichiban takai desu ka.
      Eberesuto san ga ichiban takai to omoimasu.
   2. Tōkyō to Rondon to Manira no naka de, dore ga ichiban atsui desu ka.
      Manira ga ichiban atsui to omoimasu.
   3. Eigo to Nihongo to Doitsugo no naka de, dore ga ichiban muzukashii desu ka.
      (free choice) ga ichiban muzukashii to omoimasu.
   4. Sake to biiru to wain no naka de, dore ga ichiban suki desu ka.
      (free choice) ga ichiban suki da to omoimasu.
   5. Eiga to supōtsu to kaimono no naka de, dore ga ichiban tanoshii desu ka.
      (free choice) ga ichiban tanoshii to omoimasu.

6. Aka to shiro to kuro no naka de, dore ga ichiban suki desu ka.
   (free choice) ga ichiban suki da to omoimasu.

4. 1. Dō shite kaigi ga san-ji ni owaranakatta n' desu ka.
   Shitsumon ga takusan atta kara.
   OR Shitsumon ga ōkatta kara.
2. Dō shite shitsumon ga takusan atta n' desu ka.
   Setsumei ga amari yoku nakatta kara.
3. Dō shite setsumei wa amari yoku nakatta n' desu ka.
   Repōto no koto o amari benkyō shinakatta kara.
4. Dō shite repōto no koto o amari benkyō shinakatta n' desu ka.
   Atama ga itakatta kara.
5. Dō shite atama ga itakatta n' desu ka.
   Kinō no ban takusan nonda kara.
6. Dō shite kinō no ban takusan nonda n' desu ka.
   Tomodachi no tanjōbi datta kara.

5. 1. Fukuda san wa san-nen mae ni kekkon shimashita.
2. Takahashi san no bōifurendo wa hansamu de, shinsetsu-sō desu ne.
3. Ichiban suki-na supōtsu wa nan desu ka.
4. Ni-ji han ni denwa shita to omoimasu.
5. Tanaka san wa kesa atama ga itai kara, kaisha ni ikanai to omoimasu.
6. Kuruma wa san-nen mae ni katta kedo, mada atarashi-sō desu.

LESSON 12:

Dialogue 7: 1. Iie, genki ja arimasen. Atama ga itai n' desu.
2. Iie, mada desu.
3. Fumiko chan ga imasu.
4. Okāsan no tanjōbi da kara (ikimasu).

Dialogue 8: 1. Ginza no depāto de kaimono o shite imasu.
2. Sūtsu o mite imasu.
3. Takai kara desu.
4. Iie, suki ja nai to omoimasu.

Dialogue 9:   1. Getsuyōbi desu.
              2. Iie, tomodachi to issho ni ikimashita.
              3. Hazukashikatta kara desu.
              4. Hai, suki da to omoimasu.

Dialogue 10: 1. San-shūkan mae kara Nihon ni imasu.
              2. Hai, dekimasu.
              3. Yakyū no chiimu o yoku kangaete imasu.
              4. Yakyū o suru to omoimasu.

Dialogue 11: 1. Nihon ryōri ya Chūkka ryōri no resutoran de
                 tsukaimasu.
              2. Iie, sō omotte imasen./Iie, jōzu ja nai to omotte
                 imasu.
              3. Ni-nen mae kara Eigo no benkyō o shite imasu.
              4. Iie, rikon shite imasu.

1. ban - yoru, buraun - chairo, chotto - sukoshi, dame - warui,
   hataraku - tsutomeru, heta - jōzu ja nai, jūgyō - kurasu,
   kangaeru - omou, minna de - issho ni, nan-sai - ikutsu, haha - o-
   kāsan, takusan - ōi, hontō - uso ja nai

2. A-6, B-5, C-2, D-4, E-1, F-7, G-3

3. 1-shumi, 2-uso, 3-owaru, 4-kao, 5-au, 6-atta, 7-kesa, 8-neru,
   9-kara, 10-asa, 11-dekita, 12-zenzen, 13-itai, 14-itsu, 15-aoi,
   16-akai, 17-ani, 18-kedo, 19-genki, 20-kangaeru, 21-kau,
   22-dake, 23-takai

4. [country name] desu.
   Senshū no kayobi ni kita n' desu.
   Ashita made desu.
   Tōkyō wa, hito ga ōi desu ne.
   [age]-sai desu.
   Hai, sō desu./Iie, kekkon shite imasu.
   Hai, muzukashii desu./Chotto muzukashii desu.
   Hai, dekimasu./Iie, dekimasen.

5. 1. [day]yōbi desu.
   2. Hai, tokidoki tsukaimasu./Iie, amari tsukaimasen.
   3. [food] desu.
   4. Hai, kekkon shite imasu./Iie, hitori desu./Iie, rikon shite
      imasu.
   5. [place name] ni sunde imasu.

6. Hai, muzukashii to omoimasu./Iie, muzukashiku nai to omoimasu.
7. Hai, mainichi benkyō shimasu./Iie, mainichi benkyō shimasen.
8. [hobby] desu.
9. Hai, dekimasu./Iie, dekimasen.
10. Hai, yoku wakarimasu./Iie, amari wakarimasen.

LESSON 13:

1. 1-T, 2-T, 3-F, 4-F, 5-T, 6-F

2. 1. San-gatsu ni-jū-hachi-nichi ni Kawasaki de tenisu o shimasu.
   2. San-gatsu san-jū-ichi-nichi wa Takahashi san no pātii desu.
   3. Shi-gatsu yokka ni Sū san wa Nihon e kimasu.
   4. Shi-gatsu jū-yokka ni Nihongo no kōsu ga owarimasu.
   5. Shi-gatsu ni-jū-ku-nichi ni "Golden Week" ga hajimarimasu.

3. 1. Akai denwa mo kuroi denwa mo tsukatte mo ii desu.
   2. Ni-ji no kaigi ni denakute mo ii desu.
   3. Yo-ji han ni kaette mo ii desu.
   4. Kono heya de kōhii o nonde mo ii desu.
   5. Neruson san ni Nihongo de hanashite mo ii desu.
   6. Minna no mae de, jiko shōkai o shinakute mo ii desu.

4. Neruson san wa, sumimasen ga, kyō no kaigi wa nan-ji ni hajimaru ka to kikimashita.
   Watashi wa, ni-ji da to kotaemashita.
   Neruson san wa, dono heya ni aru ka to kikimashita.
   Watashi wa, sumimasen ga, wakaranai to kotaemashita.
   Neruson san wa, ā, hiru-gohan no jikan da to iimashita. Obata san mo iku ka to kikimashita.
   Watashi wa, iie, mada ikanai to iimashita.

5. 1. "Kochira koso" o Eigo de nan to iimasu ka.
   2. Tanaka san wa roku-ji made kaisha ni iru to iimashita.
   3. Sonna kotoba o tsukatte wa ikemasen.
   4. Raigetsu no shutchō wa mikka kara nanoka made desu.
   5. Kono tsukue o tsukatte mo ii desu ka.
   6. Iroiro arigatō gozaimashita. Taihen/Totemo tanoshikatta desu.

1. 1-T, 2-T, 3-F, 4-T, 5-F, 6-F

2. Sports: bowling, golf, basketball, ice skating, hiking, surfing, windsurfing
   Countries: Ireland, Australia, India, New Zealand, Brazil, Italy, Austria

3. 1. Osoi kara, takushii de kaetta hō ga ii desu.
   2. Mō sugu kaetta hō ga ii desu.
   3. Supagetti ya piza tōsuto o tabeta hō ga ii desu.
   4. Atarashii no o katta hō ga ii desu.
   5. Rikon shita hō ga ii desu.
   6. Chokorēto o sonna ni takusan tabenai hō ga ii desu.

4. 1. Kinō, shinbun ga tēburu no ue ni atta kedo, ima wa tsukue no shita ni arimasu.
   2. Kinō, ranpu ga tsukue no tonari/soba ni atta kedo, ima wa tsukue no ue ni arimasu.
   3. Kinō, rajio ga wāpuro to hon no aida ni atta kedo, ima wa tēburu no ue ni arimasu.
   4. Kinō, sūtsukēsu ga tēburu no mae ni atta kedo, ima wa tēburu no ushiro ni arimasu.
   5. Kinō tenki ga yokatta kedo, kyō wa warui desu.
   6. Kinō, kāten ga nakatta kedo, kyō wa arimasu.

5. 1. Hotto futatsu, hambāgā hitotsu to supagetti o hitotsu kudasai.
   2. Atama ga itai kara, uchi ni ite, terebi o mita hō ga ii to omoimasu.
   3. Kono eiga ga omoshiro-sō desu ne. Konban mi ni ikimashō ka.
   4. Yūbinkyoku no tonari no ōkii uchi ni, dare ga sunde imasu ka.
   5. Wada san ni denwa shinai hō ga ii to omoimasu ka.
   6. Watanabe san wa, gakkō no naka ni tsukue ga zenbu de ikutsu aru ka to kikimashita.

1. 1-F, 2-T, 3-T, 4-T, 5-F, 6-T

2. 1. Takahashi san wa natsu yasumi no koto ni tsuite hanashitai n' desu ga, Kenji san wa hanashitaku arimasen.
   2. Takahashi san mo Kenji san mo Itaria ryōri no resutoran de tabetai n' desu.
   3. Takahashi san wa nichiyōbi ni umi e ikitai n' desu ga, Kenji san wa ikitaku arimasen.
   4. Takahashi san wa Eigo no kurasu ni hairitai n' desu ga, Kenji san wa hairitaku arimasen.
   5. Takahashi san wa konban eiga o mitaku arimasen ga, Kenji san wa mitai n' desu.
   6. Takahashi san wa rainen kekkon shitai n' desu ga, Kenji san wa kekkon shitaku arimasen.

3. 1. Kono heya de sando o tabenaide kudasai.
   2. Denwa de bōifurendo to hanasanaide kudasai.
   3. Sono purintā o tsukawanaide kudasai.
   4. Sensei no wāpuro de repōto o kakanaide kudasai.
   5. Tsukue de shinbun o yomanaide kudasai.
   6. Gakkō no naka de, "Walkman" o kikanaide kudasai.

4. 1. Nanoka no gogo, kōchō sensei to uchiawase o suru yotei desu.
   2. Kokonoka no asa, kyōiku iinkai no kaigi ni deru yotei desu.
   3. Jū-ichi-nichi no yoru, gakkō no sutaffu to bōringu ni iku (OR o suru) yotei desu.
   4. Jū-yokka no asa, kōchō sensei ni repōto o dasu yotei desu.
   5. Jū-go-nichi no gogo, Sū san ni denwa shite, natsu yasumi ni tsuite sōdan suru yotei desu.
   6. Jū-hachi-nichi no asa, Tōkyō ni itte, atarashii sūtsu o kau yotei desu.

5. 1. Watashi no kyūryō ni tsuite shitsumon shite mo ii desu ka.
   2. Kayōbi no gogo wa aite imasu ka.
   3. Kotoshi no natsu, atarashii kuruma o kau tsumori desu.
   4. Tonari no heya de kaigi ga aru kara, hairanaide kudasai.
   5. O-naka ga suita kara, takusan tabetai n' desu!
   6. Rainen no haru (ni), kazoku to issho ni Amerika e iku yotei desu.

Dialogue 13: 1. Hai, ikitai to omoimasu.
2. "Spring equinox" to iimasu.
3. Hiro kun wa mada wakai kara desu. OR Hirokun wa mada jū-san sai dakara desu.
4. Maiku san wa konban kite iru kara desu.
Dialogue 14: 1. Takahashi san ga chūmon o shimasu.
2. Kōshū denwa ga arimasu.
3. Iie, kyō Kenji san to hanashitaku nai n' desu.
4. Gakkō no sutaffu to issho ni eiga o mi ni ikimasu.

Dialogue 15: 1. Kōchō sensei ga yoku wakarimasu.
2. Iie, ichi-nichi yasumi dake toritai n' desu.
3. Kore kara no keikaku ni tsuite hanasu yotei desu.
4. Saitō san wa ima kōchō sensei no sukejūru o motte iru kara desu.

1. 1. itsu (the others are all numbers)
2. shunbun (the others are all seasons)
3. wain (the others are all foods)
4. toki (the others all refer to parts of the day)
5. shisha (the others all show location)
6. onna (the others are all personal pronouns)
7. anna (the others are all question words)
8. shutchō (the others are all people)

2. 1. Maiku san wa ashita no asa yakyū o suru yotei desu. (rainen)
2. Konban takusan nomanai hō ga ii to omoimasu. (dekiru)
3. Kotoshi no natsu gaikoku e ikitai to omoimasu. (tsuite)
4. Shitsumon o kiite mo ii desu ka. (dare)
5. Konna ni muzukashii to omoimasen deshita. (nakatta)
6. Takahashi san ni kyūryō no koto ni tsuite hanasanaide kudasai. (tsumori)

3. Moshi moshi, [your name] desu.
Keiyaku ni tsuite desu ga.
Kyō no gogo wa aite imasu ka.
Asa jū-ji kara kaigi ni deru yotei desu.
Hai, gogo wa aite imasu.
Hai, ni-ji ni shimashō.

4. Across: 1-shita, 5-mo, 7-tsuite, 9-tonari, 10-sonna, 12-gatsu, 13-ikemasen
   Down: 2-ikitai, 3-aki, 4-motto, 6-futatsu, 8-aida, 9-tegami, 11-natsu

5. 1. Hai, dekimasu./Iie, dekimasen. Hai, jōzu desu./Iie, amari jōzu ja arimasen.
   2. Tanjōbi wa __-gatsu ___-nichi desu.
   3. Hai, takusan arimasu./Iie, sonna ni takusan arimasen.
   4. ___ ga suki desu./Supōtsu ga suki ja arimasen.
   5. Hai, totte mo ii desu./Iie, totte wa ikemasen.
   6. ____-sai desu.
   7. ___-ji made okite imashita.
   8. Ichiban atsui toki wa ___-gatsu desu.
   9. Hai, kekkon shite imasu./Iie, kekkon shite imasen./Iie, rikon shite imasu. Hai, imasu./Iie, imasen.
   10. Hai, yoku okorimasu./Iie, amari okorimasen.
   11. _____ [number] arimasu.
   12. Hai, _____ e iku yotei ga arimasu./Iie, arimasen.

LESSON 17:

1. 1-T, 2-T, 3-F, 4-F, 5-T, 6-T

2. 1. Wada san wa kuruma o motta koto ga arimasu ga, Saitō san wa arimasen.
   2. Wada san mo Saitō san mo Fuji san ni nobotta koto ga arimasu.
   3. Wada san wa Tōkyō ni sunda koto ga arimasen ga, Saitō san wa arimasu.
   4. Wada san mo Saitō san mo Hokkaidō e itta koto ga arimasen.
   5. Wada san wa Watanabe san no okusan ni atta koto ga arimasu ga, Saitō san wa arimasen.
   6. Wada san mo Saitō san mo bideo o totta koto ga arimasu.

3. 1-b, 2-a, 3-a, 4-b, 5-b, 6-a

4. 1. Amazon to Nairu to, dochira (no hō) ga nagai desu ka. Amazon (no ho) ga nagai desu.
   2. Fuji san to Makkinrii to, dochira (no hō) ga takai desu ka. Makkinri (no hō) ga takai desu.

3. Honkon to Taiwan to, Nihon kara dochira (no hō) ga tōi desu ka.
   Honkon (no hō) ga tōi desu.
4. Nihon to Firipin to, dochira (no hō) ga hiroi desu ka.
   Nihon (no hō) ga hiroi desu.
5. Tōkyō to Nyū Yōku to, dochira (no hō) ga hito ga ōi desu ka.
   Tōkyō (no hō) ga hito ga ōi desu.
6. Yama to umi to, dochira (no hō) ga suki desu ka.
7. Denwa to fakkusu to, dochira (no hō) o yoku tsukaimasu ka.
8. Mekishiko ryōri to Chūka ryōri to, dochira (no hō) o yoku tabemasu ka.
9. Benkyō to shigoto to, dochira (no hō) ga suki desu ka.
10. Shinbun to hon to, dochira (no hō) o yoku yomimasu ka.
   (Free answers)

5. 1. Ame ga furanakattara, nichiyōbi ni dokoka e ikimashō ka.
   2. Sono resutoran de tabeta koto ga arimasu ka.
   3. Natsu to fuyu to, dochira (no hō) ga suki desu ka.
   4. O-naka ga itai kara, nani mo tabetaku arimasen.
   5. Dandan atatakaku natte imasu ne. Mo sorosoro haru deshō.
   6. Jikan ga attara, Fukuda san ni denwa shite, kaigi no jikan o oshiete kudasai.

LESSON 18:

1. 1-F, 2-T, 3-T, 4-F, 5-T, 6-F

2. Denki-dai o haratte kara, chichi no tanjōbi no purezento o kau tame ni depāto e ikimasu.
   Chichi no tanjōbi no purezento o katte kara, kissaten de Itō san ni aimasu.
   Itō san ni atte kara, eiga o mi ni ikimasu.
   Eiga o mite kara, Kyōto made no Shinkansen no kippu o kaimasu.
   Shinkansen no kippu o katte kara, uchi e kaerimasu.
   Uchi e kaette kara, Sūzan san ni tegami o kakimasu.
   Tegami o kaite kara, Nihongo o benkyō shimasu.
   Nihongo o benkyō shite kara, Katō san to issho ni nomi ni ikimasu.
   Shinkansen no kippu o kau mae ni, eiga o mi ni ikimashita.

Eiga o mi ni iku mae ni, kissaten de Itō san ni aimashita.
Itō san ni au mae ni, chichi no tanjōbi no purezento o kau tame
ni depāto e ikimashita.
Chichi no tanjōbi no purezento o kau mae ni, denki-dai o harau
tame ni ginkō e ikimashita.
Ginkō e iku mae ni, Kawasaki de tenisu o shimashita.

3. Kono kozutsumi o Igirisu made okuritai n' desu ga, ikura
   deshō ka. Kōkūbin de.
   Sore kara, Ōsutoraria made no hagaki wa ikura desu ka.
   Hyaku-go-jū en kitte o san-mai kudasai.
   Kono tegami wa ikura desu ka.
   Amerika desu.

4. 1-g, 2-b, 3-i, 4-a, 5-h, 6-f, 7-d

5. 1. Ashita kabuki no kippu o kau tame ni Tōkyō e ikimasu.
   2. (Moshi) wakaranakereba, Saitō san ni kiite kudasai.
   3. Dekakeru mae ni, ranchi o tabemashō.
   4. Jikan ga jūbun nakereba, konakute mo ii desu.
   5. Kono kozutsumi o kōkūbin de okurimasu ka.
   6. Takeda san wa shigoto o yametai to iimashita.

LESSON 19:

1. 1-T, 2-F, 3-F, 4-T, 5-T, 6-F

2. Apāto o sōji shinakereba narimasen.
   Denwa-dai o harawanakereba narimasen.
   Kabuki no kippu o ni-mai kawanakereba narimasen.
   Atarashii yōfuku o kawanakereba narimasen.
   Shirazawa ryōkan ni denwa shinakereba narimasen.
   Narita kūkō e no densha no jikan o shirabenakereba narimasen.

3. Free answers.

4. 1. Asa-gohan o tabete ita toki, sono nyūsu o kikimashita.
   2. Terebi o mite ita toki, atama wa itaku narimashita.
   3. Ginkō ni tsutomete ita toki, kanai ni hajimete atta n' desu.
      OR Ginkō de hataraite ita toki, ...
   4. Densha ga konde iru toki, takushii ni norimasu.
   5. Watashi ga sōji o shite ita toki, Watanabe san ga uchi ni
      yorimashita.

6. Eki no mae de atta toki, kare to sono koto ni tsuite hanashimashita.

5. 1. Minna jibun no kippu o kawanakereba narimasen.
2. Tōkyō kara Ōsaka made no kippu wa ichi-man san-zen go-hyaku en gurai desu.
3. Kare wa hayaku hanasu kara, yoku wakarimasen.
4. Shinkansen ni notte, yokatta desu.
5. Rondon to ieba, Wada san wa itta koto ga arimasu ka.
6. Kyonen Nihon ni ita toki, Fuji san ni noborimashita.

LESSON 20:

Dialogue 17: 1. Yo-nin ga ikimasu.
2. Densha de ikimasu.
3. Kaidan no ue ni suwarimasu.
4. Daibutsu no naka ni hairu tsumori desu.

Dialogue 18: 1. Iroiro-na yōji ga arimasu kara.
2. Gasu-dai to denki-dai o harau tame ni ikimasu.
3. Yōshi ni kakikomanakereba narimasen.
4. Hai, konde imasu.

Dialogue 19: 1. Densha no naka ni imasu.
2. Kodomo ga san-nin iru kara.
3. Shiteiseki no kippu o kaimashita.
4. Biiru ni-hon to kōra yon-hon o kaimashita.

1. 1-ichi-mai, 2-hayaku, 3-denki-dai, 4-dō shite, 5-tōi, 6-keiyaku

2. 1. san-man roku-sen go-hyaku en
2. kitte go-mai/go-mai no kitte
3. biiru nana-hon/nana-hon no biiru
4. rok-kagetsu
5. jū-ni-ji yon-jū-go-fun
6. hachi-gatsu tōka

3. 1. Shikata ga arimasen.
2. Ii kagen ni shi nasai.
3. Hajimemashite.
4. Itadakimasu.
5. Kanpai.
6. O-jama shimasu/shimashita.

7. O-yasumi nasai.
8. Abunai.
9. Ki o tsukete kudasai.
10. Sore wa zannen desu.

4. 1-hon, 2-nobotta, 3-akaku, 4-kippu, 5-narimasen, 6-kibun, 7-dake, 8-byōki [=Hokkaidō]

5. 1-c, 2-f, 3-g, 4-b, 5-h, 6-a, 7-e, 8-d

6. 1. Hai, arimasu/Iie, arimasen.
   2. [placename] ni sunde imashita.
   3. ____ o kaitai n' desu.
   4. ____ no hō ga muzukashii to omoimasu.
   5. ____-gatsu ni samuku narimasu.
   6. ____ -nakereba narimasen.
   7. ____-mai motte imasu.
   8. Is-shūkan ni ___-kai gurai Nihongo no benkyō o shimasu.

VERBS

This is a list of all verbs which have appeared in *Essential Japanese*, showing the -**masu** form and the -**te** form.

Dictionary form	-**masu** form	-**te** form	Meaning
agaru	agarimasu	agatte	go/come up
aku	akimasu	aite	be open, free
aru	arimasu	atte	be, exist, have
aruku	arukimasu	aruite	walk
au	aimasu	atte	meet
azukaru	azukarimasu	azukatte	receive, be entrusted with
chigau	chigaimasu	chigatte	differ, be mistaken
dasu	dashimasu	dashite	put out, send, submit
dekakeru	dekakemasu	dekakete	go out
dekiru	dekimasu	dekite	can, be able to
deru	demasu	dete	go out, appear
furu	furimasu	futte	fall, drop
ganbaru	ganbarimasu	ganbatte	try hard, do one's best
hairu	hairimasu	haitte	go in, enter
hajimaru	hajimarimasu	hajimatte	begin
hanasu	hanashimasu	hanashite	speak, talk
harau	haraimasu	haratte	pay
hashiru	hashirimasu	hashitte	run
hataraku	hatarakimasu	hataraite	work, labor
iku	ikimasu	itte	go
irassharu	irasshaimasu	irasshatte	be [formal]
iru	imasu	ite	be, exist
itadaku	itadakimasu	itadaite	receive
iu	iimasu	itte	say, relate
kaeru	kaerimasu	kaette	return, go/come home
kakaru	kakarimasu	kakatte	take (time), last
kakikomu	kakikomimasu	kakikonde	fill in/out (a form)
kaku	kakimasu	kaite	write

kangaeru	kangaemasu	kangaete	think about, consider
kau	kaimasu	katte	buy
ki o tsukeru	ki o tsukemasu	ki o tsukete	take care
kiku	kikimasu	kiite	hear, ask
kimeru	kimemasu	kimete	decide
komu	komimasu	konde	be crowded
kotaeru	kotaemasu	kotaete	answer, reply
kuru	kimasu	kite	come
magaru	magarimasu	magatte	turn
matsu	machimasu	matte	wait
miru	mimasu	mite	see, watch
miseru	misemasu	misete	show
mōsu	mōshimasu	mōshite	be called, named
narabu	narabimasu	narande	line up, queue
naru	narimasu	natte	become, get
neru	nemasu	nete	sleep, go to bed
noboru	noborimasu	nobotte	climb, go up
nomu	nomimasu	nonde	drink
noru	norimasu	notte	get in/on, ride
oboeru	oboemasu	oboete	remember, recall
okiru	okimasu	okite	get up
okoru	okorimasu	okotte	get angry
okuru	okurimasu	okutte	send
omou	omoimasu	omotte	think
oshieru	oshiemasu	oshiete	teach, tell
owaru	owarimasu	owatte	end, finish
shiraberu	shirabemasu	shirabete	investigate, look into
suku	sukimasu	suite	become empty
sumu	sumimasu	sunde	live, reside
suru	shimasu	shite	do
suwaru	suwarimasu	suwatte	sit down
taberu	tabemasu	tabete	eat
tatsu	tachimasu	tatte	stand up
tomaru	tomarimasu	tomatte	stay over
tomeru	tomemasu	tomete	stop, halt
toru	torimasu	totte	take
tsukareru	tsukaremasu	tsukarete	become tired
tsukau	tsukaimasu	tsukatte	use
tsutomeru	tsutomemasu	tsutomete	be employed
uru	urimasu	utte	sell
wakaru	wakarimasu	wakatte	understand
wasureru	wasuremasu	wasurete	forget

APPENDIX 1

yameru	yamemasu	yamete	quit, stop
yaru	yarimasu	yatte	do, try
yobu	yobimasu	yonde	call, summon
yomu	yomimasu	yonde	read
yoru	yorimasu	yotte	call in, drop by

THE JAPANESE WRITING SYSTEM

As we explained in the Introduction, written Japanese is made up of three quite different writing systems, **kanji, hiragana** and **katakana** characters, which are used in combination.

As there is not enough space in this book to teach the written language, we have instead used what is commonly known as the modified Hepburn system, which is the most widely used way of writing Japanese in the Roman alphabet.

Kanji characters were developed in China over three thousand years ago, and were first introduced into Japan in the third century. Where the letters of our Roman alphabet represent sounds, kanji represent meanings. Each kanji is rather like a picture or symbol, representing just one thing or idea, so it follows that thousands and thousands of individual kanji must be learned in order to be able to read a newspaper, or write a letter. In everday life it is necessary to know around three thousand different kanji, although specialists need to know far more for their particular field.

An added complication of kanji characters is that they may be pronounced in several completely different ways, depending on which other characters they are combined with in compound words. For example, the kanji character for "east," when by itself, is pronounced **higashi,** and the character for "capital city" is pronounced **kei,** but when the two are combined in a compound word meaning "eastern capital," they are pronounced **tō** and **kyō** – Tokyo. Some examples of kanji characters and the way they are pronounced have been given in each lesson.

In addition to kanji, there are two sets of phonetic characters, **hiragana** and **katakana.** These are two separate ways of representing the same sounds. There are 46 characters in each set, and apart from the five vowels and a single "n" sound, all the rest represent syllables made up of a consonant and a vowel. In other words, there is no character for the sound "k," but there *are* characters for the sounds **ka, ki, ku, ke** and **ko.** When you say Japanese words slowly, you will see that most of them can be split easily into syllables, and each of these would be written with one hiragana or katakana character. For example **hi-ra-ga-na** would be written with four characters, **ki-mo-no** with three, and **su-shi** with two.

Hiragana characters are used in a number of ways. They are joined to the end of words written in kanji to indicate grammatical function, such as different verb endings to show past or present tense. Hiragana characters are also used for small words such as those meaning "in," "at," "to," which do not have kanji equivalents, and for words whose kanji characters are very complex, or which have become obsolete over the years.

Katakana characters represent exactly the same sounds as hiragana, so in principle all words can be written in katakana, but in fact they are used in much the same way as we use italics, that is, to show stress, and to write foreign words which have been imported into Japanese. There are a great number of such words, mostly taken from American English, and it is easy to recognize them in written form as they are always written in katakana. Hiragana are cursive and flowing characters, whereas katakana tend to be squarer, with more straight lines and corners.

The complete set of hiragana and katakana characters are shown in the table overleaf.

Here is an example of how kanji, hiragana and katakana are used together in a sentence. The sentence means "Mike's school is in Yokohama."

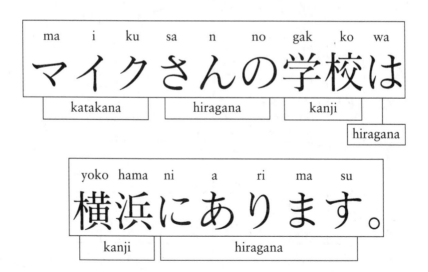

Hiragana					Katakana				
あ a	い i	う u	え e	お o	ア a	イ i	ウ u	エ e	オ o
か ka	き ki	く ku	け ke	こ ko	カ ka	キ ki	ク ku	ケ ke	コ ko
さ sa	し shi	す su	せ se	そ so	サ sa	シ shi	ス su	セ se	ソ so
た ta	ち chi	つ tsu	て te	と to	タ ta	チ chi	ツ tsu	テ te	ト to
な na	に ni	ぬ nu	ね ne	の no	ナ na	ニ ni	ヌ nu	ネ ne	ノ no
は ha	ひ hi	ふ fu	へ he	ほ ho	ハ ha	ヒ hi	フ fu	ヘ he	ホ ho
ま ma	み mi	む mu	め me	も mo	マ ma	ミ mi	ム mu	メ me	モ mo
や ya		ゆ yu		よ yo	ヤ ya		ユ yu		ヨ yo
ら ra	り ri	る ru	れ re	ろ ro	ラ ra	リ ri	ル ru	レ re	ロ ro
わ wa				を o	ワ wa				ヲ o
ん n					ン n				

about, approximately: **gurai** (19)
above, on: **ue** (14)
academy, school: **gakuin** (1)
address: **jūsho** (5)
after: **ato** (15); **kara** (18)
afternoon: **gogo** (7)
again, once more: **mata** (4)
ahead, before: **saki ni** (17)
air conditioner: **eakon** (14)
airmail: **kōkūbin** (18)
airport: **kūkō** (15)
all: **zenbu** (10)
all day long: **ichi-nichi-jū** (19)
all kinds of: **iroiro(-na)** (11)
already, (not) any longer: **mō** (5)
always: **itsumo** (8)
amazing, incredible: **sugoi** (17)
American person: **Amerikajin** (1)
among, within: **naka** (11)
and: **to** (1); **ya** (10)
answer, respond: **kotaeru** (13)
answer, response: **kotae** (10)
apartment: **apāto** (14)
April: **shi-gatsu** (13)
argument: **kenka** (14)
as far as: **made** (5)
at: **ni** [with time] (4)
at, in: **de** [place where action occurs] (5)
attend a meeting: **kaigi ni deru** (13)
August: **hachi-gatsu** (13)
Australia: **Ōsutoraria** (14)
Austria: **Ōsutoria** (14)
autumn/fall: **aki** (13)
Autumnal Equinox Day: **shūbun no hi** (13)
bad, wrong: **warui** (7)
bank: **ginkō** (2)
baseball: **yakyū** (7)
basketball: **basukettobōru** (10)

be, exist: **aru** [inanimate objects] (2); **iru** [animate objects] (4)
be called, named: **mōsu** (10)
be crowded: **komu** (8)
be employed: **tsutomeru** (10)
be excited: **kōfun suru** (19)
be incorrect, wrong: **chigau** (1)
be married: **kekkon suru** (11)
be open, free, have no engagements: **aku** (15)
because: **kara** (11)
become, get: **naru** (17)
become empty: **suku** (14)
become hungry: **o-naka ga suku** (14)
become tired: **tsukareru** (9)
bed: **beddo** (14)
beer: **biiru** (9)
before, in front of: **mae** (7)
behave yourselves: **ii kagen ni shi nasai** (19)
behind, in back of: **ushiro** (14)
below, under: **shita** (14)
belt: **beruto** (8)
between: **aida** (14)
big: **ōkii** (2)
birthday: **tanjōbi** (7)
black: **kuro(i)** (8)
blue: **burū** (8)
blue-green: **ao(i)** (8)
bon appetit: **itadakimasu** (3)
book: **hon** (5)
both - and -: **- mo - mo** (9)
bowling: **bōringu** (14)
boyfriend: **bōifurendo** (10)
branch office: **shisha** (14)
Brazil: **Burajiru** (14)
brief, simple: **kantan(-na)** (8)
bring: **motte kuru** (19)
brown: **buraun** (8); **chaiiro** (8)
building: **tatemono** (5)
Bullet Train: **Shinkansen** (11)
bus: **basu** (10)
business card: **meishi** (1)
business trip: **shutchō** (13)
busy: **isogashii** (13)
but: **ga** (1)
but, although: **kedo** (9)

buy: **kau** (8)
by: **de** [means by which something is done] (4); **made ni** [date or time] (15)
by the way: **tokorode** (5)
cake: **kēki** (14)
call, summon: **yobu** (7)
call in, drop by: **yoru** (15)
can, be able to: **dekiru** (10)
Canada: **Kanada** (1)
Canadian person: **Kanadajin** (1)
can't be helped: **shikata ga arimasen** (17)
car: **kuruma** (1)
carpet: **kāpetto** (14)
CD, compact disc: **shii dii** (14)
certainly, very good: **kashikomarimashita** [formal] (14)
chance, opportunity: **chansu** (9)
change [money]: **o-tsuri** (5)
cheap: **yasui** (7)
cheese: **chiizu** (17)
child: **kodomo** (8)
children: **kodomotachi** (11)
Children's Day: **kodomo no hi** (13)
Chinese cuisine: **Chūka ryōri** (11)
Chinese written characters: **kanji** (9)
chocolate: **chokorēto** (14)
chopsticks: **hashi** (4)
city, town: **machi** (9)
class: **kurasu** (9)
clerk, office worker: **jimu no hito** (2)
climb, go up: **noboru** (17)
close, nearby: **chikai** (17)
clothes: **yōfuku** (19)
coat: **kōto** (8)
coffee shop: **kissaten** (9)
cola: **kōra** (14)
cold: **samui** (7)
come: **kuru** (3)
Coming-of-Age Day: **seijin no hi** (13)
committee: **iinkai** (15)
company, office: **kaisha** (1)
computer: **konpyūtā** (2)
concerning, regarding: **ni tsuite** (15)
Constitution Day: **kenpō kinenbi** (13)
consult, talk over: **sōdan suru** (15)

contract: **keiyaku** (15)
conversation: **kaiwa** (14)
conversation, chat: **hanashi** (4)
cooking, cuisine: **ryōri** (10)
cool: **suzushii** (17)
corner: **kado** (5)
could I speak to -?: **-san onegai shimasu** (4)
country: **kuni** (10)
course [of study]: **kōsu** (13)
Culture Day: **bunka no hi** (13)
curtain: **kāten** (14)
cushion: **kusshon** (14)
dangerous: **abunai** (19)
dark: **kurai** (17)
date [of the month]: **-nichi** (13)
day: **hi** (13)
day after tomorrow: **asatte** (3)
day off, vacation: **yasumi no hi** (13)
daytime: **hiruma** (13)
December: **jū-ni-gatsu** (13)
decide: **kimeru** (15)
definitely, without fail: **kitto** (17)
department head: **buchō** (15)
department store: **depāto** (8)
design: **dezain** (8)
designer: **dezainā** (8)
desk: **tsukue** (2)
dictionary: **jisho** (18)
difficult: **muzukashii** (7)
direction, side: **hō** (17)
dirty: **kitanai** (14)
dislike: **kirai(-na)** (3)
divorce: **rikon** (11)
do: **suru** (3); **yaru** (19)
do the cleaning: **sōji suru** (19)
dog: **inu** (4)
dollars: **doru** (5)
dress [noun]: **wanpiisu** (8)
drink [verb]: **nomu** (3)
early: **hayai** (7)
eat: **taberu** (3)
education: **kyōiku** (15)
egg: **tamago** (18)
eight: **hachi** (4)

eight (objects): **yattsu** (14)
electricity: **denki** (18)
electricity charges: **denki-dai** (18)
eleven: **jū-ichi** (4)
embarrassed, shy: **hazukashii** (9)
Emperor's Birthday: **tennō tanjōbi** (13)
engineer: **enjinia** (1)
England, Great Britain: **Igirisu** (2)
English conversation: **Eikaiwa** (18)
English language: **Eigo** (3)
English/British person: **Igirisujin** (2)
enjoyable, fun: **tanoshii** (9)
enough, sufficient: **jūbun** (18)
entrance area [in a house]: **genkan** (5)
envelope: **fūtō** (18)
errand, chore: **yōji** (18)
et cetera, and so on: **nado** (10)
Europe: **Yōroppa** (13)
evening: **yoru** (9), **ban** (11)
every day: **mainichi** (3)
everyone: **mina san, minna** (2)
everyone together: **minna de** (7)
exactly, precisely: **chōdo** (11)
excuse me, I beg your pardon: **gomen nasai** (13)
excuse me for disturbing you: **o-jama shimasu** (5)
excuse me, goodbye: **shitsurei shimasu** (2)
expensive: **takai** (7)
explain: **setsumei suru** (11)
explanation: **setsumei** (11)
face: **kao** (10)
fall, drop: **furu** (17)
family: **kazoku** (7)
family (your): **go-kazoku** (7)
family computer: **famikon** (14)
famous: **yūmei(-na)** (8)
far, distant: **tōi** (17)
father (my): **chichi** (7)
father (your): **o-tōsan** (7)
fax: **fakkusu** (8)
February: **ni-gatsu** (13)
females, women: **jōsei** (11)
fill in/out [a form]: **kakikomu** (18)
finally, at the end: **saigo ni** (18)
fine, all right: **daijōbu(-na)** (8)

finish, end [verb]: **owaru** (10)
first of all, to begin with: **mazu** (18)
first time: **hajimete** (15)
fish: **sakana** (3)
five: **go** (4)
five (objects): **itsutsu** (14)
floppy disk: **furoppi** (14)
flower: **hana** (3)
food: **tabemono** (10)
foreign country, abroad: **gaikoku** (15)
foreigner: **gaijin** (4)
forget: **wasureru** (9)
form, a blank: **yōshi** (15)
four: **shi/yo/yon** (4)
four (objects): **yottsu** (14)
France: **Furansu** (10)
French language: **Furansugo** (10)
frequently occurring: **yoku aru** (11)
Friday: **kinyōbi** (9)
friend: **tomodachi** (3)
from: **kara** (2)
game: **gēmu** (10)
gas: **gasu** (18)
gas charges: **gasu-dai** (18)
German language: **Doitsugo** (10)
get angry: **okoru** (14)
get up, get out of bed: **okiru** (13)
girlfriend: **gārufurendo** (11)
go: **iku** (3)
go in, enter: **hairu** (9)
go out: **dekakeru** (18)
go out, appear: **deru** (13)
go skiing: **sukii ni iku** (13)
go to meet: **mukae ni iku** (15)
go up: **agaru** (5)
golf: **gorufu** (9)
good, fine: **ii** (3)
good evening: **konbanwa** (2)
good morning: **ohayō gozaimasu** (2)
good night: **oyasumi nasai** (2)
gradually, little by little: **dandan** (17)
gray: **gurē** (8)
green: **guriin, midori** (8)
green tea: **o-cha** (3)

Greenery Day: **midori no hi** (13)
grilled fish: **yaki-zakana** (3)
guest, customer: **kyaku, o-kyaku san** (14)
half past -: **-han** (4)
ham: **hamu** (14)
hamburger: **hanbāgā** (14)
handsome: **hansamu(-na)**: (11)
happen, be completed: **dekiru** (15)
happy: **ureshii** (11)
happy to meet you: **dōzo yoroshiku** (2)
hate, loathe: **dai-kirai(-na)** (3)
have: **gozaimasu** [formal] (8)
have, hold: **motsu** (15)
have a headache: **atama ga itai** (7)
have a talk, chat: **hanashi o suru** (4)
have you ever ...?: **koto ga arimasu ka** (17)
he, him: **kare** (14)
head: **atama** (7)
healthy, energetic: **genki(-na)** (8)
hear, listen, ask: **kiku** (3)
hello: **konnichiwa** (2); [on the telephone] **moshi moshi** (4)
her, she: **kanojo** (15)
here: **koko** (2)
high: **takai** (7)
high school: **kōkō** [short for **kōtō gakkō**] (1)
hiking: **haikingu** (14)
him, he: **kare** (14)
history: **rekishi** (10)
hobby: **shumi** (10)
homework: **shukudai** (7)
horrible: **iya(-na)** (8)
hot: **atsui** (7)
hot and humid: **mushiatsui** (17)
hot coffee: **hotto (kōhii)** (14)
hot spring: **onsen** (9)
hotel: **hoteru** (8)
hour: **jikan** (9)
house, home: **uchi** (2)
how?: **dō** (3)
how about -?: **dō desu ka** (3)
how are you?: **o-genki desu ka** (8)
how do you do?: **hajimemashite** (1)
how many?: **ikutsu** (14)
how many people?: **nan-nin** (9)

how much (money)?: **ikura** (5)
how old?: **ikutsu, nan-sai** (11)
however, but: **demo** (4)
hundred: **hyaku** (5)
hundred million: **oku** (19)
husband (my): **otto/shujin** (7)
husband (your): **go-shujin** (7)
I, me: **watashi** (1); **boku** [used by boys and men] (11)
ice skating: **aisu skēto** (14)
ill: **byōki(-na)** (17)
in, at [location]: **ni** (2)
in fact: **jitsu wa** (11)
India: **Indo** (14)
inside: **naka** (14)
inside the train: **shanai** (19)
intention: **tsumori** (15)
interest, hobby: **shumi** (10)
interesting, amusing: **omoshiroi** (9)
interference, obstruction: **jama** (5)
introduce: **shōkai suru** (10)
investigate, look into: **shiraberu** (19)
Ireland: **Airurando** (14)
iron: **airon** (14)
is/are: **desu** (1); **aru** [inanimate objects] (2); **iru** [animate objects] (4);
    irassharu [polite form of **iru**] (4); **de gozaimasu** [formal] (8)
isn't/aren't: **ja arimasen** (2)
Italy: **Itaria** (14)
jacket: **jaketto** (8)
January: **ichi-gatsu** (13)
Japan: **Nihon** (1)
Japan Alps: **Nihon Arupusu** (9)
Japanese language: **Nihongo** (1)
Japanese-style inn: **ryokan** (9)
jeans: **G-pan** (8)
July: **shichi-gatsu** (13)
June: **roku-gatsu** (13)
just, only: **tada** (15)
keyboard: **kiibōdo** (14)
kind, gentle: **shinsetsu(-na)** (8)
Labor Thanksgiving Day: **kinrō kansha no hi** (13)
lamp: **ranpu** (14)
large [in area], spacious: **hiroi** (17)
last month: **sengetsu** (13)
last week: **senshū** (9)

last year: **kyonen** (15)
late: **osoi** (7)
left (side): **hidari** (5)
left-hand side: **hidari-gawa** (5)
leg, foot: **ashi** (19)
lemon tea: **remon tii** (14)
lesson, class: **jūgyō** (10)
lesson one: **dai ik-ka** (1)
letter: **tegami** (13)
lie, untruth, story: **uso** (10)
life, living: **seikatsu** (10)
like: **suki(-na)** (3)
like very much, love: **dai-suki(-na)** (3)
line up, queue: **narabu** (17)
little, a bit: **sukoshi** (5), **chotto** (7)
lonely: **sabishii** (11)
long: **nagai** (10)
look forward to: **tanoshimi ni suru** (19)
look out!: **abunai!** (19)
luggage: **nimotsu** (19)
lunch: **hiru-gohan** (7), **ranchi** (18)
make: **tsukuru** (18)
males, men: **dansei** (11)
man: **otoko no hito** (9)
manager: **manejā** (10)
many, abundant: **ōi** (11)
many, much: **takusan** (4)
March: **san-gatsu** (13)
marriage: **kekkon** (11)
mathematics: **sūgaku** (10)
May: **go-gatsu** (13)
meet: **au** (4.)
meeting: **kaigi** (3)
meeting, consultation: **uchiawase** (15)
memo: **memo** (15)
menu: **menyū** (14)
message: **messēji** (15)
minute: **-fun/pun** (4)
miso soup: **miso shiru** (3)
Monday: **getsuyōbi** (9)
money: **o-kane** (15)
monitor: **monitā** (14)
mood, feeling: **kibun** (17)
more: **motto** (8)

morning: **asa** (9)
most, -est: **ichiban** (11)
mother (my): **haha** (7)
mother (your): **o-kāsan** (7)
Mount Fuji: **Fuji san** (11)
mountain: **yama** (9)
movie, film: **eiga** (3)
Mr., Mrs., Ms., Miss: **san** (1); **sama** [very polite] (4)
music: **ongaku** (19)
my: **watashi no** (1)
name: **namae** (1)
National Foundation Day: **kenkoku kinenbi** (13)
near, close [adverb]: **chikaku** (14)
near, next to: **soba** (14)
necktie: **nekutai** (8)
neither - nor -: **- mo - mo** (9)
never: **zenzen** (8)
new: **atarashii** (2)
New Year's Day: **ganjitsu** (13)
New Zealand: **Nyū Jiirando** (14)
news: **nyūsu** (4)
newspaper: **shinbun** (2)
next: **tsugi no** (5)
next month: **raigetsu** (13)
next to, by the side: **tonari** (7)
next week: **raishū** (9)
next year: **rainen** (15)
nine: **kyū/ku** (4)
nine (objects): **kokonotsu** (14)
no: **iie** (1)
no good, useless: **dame(-na)** (8)
no one: **dare mo** (17)
noisy: **urusai** (19)
noodles: **soba** (10)
not very: **amari** (3)
November: **jū-ichi-gatsu** (13)
now, at the moment: **ima** (4)
ocean: **umi** (9)
__ o'clock: **-ji** (4)
October: **jū-gatsu** (13)
octopus: **tako** (19)
odd, strange: **hen(-na)** (8)
of course, naturally: **mochiron** (17)
office work: **jimu** (2)

often: **yoku** (8)
older brother (my): **ani** (7)
older brother (your): **o-niisan** (7)
older sister (my): **ane** (7)
older sister (your): **o-nēsan** (7)
on, on top, above: **ue** (14)
once, one time: **ichido** (11); **ik-kai** (19)
once more: **mō ichido** (11)
one: **ichi** (4)
one (object): **hitotsu** (14)
one day: **ichi-nichi** (15)
one month: **ik-kagetsu** (19)
one person: **hitori:** (9)
one-year period: **ichi-nen-kan** (11)
only: **dake** (9)
or: **ka** (15)
orange: **orenji** (8)
order, request [noun]: **chūmon** (14)
other, another, else: **hoka ni:** (17)
outside: **soto** (9)
over there: **asoko** (2)
over there, the other direction: **mukō** (14)
own, my own, your own: **jibun no** (19)
painful: **itai** (7)
parcel: **kozutsumi** (18)
pardon me: **gomen kudasai** (4)
part-time worker: **pāto** (2)
party: **pātii** (9)
past, after: **sugi** (7)
pay: **harau** (18)
people: **hitotachi** (9)
person, people: **hito** (2)
photocopy: **kopii** (14)
photograph: **shashin** (17)
physical education: **taiiku** (10)
piano: **piano** (10)
pickles: **tsukemono** (3)
picnic: **pikkunikku** (17)
picture postcard: **e-hagaki** (19)
pink: **pinku** (8)
pity, unfortunate: **zannen(-na)** (9)
pizza: **piza** (14)
place: **tokoro** (9)
plan, schedule: **yotei** (15)

please: **onegai shimasu** (5)
pleased to meet you: **yoroshiku onegai shimasu** (2)
post office: **yūbinkyoku** (14)
postcard: **hagaki** (18)
practice: **renshū** (7)
present, gift: **purezento** (18)
president [of a company]: **shachō** (15)
pretty, clean: **kirei(-na)** (8)
principal, head teacher: **kōchō** (15)
printer: **purintā** (2)
probably, must be: **deshō** (8)
problem: **mondai** (5)
project, plan: **keikaku** (15)
public telephone: **kōshū denwa** (14)
purple: **murasaki** (8)
purpose/benefit of: **tame ni** (18)
question: **shitsumon** (11)
quick: **hayai** (7)
quiet, peaceful: **shizuka(-na)** (8)
quit, cease: **yameru** (18)
radio: **rajio** (3)
rain: **ame** [noun], **ame ga furu** [verb] (17)
raw fish: **sashimi** (3)
raw fish on rice: **sushi** (10)
read: **yomu** (3)
really, truly: **hontō ni** (9)
receive, be entrusted with: **azukaru** (18)
recently: **saikin** (19)
red: **aka(i)** (8)
remember, recall: **oboeru** (7)
report [noun]: **repōto** (8)
reserved seat: **shiteiseki** (19)
reside, live: **sumu** (7)
Respect for the Aged Day: **keirō no hi** (13)
restaurant: **resutoran** (3)
restroom: **o-tearai, tearai** (17)
return, go/come home: **kaeru** (7)
review: **fukushū** (6)
rice (cooked): **gohan** (3)
rich person: **kanemochi** (17)
right (side): **migi** (5)
right-hand side: **migi-gawa** (5)
room: **heya** (13)
run: **hashiru** (10)

sake, rice wine: **o-sake, sake** (9)
salad: **sarada** (14)
salary, wages: **kyūryō** (15)
sales, selling: **hanbai** (19)
same: **onaji** (13)
sandwich: **sando** (14)
Saturday: **doyōbi** (9)
say, relate: **iu** (13)
schedule: **sukejūru** (15)
school: **gakkō** (1)
science: **kagaku** (10)
science-fiction: **SF (ess efu)** (4)
sea: **umi** (9)
second floor, upstairs: **ni-kai** (7)
section head, assistant manager: **kachō** (15)
see, watch: **miru** (3)
self, oneself: **jibun** (19)
self-introduction: **jiko shōkai** (10)
sell: **uru** (15)
send: **okuru** (18)
September: **ku-gatsu** (13)
set meal: **teishoku** (3)
seven: **nana/shichi** (4)
seven (objects): **nanatsu** (14)
share, portion: **-bun** (19)
she, her: **kanojo** (15)
shirt: **shatsu** (8)
shoes: **kutsu** (8)
shop: **mise** (14)
shopping [noun]: **kaimono** (8)
show: **miseru** (18)
shy, embarrassed: **hazukashii** (9)
__ side: **-gawa** (5)
single: **o-hitori** (11)
sit down: **suwaru** (5)
six: **roku** (4)
six (objects): **muttsu** (14)
size: **saizu** (8)
ski resort: **sukii-jō** (13)
skiing: **sukii** (13)
skillful, good at: **jōzu(-na)** (9)
skirt: **sukāto** (8)
ski-wear: **sukii-uea** (19)
sky: **sora** (8)

sleep, go to bed: **neru** (7)
slippers: **surippa** (5)
slow: **osoi** (7)
slowly: **yukkuri** (5)
slowly, gradually: **sorosoro** (13)
small: **chiisai** (7)
smart, clever: **atama ga ii** (10)
snow: **yuki** (17)
so, therefore: **dakara** (9)
someone: **dareka** (17)
something, anything: **nanika** (9)
sometimes: **tokidoki** (3)
somewhere, anywhere: **dokoka** (9)
soon: **sugu** (4)
sorry: **sumimasen** (1)
sorry, I apologize: **dōmo sumimasen** (1)
spaghetti: **supagetti** (14)
speak, talk: **hanasu** (3)
special, particular: **tokubetsu no** (15)
sport: **supōtsu** (10)
Sports Health Day: **taiiku no hi** (13)
spring: **haru** (13)
Spring Equinox Day: **shunbun no hi** (13)
staff: **sutaffu** (14)
stamp: **kitte** (18)
stand: **tatsu** (17)
stay (overnight): **tomaru** (9)
steak: **sutēki** (14)
steps, stairs: **kaidan** (17)
still, (not) yet: **mada** (4)
stomach: **o-naka** (14)
stop, halt [transitive]: **tomeru** (5)
straight ahead: **massugu** (5)
strong: **tsuyoi** (17)
student: **gakusei** (1)
study : **benkyō** [noun], **benkyō (o) suru** [verb] (4)
suit: **sūtsu** (8)
suitcase: **sūtsukēsu** (1)
summer: **natsu** (13)
summer vacation: **natsu-yasumi** (13)
Sunday: **nichiyōbi** (9)
surfing: **sāfingu** (14)
sweater: **sētā** (8)
T-shirt: **T-shatsu** (8)

table: **tēburu** (14)
take: **toru** (15)
take (time), last: **kakaru** (9)
take care, be careful: **ki o tsukeru** (7)
talk, speak: **hanasu** (3)
tasty, delicious: **oishii** (3)
taxi: **takushii** (4)
teacher, professor: **sensei** (1)
team: **chiimu** (10)
telephone: **denwa** (2)
telephone charges: **denwa-dai** (18)
television, TV: **terebi** (4)
tell, teach: **oshieru** (3)
ten: **jū** (4)
ten (objects): **tō** (14)
ten thousand: **ichi-man** (19)
tennis: **tenisu** (4)
terrible, awful: **taihen(-na)** (8)
test [noun]: **tesuto** (4)
thank you: **dōmo arigatō, arigatō** (1)
thank you for the meal: **go-chisō sama deshita** (3)
that [adjective]: **sono** (3)
that [noun]: **sore** (2)
that - over there [adjective]: **ano** (3)
that kind of: **sonna, anna** (13)
that one [of two]: **sochira, sotchi** (17)
that over there [noun]: **are** (2)
then: **soshite** (18)
there: **soko** (2)
thing, event, fact: **koto** (10)
think: **omou** (10)
think about, consider: **kangaeru** (10)
this [adjective]: **kono** (3)
this [noun]: **kore** (2)
this evening: **konban** (3)
this kind of: **konna** (13)
this month: **kongetsu** (13)
this morning: **kesa** (9)
this one [of two]: **kochira, kotchi** (17)
this year: **kotoshi** (15)
thousand: **sen** (5)
three: **san** (4)
three (objects): **mittsu** (14)
Thursday: **mokuyōbi** (9)

ticket: **kippu** (18)
time, hour: **jikan** (4)
time, period: **toki** (13)
to begin [intransitive]: **hajimaru** (4)
to get older [of people]: **toshi o toru** (19)
to get on/in [transportation]: **noru** (19)
to put out, send, submit: **dasu** (15)
to, towards: **e** (1), **ni** (9)
toast: **tōsuto** (14)
today: **kyō** (2)
together: **issho ni** (7)
tomorrow: **ashita** (3)
too, also: **mo** (8)
town, city: **machi** (9)
traffic signals: **shingō** (5)
train: **densha** (4)
train station: **eki** (2)
trip, journey: **ryokō** (19)
try hard, do one's best: **ganbaru** (10)
Tuesday: **kayōbi** (9)
tuna: **tsuna** (14)
turn [verb]: **magaru** (5)
twelve: **jū-ni** (4)
two: **ni** (4)
two (objects): **futatsu** (14)
two people: **futari** (9)
umbrella: **kasa** (17)
understand: **wakaru** (2)
United States: **Amerika** (1)
university: **daigaku** (2)
university student: **daigakusei** (5)
umarried: **o-hitori** (11)
unskillful, bad at: **heta(-na)** (9)
until: **made** (4)
us, we: **watashitachi** (9)
use: **tsukau** (11)
vacation, holiday, rest: **yasumi** (13)
various: **iroiro(-na)** (11)
very, extremely: **totemo** (8)
video: **bideo** (9)
wait: **matsu** (5)
walk: **aruku** (14)
want: **hoshii** (15)
warm: **atatakai** (17)

water: **mizu** (3)
weather: **tenki** (9)
Wednesday: **suiyōbi** (9)
week: **shūkan** (10)
weekend: **shūmatsu** (9)
welcome: **yōkoso** (1)
well, in that case: **ja** (1)
what?: **nan/nani** (3)
what date?: **nan-nichi** (13)
what day?: **nan-yōbi** (9)
what kind of?: **donna** (13)
what time?: **nan-ji** (4)
when?: **itsu** (9)
where?: **doko** (2)
which?: **dono** (3)
which month?: **nan-gatsu** (13)
which one?: **dore** (2); **dochira, dotchi** [of two] (17)
white: **shiro(i)** (8)
who?: **dare** (2)
why?: **dō shite** (4)
wife (my): **kanai/tsuma** (7)
wife (your): **okusan** (7)
wind: **kaze** (17)
windsurfing: **uindo sāfingu** (14)
wine: **wain** (3)
winter: **fuyu** (13)
without standing on ceremony: **go-enryo naku** (11)
woman: **onna no hito** (9)
women: **onna no hitotachi** (9)
word: **kotoba** (13)
word processor: **wāpuro** (14)
work [verb]: **shigoto (o) suru** (4)
work, employment: **shigoto** (4)
work, labor [verb]: **hataraku** (7)
worry, anxiety: **shinpai** (15)
write: **kaku** (5)
year: **nen** (11)
year, age: **toshi** (19)
__ years old: **-sai** (11)
yellow: **kiiro(i)** (8)
yen: **en** (5)
yes: **hai** (1); **ē** [informal] (9)
yes, please: **itadakimasu** [when offered food and drink] (5)
yesterday: **kinō** (9)

yesterday evening: **kinō no ban** (11)
you: **anata** (2)
young: **wakai** (9)
younger brother (my): **otōto** (7)
younger brother (your): **otōtosan** (7)
younger sister (my): **imōto** (7)
younger sister (your): **imōtosan** (7)

JAPANESE–ENGLISH GLOSSARY

abunai: dangerous, look out! (19)
agaru: go up (5)
aida: between (14)
airon: iron (14)
Airurando: Ireland (14)
aisu skēto: ice skating (14)
aka(i): red (8)
aki: fall/autumn (13)
aku: be open, free, have no engagements (15)
amari: not very [+ negative verb] (3)
ame: rain [noun] (17)
ame ga furu: rain [verb] (17)
Amerika: the United States (1)
Amerikajin: an American (1)
anata: you (2)
ane: (my) older sister (7)
ani: (my) older brother (7)
anna: that kind of (13)
ano: that – over there [adjective] (3)
ao(i): blue-green (8)
apāto: apartment (14)
appurupai: apple pie (14)
ara: oh! [used mostly by women] (14)
are: look! listen! (17)
are: that over there [noun] (2)
arigatō: thank you [more informal than **dōmo arigatō**] (1)
aru: be, exist, there is/are, have [used with inanimate objects] (2)
aruku: walk (14)
asa: morning (9)
asatte: the day after tomorrow (3)
ashi: leg, foot (19)
ashita: tomorrow (3)
asoko: over there (2)
atama: head (7)
atama ga ii: smart, clever (10)
atama ga itai: have a headache (7)
atarashii: new (2)
atatakai: warm (17)

ato: after (15)
atsui: hot (7)
au: meet (4)
azukaru: receive, be entrusted with (18)
ban: evening (11)
basu: bus (10)
basukettobōru: basketball (10)
beddo: bed (14)
benkyō: study [noun] (4)
benkyō (o) suru: study [verb] (4)
beruto: belt (8)
bideo: video (9)
biiru: beer (9)
bōifurendo: boyfriend (10)
boku: I [used by boys and men](11)
bōringu: bowling (14)
buchō: department head, manager (15)
-bun: quantity, share, portion (19)
bunka no hi: Culture Day (13)
Burajiru: Brazil (14)
buraun: brown (8)
burū: blue (8)
byōki(-na): ill (17)
chaiiro: brown (8)
chan: [term of address used instead of san for girls and small
    children] (4)
chansu: chance, opportunity (9)
chichi: (my) father (7)
chigau: be incorrect, wrong (1)
chiimu: team (10)
chiisai: small (7)
chiizu: cheese (17)
chikai: close, nearby (17)
chikaku: near, close [adverb] (14)
chōdo: exactly, precisely (11)
chokorēto: chocolate (14)
chotto: a little, a bit (7)
Chūka ryōri: Chinese cuisine (11)
chūmon: an order, request (14)
da: is/are [plain form of desu] (10)
dai ik-ka: lesson one (1)
dai-kirai(-na): hate, loathe (3)
dai-suki(-na): like very much, love (3)
daibutsu: large statue of Buddha (17)

daigaku: university (2)
daigakusei: university student (5)
daijōbu(-na): fine, all right (8)
dakara: so, therefore (9)
dake: only (9)
dame(-na): no good, useless (8)
dandan: gradually, little by little (17)
dansei: males, men (11)
dare: who? (2)
dare mo: no one (17)
dareka: someone (17)
dasu: to put out, send, submit (15)
de: at, in [particle indicating place where an action occurs] (5)
de: by [particle indicating means by which something is done] (4)
de gozaimasu: is, are [formal] (8)
dekakeru: go out (18)
dekiru: can, be able to (10); happen, be completed (15)
demo: - or something (19)
demo: however, but [at the beginning of a sentence] (4)
denki: electricity (18)
denki-dai electricity charges (18)
densha: train (4)
denwa: telephone (2)
denwa-dai: telephone charges (18)
depāto: department store (8)
deru: go out, appear (13)
deshō: I wonder if, probably, must be (8)
desu: am/is/are (1)
dezain: design (8)
dezainā: designer (8)
dō: how? (3)
dō shimashita ka: what happened?(9)
dō shimashō ka: what shall I do? (5)
dō shite: why? (4)
dochira: where? [formal] (11); which one? [of two] (17)
Doitsugo: German language (10)
doko: where? (2)
dokoka: somewhere, anywhere (9)
dōmo arigatō: thank you (1)
dōmo sumimasen: I'm sorry, I apologize (1)
donna: what kind of? (13)
dono: which? [adjective] (3)
dore: which one? (2)
doru: dollars (5)

dotchi: which one? [of two] [short form of **dochira**] (17)
doyōbi: Saturday (9)
dōzo: here you are [when giving something] (1)
dōzo dōzo: please do so, please go ahead (4)
dōzo yoroshiku: happy to meet you (2)
e: to, towards (1)
ē: yes [informal] (9)
e-hagaki: picture postcard (20)
eakon: air conditioner (14)
eiga: movie, film (3)
Eigo: English language (3)
Eikaiwa: English conversation (18)
eki: train station (2)
en: yen (5)
enjinia: engineer (1)
fakkusu: fax (8)
famikon: family computer (14)
Fuji san: Mount Fuji (11)
fukushū: review (6)
-fun/pun: minute (4)
Furansu: France (10)
Furansugo: French language (10)
furoppi: floppy disk (14)
furu: fall, drop (17)
futari: two (people)(9)
futatsu: two (objects) (14)
fūtō: envelope (18)
fuyu: winter (13)
G-pan: jeans (8)
ga: [particle indicating subject of verb] (3)
ga: but (1); but [when joining two sentences] (8)
gaijin: foreigner (4)
gaikoku: foreign country, abroad (15)
gairaigo: words borrowed from other languages (14)
gakkō: school (1)
gakuin: academy, school, place of learning (1)
gakusei: student (1)
ganbaru: try hard, do one's best (10)
ganjitsu: New Year's Day (13)
gārufurendo: girlfriend (11)
gasu: gas (18)
gasu-dai: gas charges (18)
-gawa: the - side (5)
gēmu: game (10)

genkan: entrance area [in a house] (5)
genki(-na): healthy, energetic (8)
getsuyōbi: Monday (9)
ginkō: bank (2)
go: five (4)
go-chisō sama deshita: thank you for the meal (3)
go-enryo naku: without standing on ceremony (11)
go-gatsu: May (13)
go-kazoku: (your) family (7)
go-shujin: (your) husband (7)
gogo: afternoon (7)
gohan: cooked rice (3)
gomen kudasai: excuse me, is anyone there? (5); pardon me for causing any inconvenience (4)
gomen nasai: excuse me, I beg your pardon (13)
gorufu: golf (9)
gozaimasu: have [formal] (8)
gurai: about, approximately (19)
gurē: gray (8)
guriin: green (8)
hachi: eight (4)
hachi-gatsu: August (13)
hagaki: postcard (18)
haha: (my) mother (7)
hai: yes (1)
haikingu: hiking (14)
hairu: go in, enter (9)
hajimaru: to begin [intransitive] (4)
hajimemashite: how do you do? (1)
hajimete: first time (15)
hamu: ham (14)
-han: half past - (4)
hana: flower (3)
hanashi: a talk, conversation, chat (4)
hanashi o suru: have a talk, chat (4)
hanasu: speak, talk (3)
hanbāgā: hamburger (14)
hanbai: sales, selling (19)
hansamu(-na) handsome (11)
harau: pay (18)
haru: spring (13)
hashi: chopsticks (4)
hashiru: run (10)
hataraku: work, labor [verb] (7)

hayai: quick, early (7)
hazukashii: shy, embarrassed (9)
hen(-na): odd, strange (8)
heta(-na): bad at, unskillful (9)
heya: room (13)
hi: day (13)
hidari: the left (5)
hidari-gawa: the left-hand side (5)
hiroi: large [in area], spacious, extensive (17)
hiru-gohan: lunch (7)
hiruma: daytime (13)
hisashiburi: it's been a long time (8)
hito: person, people (2)
hitori: one (person) (9)
hitotachi: people (9)
hitotsu: one (object) (14)
hō ga ii: - would be best (14)
hō: direction, side (17)
hoka ni: other, another, else (17)
Hokkaidō: the northernmost of the four main islands of Japan (8)
hon: book (5)
-hon: [counter for long, thin objects] (19)
hontō ni: really, truly (9)
hoshii: want (15)
hoteru: hotel (8)
hotto (kōhii): hot coffee (14)
hyaku: hundred (5)
ichi: one (4)
ichi-gatsu: January (13)
ichi-man: ten thousand (19)
ichi-nen-kan: a one-year period (11)
ichi-nichi-jū: all day long (19)
ichi-nichi: one day (15)
ichiban: most, the first, number one (11)
ichido: once, one time (11)
Igirisu: England, Great Britain (2)
Igirisujin: an English/British person (2)
ii: good, fine (3)
ii kagen ni shi nasai: please behave yourselves (19)
iie: no (1)
iinkai: committee (15)
ik-kagetsu: one month (19)
ik-kai: once, one time (19)
ikaga: how about -? [polite form of dō] (5)

iku: go (3)
ikura: how much (money)? (5)
ikutsu: how old? (11); how many? (14)
ima: now, at the moment (4)
imōto: (my) younger sister (7)
imōtosan: (your) younger sister (7)
Indo: India (14)
inu: dog (4)
irassharu: is, are [very polite form of **iru**] (4)
iroiro(-na): all kinds of, various (11)
iru: am, is, are [used with animate objects] (4)
isogashii: busy (13)
issho ni: together (7)
itadakimasu: bon appetit (3); yes, please [when offered food or drink] (5)
itai: painful (7)
Itaria: Italy (14)
itsu: when?(9)
itsumo: always (8)
itsutsu: five (objects) (14)
iu: say, relate (13)
iya(-na): horrible (8)
ja: well, in that case (1)
ja arimasen: isn't, aren't (2)
jaketto: jacket (8)
jama: interference, obstruction (5)
-ji: - o'clock (4)
jibun: self, oneself (19)
jibun no: one's own, my own, your own (19)
jikan: time, hour (4)
-jikan: - hours (9)
jikō shōkai: self-introduction (10)
jimu: office work (2)
jimu no hito: clerk, office worker (2)
-jin: person (of a country) (1)
jisho: dictionary (18)
jitsu wa: in fact (11)
josei: females, women (11)
jōzu(-na): skillful, good at (9)
jū: ten (4)
jū-gatsu: October (13)
jū-ichi-gatsu: November (13)
jū-ichi: eleven (4)
jū-ni-gatsu: December (13)

jū-ni: twelve (4)
jūbun: enough, sufficient (18)
jūgyō: lesson, class (10)
juppun: 10 minutes (4)
jūsho: address (5)
ka: [sentence ending to indicate a question] (1)
ka: or (15)
kabuki: Japanese classical play (18)
kachō: section head, assistant manager (15)
kado: corner (5)
kaeru: return, go/come home (7)
kagaku: science (10)
kaidan: steps, stairs (17)
kaigi: a meeting (3)
kaigi ni deru: attend a meeting (13)
kaimono: shopping [noun] (8)
kaisha: company, office (1)
kaiwa: conversation (14)
kakaru: take (time), last (9)
kakikomu: fill in/out [a form] (18)
kaku: write (5)
Kamakura: city close to Yokohama, famous for its large statue of
         Buddha (17)
Kanada: Canada (1)
Kanadajin: a Canadian (1)
kanai/tsuma: (my) wife (7)
kanemochi: rich person (17)
kangaeru: think about, consider (10)
kanji: Chinese written characters (9)
kanojo: she, her (15)
kantan(-na): brief, simple (8)
kao: face (10)
kāpetto: carpet (14)
kara: from (2); because (11); after (18)
kare: him, he (14)
kasa: umbrella (17)
kashikomarimashita: certainly, very good [formal] (14)
kāten: curtain (14)
kau: buy (8)
Kawasaki: industrial city near Tokyo (7)
kayōbi: Tuesday (9)
kaze: wind (17)
kazoku: family (7)
kedo: but, although (9)

keikaku: plan, project, scheme (15)
keirō no hi: Respect for the Aged Day (13)
keiyaku: contract (15)
kēki: cake (14)
kekkon: marriage (11)
kekkon suru: be married (11)
kenka: argument (14)
kenkoku kinenbi: National Foundation Day (13)
kenpō kinenbi: Constitution Day (13)
kesa: this morning (9)
ki o tsukeru: take care, be careful (7)
kibun: mood, feeling (17)
kiibōdo: keyboard (14)
kiiro(i): yellow (8)
kiku: chrysanthemum (3)
kiku: hear, listen, ask (3)
kimeru: decide (15)
kinō: yesterday (9)
kinō no ban: yesterday evening (11)
kinrō kansha no hi: Labor Thanksgiving Day (13)
kinyōbi: Friday (9)
kippu: ticket (18)
kirai(-na): dislike (3)
kirei(-na): pretty, clean (8)
kissaten: coffee shop (9)
kitanai: dirty (14)
kitte: stamp (18)
kitto: definitely, without fail (17)
kochira: this way (1); this person [used with introductions] (2); this one [of two] (17)
kochira koso: the pleasure's mine (13)
kōchō: principal, head teacher (15)
kodomo no hi: Children's Day (13)
kodomo: child (8)
kodomotachi: children (11)
kōfun suru: be excited (19)
koko: here (2)
kōkō: high school [short for **kōtō gakkō**] (1)
kokonotsu: nine (objects) (14)
kōkūbin: airmail (18)
komu: be crowded (8)
konban: this evening (3)
konbanwa: good evening (2)
kongetsu: this month (13)

konna: this kind of (13)
konnichiwa: good day, hello [not used early in the morning] (2)
kono: this [adjective] (3)
konpyūtā: computer (2)
kopii: photocopy (14)
kōra: cola (14)
kore: this [noun] (2)
kōshū denwa: public telephone (14)
kōsu: course [of study] (13)
kotae: answer, response (10)
kotaeru: answer, respond (13)
kotchi: this side, this one [of two] [from **kochira**] (17)
kōto: coat (8)
koto: thing, event, fact (10)
koto ga arimasu ka: have you ever …? (17)
kotoba: word (13)
kotoshi: this year (15)
kozutsumi: parcel (18)
ku-gatsu: September (13)
kūkō: airport (15)
kuni: country (10)
kurai: dark (17)
kurasu: class (9)
kuro(i): black (8)
kuru: come (3)
kuruma: car (1)
kusshon: cushion (14)
kutsu: shoes (8)
kyaku: guest, customer (14)
kyō: today (2)
kyōiku: education (15)
kyonen: last year (15)
kyū/ku: nine (4)
kyūryō: salary, wages (15)
machi: town, city (9)
mada: still, (not) yet (4)
made: until (4); as far as (5)
made ni: by [date or time] (15)
mae: before, in front of (7)
magaru: turn [verb] (5)
-mai: [counter for flat objects] (18)
mainichi: every day (3)
-man: ten thousand (19)
manejā: manager (10)

massugu: straight ahead (5)
mata: again, once more, another time (4)
mata ashita: until tomorrow, see you tomorrow [informal] (4)
mata dōzo: please come again (13)
matsu: wait (5)
mazu: first of all, to begin with (18)
meishi: business card (1)
memo: memo (15)
menyū: menu (14)
messēji: message (15)
midori: green (8)
midori no hi: Greenery Day (13)
migi: the right (5)
migi-gawa: right-hand side (5)
mina san, minna: everyone (2)
minna de: altogether, everyone together (7)
miru: see, watch (3)
mise: shop (14)
miseru: show (18)
miso shiru: miso soup (3)
mittsu: three (objects) (14)
mizu: water (3)
mō: already, (not) any longer, another, further (5)
mo: too, also (8)
mō ichido: once more (11)
- mo - mo: both - and -/neither - nor - (9)
mochiron: of course, naturally (17)
mokuyōbi: Thursday (9)
mondai: problem (5)
monitā: a monitor (14)
moshi moshi: hello? [on the telephone] (4)
moshi yokattara: if it's allright (13)
moshi: if (17)
mōsu: be called, named (10)
motsu: have, hold (15)
motte kuru: bring (19)
motto: more (8)
mukae ni iku: go to meet (15)
mukō: the other direction, over there (14)
murasaki: purple (8)
mushiatsui: hot and humid (17)
muttsu: six (objects) (14)
muzukashii: difficult (7)
nado: and so on, et cetera (10)

nagai: long (10)
naka: among, within (11); inside (14)
namae: name (1)
nan/nani: what? (3)
nan-gatsu: which month? (13)
nan-ji: what time? (4)
nan-nichi: what date? (13)
nan-nin: how many people? (9)
nan-sai: how old? (11)
nan-yōbi: what day? (9)
nana/shichi: seven (4)
nanatsu: seven (objects) (14)
nanika: something, anything (9)
narabu: line up, queue (17)
naru: become, get (17)
natsu: summer (13)
natsu-yasumi: summer vacation (13)
ne: isn't it? aren't they? don't you? etc. (3)
nekutai: necktie (8)
nen: year (11)
neru: sleep, go to bed (7)
ni: in, at [location] (2); at [when giving the time] (4); to, towards (9)
ni: two (4)
-nichi: [added to numbers to give the date] (13)
ni-gatsu: February (13)
ni-kai: second floor, upstairs (7)
ni tsuite: concerning, regarding (15)
nichiyōbi: Sunday (9)
Nihon: Japan (1)
Nihon Arupusu: Japan Alps, mountain range in central Japan (9)
Nihongo: Japanese language (1)
nimotsu: luggage (19)
-nin: [counter for people] (9)
no: [particle showing possession, similar to English "__'s"] (1)
noboru: climb, go up (17)
nomu: drink [verb] (3)
noru: to get on/in [transportation] (19)
Nyū Jiirando: New Zealand (14)
Nyū Yōku: New York (9)
nyūsu: the news (4)
o: [particle to indicate object of verb] (3)
- o kudasai: could I have -, please (3)
o-cha: green tea (3)
o-genki desu ka: how are you? (8)

o-hisashiburi: it's been a long time (8)

o-hitori: single, unmarried (11)

o-jama shimasu: excuse me for disturbing you (5)

o-kage sama de: thank you for asking [set phrase in response to o-genki desu ka] (8)

o-kake kudasai: please take a seat (5)

o-kane: money (15)

o-kanemochi: rich person (17)

o-kāsan: (your) mother [or when addressing one's own mother] (7)

o-kyaku san: guest, customer [formal] (14)

o-naka ga suku: become hungry (14)

o-naka: stomach (14)

o-nēsan: (your) older sister [or when addressing one's own older sister] (7)

o-niisan: (your) older brother [or when addressing one's own older brother] (7)

o-sake: sake, rice wine (9)

o-tearai: restroom (17)

o-tōsan: (your) father [or when addressing one's own father] (7)

o-tsuri: the change [money] (5)

oboeru: remember, recall (7)

Ohaio-shu: the state of Ohio (10)

ohayō gozaimasu: good morning (2)

ōi: many, abundant, a lot of (11)

oishii: tasty, delicious (3)

ōkii: big (2)

okiru: get up, get out of bed (13)

okoru: get angry (14)

oku: hundred million (19)

okuru: send (18)

okusan: (your) wife (7)

omoshiroi: interesting, amusing (9)

omou: think (10)

onaji: same (13)

onegai shimasu: Could I speak to-? (4); please [Lit: I have a request/favor] (5); please do that (15)

ongaku: music (19)

onna no hito: woman (9)

onna no hitotachi: women (9)

onsen: hot spring (9)

orenji: orange (8)

oshieru: tell, teach (3)

osoi: late, slow (7)

Ōsutoraria: Australia (14)

Ōsutoria: Austria (14)
otoko no hito: man (9)
otōto: (my) younger brother (7)
otōtosan: (your) younger brother (7)
otto/shujin: (my) husband (7)
owaru: finish, end [verb] (10)
oyasumi nasai: good night (2)
pātii: party (9)
pāto: part-time worker (2)
piano: piano (10)
pikkunikku: picnic (17)
pinku: pink (8)
piza: pizza (14)
purezento: present (18)
purintā: printer (2)
raigetsu: next month (13)
rainen: next year (15)
raishū: next week (9)
rajio: radio (3)
ranchi: lunch (18)
ranpu: lamp (14)
rekishi: history (10)
remon tii: lemon tea (14)
renshū: practice (7)
repōto: report [noun] (8)
resutoran: restaurant (3)
rikon: divorce (11)
roku: six (4)
roku-gatsu: June (13)
ryokan: Japanese-style inn (9)
ryokō: trip, journey (19)
ryōri: cooking, cuisine (10)
sabishii: lonely (11)
sāfingu: surfing (14)
-sai: – years old (11)
saigo ni: finally, at the end (18)
saikin: recently (19)
saizu: size (8)
sakana: fish (3)
sake: sake, rice wine (9)
saki ni: in advance, ahead, before (17)
sama: Mr., Mrs., Ms., Miss [very polite] (4)
samui: cold
san: Mr., Mrs., Ms., Miss (1)

san: three (4)
san-gatsu: March (13)
sando: sandwich (14)
sarada: salad (14)
sashimi: raw fish (3)
seijin no hi: Coming-of-Age Day (13)
seikatsu: life, living (10)
sen: thousand (5)
sengetsu: last month (13)
sensei: teacher, professor [used instead of **san** as a term of address to teachers, professors and doctors] (1)
senshū: last week (9)
sētā: sweater (8)
setsumei: explanation (11)
setsumei suru: explain (11)
SF (ess efu): science-fiction (4)
shachō: president (15)
shanai: inside the train (19)
shashin: photograph (17)
shatsu: shirt (8)
shi/yo/yon: four (4)
shi-gatsu: April (13)
shichi-gatsu: July (13)
shichi/nana: seven (4)
shigoto: work, employment (4)
shigoto suru: work [verb] (4)
shii dii: CD, compact disc (14)
shikata ga arimasen: it can't be helped (17)
shinbun: newspaper (2)
shingō: traffic signals (5)
Shinkansen: Bullet Train (11)
shinpai: worry, anxiety (15)
shinsetsu(-na): kind, gentle (8)
shiraberu: investigate, look into (19)
shiro(i): white (8)
shisha: branch office (14)
shita: below, under (14)
shiteiseki: reserved seat (19)
shitsumon: question (11)
shitsurei desu ga: I'm sorry to trouble you, but ...; excuse me, but ... (1)
shitsurei shimasu: excuse me (2); goodbye (4)
shizuka(-na): quiet, peaceful (8)
shōkai suru: introduce (10)

shūbun no hi: Autumnal Equinox Day (13)
shūkan: week (10)
shukudai: homework (7)
shūmatsu: weekend (9)
shumi: interest, hobby (10)
shunbun no hi: Spring Equinox Day (13)
shutchō: business trip (13)
sō desu: that's right, that's so (1)
sō desu ka: I see, is that so? (1)
soba: near, next to (14)
soba: noodles (10)
sochira: that side, that one [of two] (17)
sōdan suru: consult, confer with, talk over (15)
sōji suru: do the cleaning (19)
soko: there (2)
sonna: that kind of (13)
sono: that [adjective] (3)
sono ato: after that (15)
sora: sky (8)
sore: that [noun] (2)
sore de: so, therefore, and then (14)
sore kara: and also (4)
sorosoro: slowly, gradually, soon (13)
soshite: then (18)
sotchi: that side, that one [of two] [from **sochira**] (17)
soto: outside (9)
sūgaku: mathematics (10)
sugi: past, after (7)
sugoi: amazing, incredible (17)
sugu: soon (4)
suiyōbi: Wednesday (9)
sukāto: skirt (8)
sukejūru: schedule (15)
suki(-na): like (3)
sukii: skiing (13)
sukii ni iku: go skiing (13)
sukii-jō: ski resort (13)
sukii-uea: ski-wear (19)
sukoshi: a little, a small amount (5)
suku: become empty (14)
sumimasen: excuse me, I'm sorry (1)
sumu: reside, live (7)
supagetti: spaghetti (14)
supōtsu: sport (10)

surippa: slippers (5)
suru: do (3); - **ni suru:** I'll have/decide on - (3)
sushi: raw fish on rice (10)
sutaffu: staff (14)
sutēki: steak (14)
sūtsu: suit (8)
sūtsukēsu: suitcase (1)
suwaru: sit down (5)
suzushii: cool (17)
T-shatsu: T-shirt (8)
tabemono: food (10)
taberu: eat (3)
-tachi: [plural ending for words associated with people] (9)
tada: just, only, simply (15)
taihen(-na): terrible, awful (8)
taiiku: physical education (10)
taiiku no hi: Sports Health Day (13)
takai: high, expensive (7)
tako: octopus (19)
takusan: a lot of, many, much (4)
takushii: taxi (4)
tamago: egg (18)
tame ni: for the purpose of, benefit of (18)
tanjōbi: birthday (7)
tanoshii: enjoyable, fun (9)
tanoshimi ni suru: look forward to (19)
tatemono: building (5)
tatsu: stand (17)
tearai: restroom (17)
tēburu: table (14)
tegami: letter (13)
teishoku: set meal (3)
tenisu: tennis (4)
tenki: weather (9)
tennō tanjōbi: Emperor's Birthday (13)
tenpura: tempura [deep fried food] (11)
terebi: television, TV (4)
tesuto: a test (4)
to: and [to join nouns] (1)
tō: ten (objects) (14)
to ieba: talking of -, that reminds me (19)
tōi: far, distant (17)
toki: time, period (13)
tokidoki: sometimes (3)

tokoro: place (9)
tokorode: by the way (5)
tokubetsu no: special, particular (15)
tomaru: stay (overnight) (9)
tomeru: stop, halt [transitive verb] (5)
tomodachi: friend (3)
tonari: next to, by the side (7)
toru: take (15)
toshi: year, age (19)
toshi o toru: get older [of people] (19)
tōsuto: toast (14)
totemo: very, extremely (8)
tsugi no: the next (5)
tsukareru: become tired (9)
tsukau: use (11)
tsukemono: pickles (3)
tsukue: desk (2)
tsukuru: make (18)
tsuma/kanai: (my) wife (7)
tsumori: intention (15)
tsuna: tuna (14)
tsutomeru: be employed (10)
tsuyoi: strong (17)
uchi: house, home (2)
uchiawase: meeting, consultation (15)
ue: above, on top (14)
uindo sāfingu: windsurfing (14)
umi: sea, ocean(9)
ureshii: happy (11)
uru: sell (15)
urusai: noisy (19)
ushiro: behind, in back of (14)
uso: untruth, story, lie (10)
wa: [particle to indicate main topic of sentence] (2)
- wa dō desu ka: how about -? (3)
wain: wine (3)
wakai: young (9)
wakarimashita: I see, I've got it, I understand [from **wakaru**] (5)
wakaru: understand (2)
wanpiisu: dress [noun] (8)
wāpuro: word processor (14)
warui: bad, wrong (7)
wasureru: forget (9)
watashi: I, me (1)

watashi no: my (1)
watashitachi: us, we (9)
ya: and (10)
yaki-zakana: grilled fish (3)
yakyū: baseball (7)
yama: mountain (9)
yameru: quit, stop, cease (18)
yaru: do, try (19)
yasui: cheap (7)
yasumi: holiday, rest, pause (13)
yasumi no hi: holiday, vacation, day off (13)
yattsu: eight (objects) (14)
yo: [sentence ending to show emphasis] (5)
yobu: call, summon (7)
yōfuku: clothes (19)
yōji: errand, chore, something to do (18)
yokattara: if it's allright (17)
yōkoso: welcome (1)
yoku: often (8); well (10)
yoku aru: frequently occurring (11)
yomu: read (3)
yon/yo/shi: four (4)
Yōroppa: Europe (13)
yoroshiku onegai shimasu: pleased to meet you [Lit: please treat me well] (2); goodbye [on the phone] (4)
yoru: call in, drop by (15)
yoru: evening (9)
yōshi: a form, a blank (15)
yotei: plan, program, schedule (15)
yottsu: four (objects) (14)
yu: hot water (9)
yūbinkyoku: post office (14)
yuki: snow (17)
yukkuri: slowly (5)
yūmei(-na): famous (8)
zannen(-na): pity, unfortunate (9)
zenbu: all (10)
zenzen: never [+ negative verb] (8)

Christopher Cassa
280 Madison St.
Franklin Sq., NY 11010-2239
USA

CCassa@hotmail.Com